FACTORY

TITAN®
COMICS

STATIX
PRESS

D1534657

STATIX PRESS

ALSO FROM TITAN COMICS AND STATIX PRESS

ALEJANDRO JODOROWSKY
ENKI BILAL
PHILIPPE DRUILLET
SEAN PHILLIPS
JUNKO MIZUNO
FABIEN NURY

STATIX
PRESS

THE GREATEST CREATORS IN THE WORLD

WRITER & ARTIST
ELGO

TRANSLATED BY:
MARC BOURBON-CROOK

EDITOR
JONATHAN STEVENSON

TITAN COMICS

MANAGING AND LAUNCH EDITOR
Andrew James

DESIGNER
Wilfred Tshikana-Ekutshu

PRODUCTION CONTROLLER
Peter James

PRODUCTION SUPERVISOR
Maria Pearson

SENIOR PRODUCTION CONTROLLER
Jackie Flook

PRODUCTION ASSISTANT
Rhiannon Roy

ART DIRECTOR
Oz Browne

SENIOR SALES MANAGER
Steve Tothill

CIRCULATION EXECUTIVE
Frances Hallam

PRESS OFFICER
Will O'Mullane

BRAND MANAGER
Chris Thompson

ADS & MARKETING ASSISTANT
Bella Hoy

DIRECT SALES & MARKETING MANAGER
Ricky Claydon

COMMERCIAL MANAGER
Michelle Fairlamb

PUBLISHING MANAGER
Darryl Tothill

PUBLISHING DIRECTOR
Chris Teather

OPERATIONS DIRECTOR
Leigh Baulch

EXECUTIVE DIRECTOR
Vivian Cheung

PUBLISHER
Nick Landau

FACTORY

9781785865985
Published by Titan Comics
A division of Titan Publishing Group Ltd.
144 Southwark St., London, SE1 0UP.
Titan Comics is a registered trademark of Titan Publishing Group, Ltd.
All rights reserved.

Originally published in French by Éditions Carabas ©Yacine Elghorri, 2007, 2008, 2009.

A CIP catalogue record for this title is available from the British Library

10 9 8 7 6 5 4 3 2 1
First Published AUGUST 2018
Printed in SPAIN.
Titan Comics.

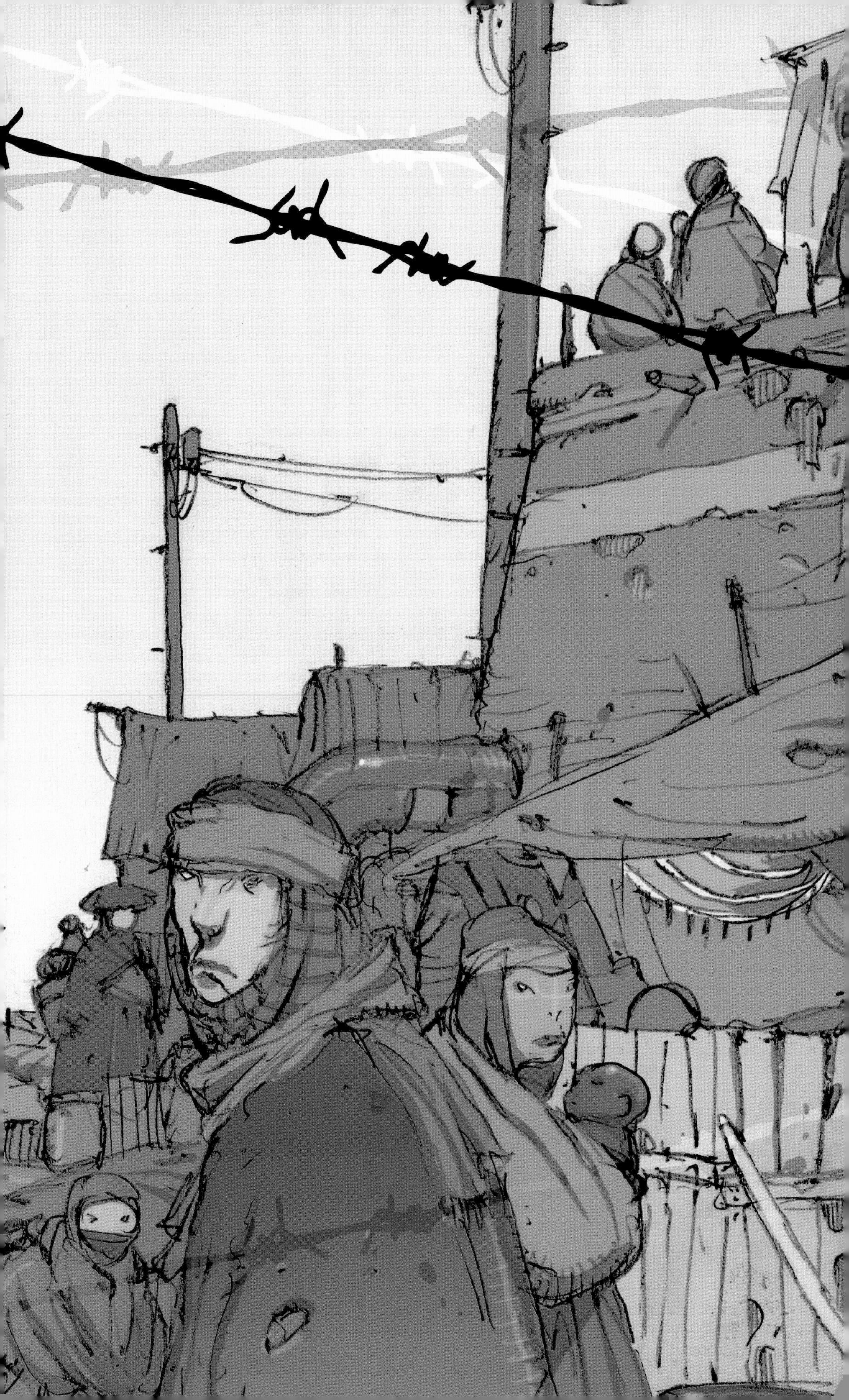

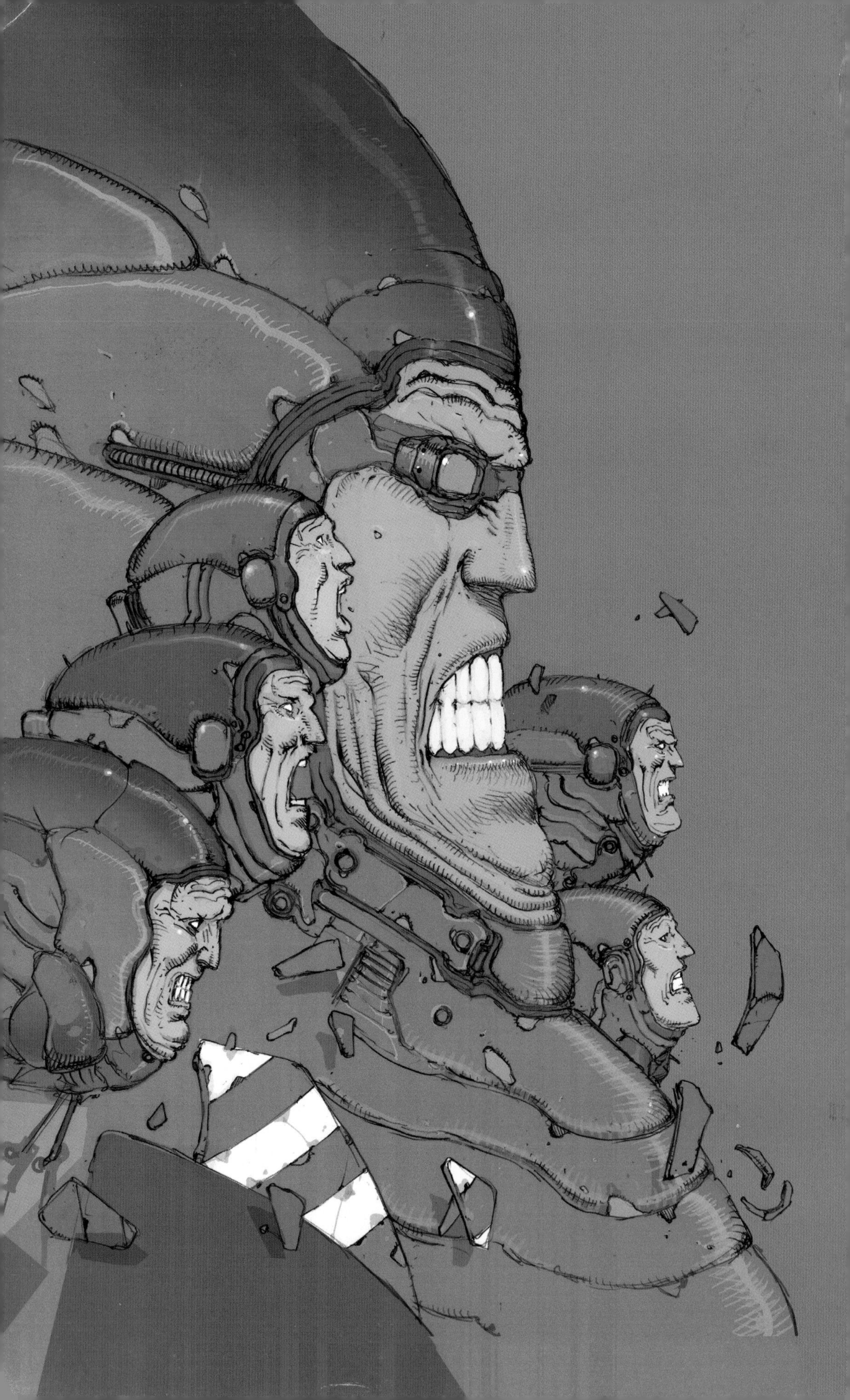

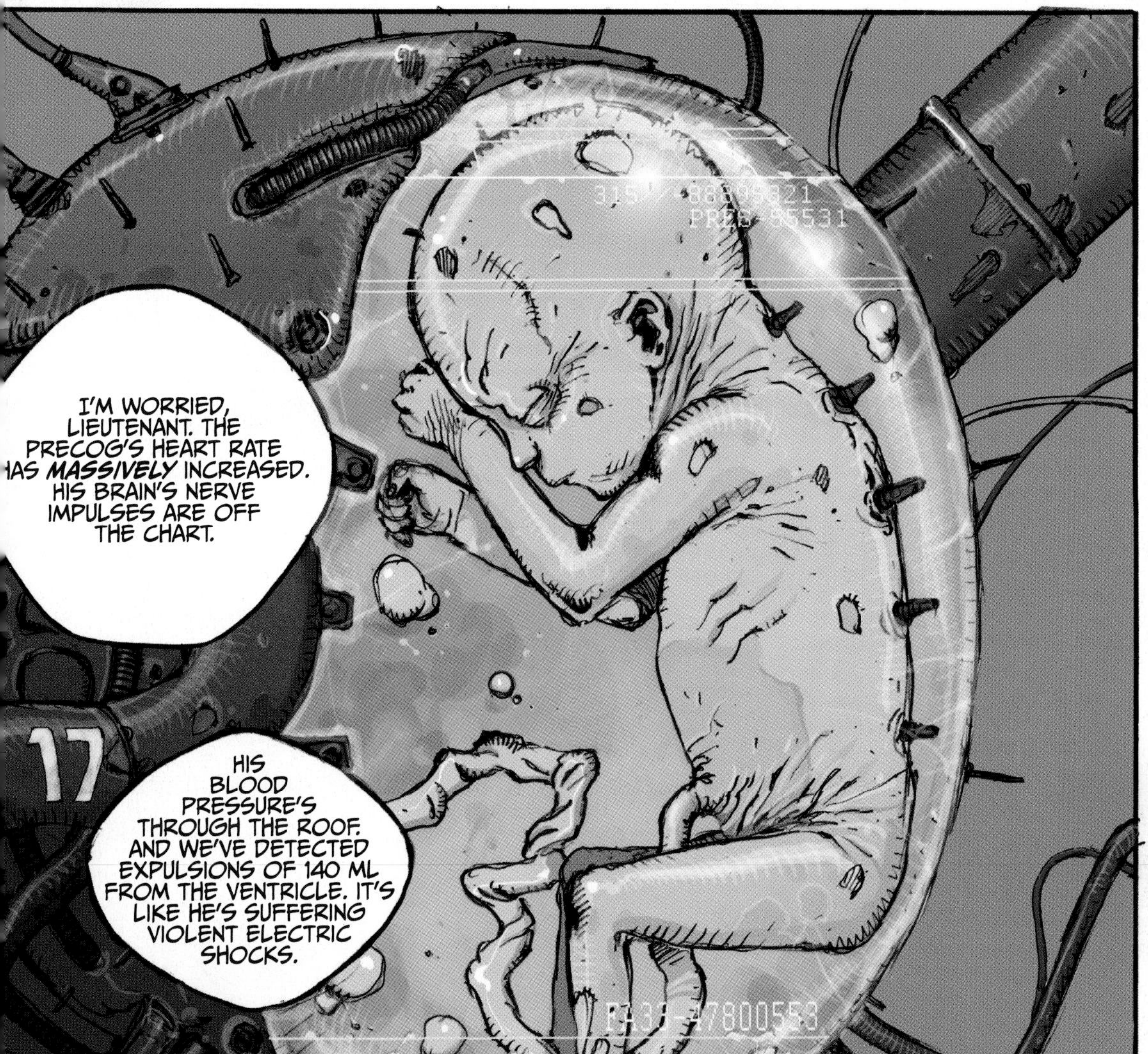
315 / 88895321
PREC-55531
I'M WORRIED, LIEUTENANT. THE PRECOG'S HEART RATE IAS *MASSIVELY* INCREASED. HIS BRAIN'S NERVE IMPULSES ARE OFF THE CHART.
17
HIS BLOOD PRESSURE'S THROUGH THE ROOF. AND WE'VE DETECTED EXPULSIONS OF 140 ML FROM THE VENTRICLE. IT'S LIKE HE'S SUFFERING VIOLENT ELECTRIC SHOCKS.
TERMINAL HB8055-

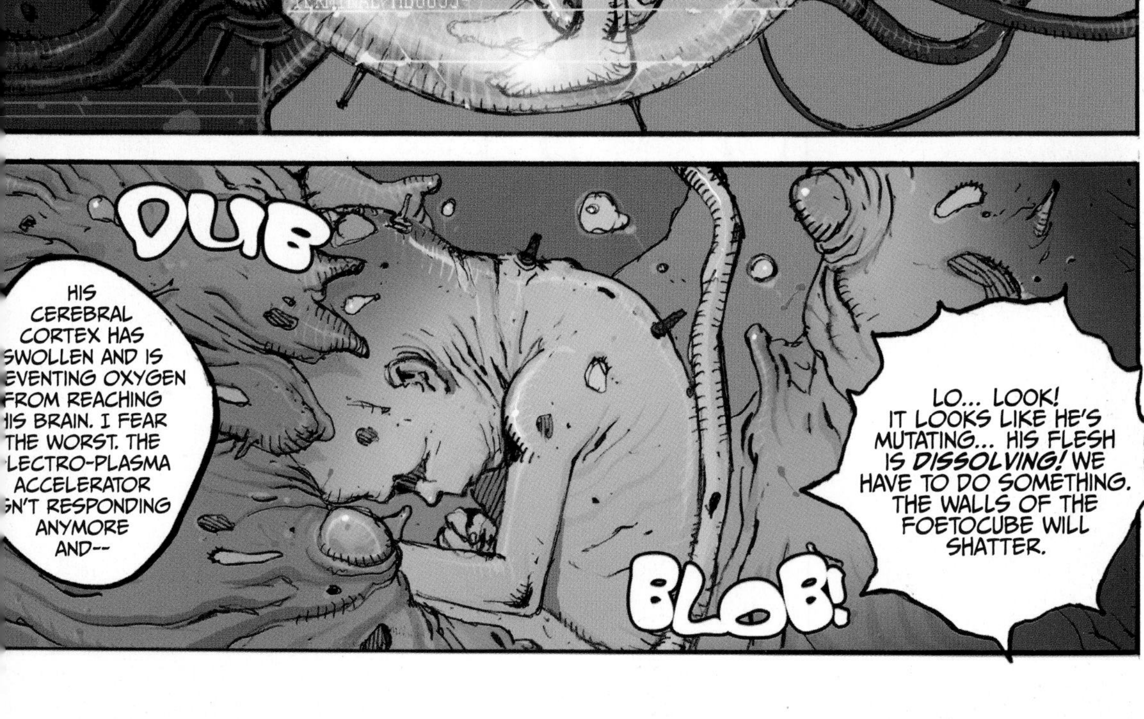
DUB
HIS CEREBRAL CORTEX HAS SWOLLEN AND IS EVENTING OXYGEN FROM REACHING IS BRAIN. I FEAR THE WORST. THE LECTRO-PLASMA ACCELERATOR SN'T RESPONDING ANYMORE AND--
LO... LOOK! IT LOOKS LIKE HE'S MUTATING... HIS FLESH IS *DISSOLVING!* WE HAVE TO DO SOMETHING. THE WALLS OF THE FOETOCUBE WILL SHATTER.
BLOB!

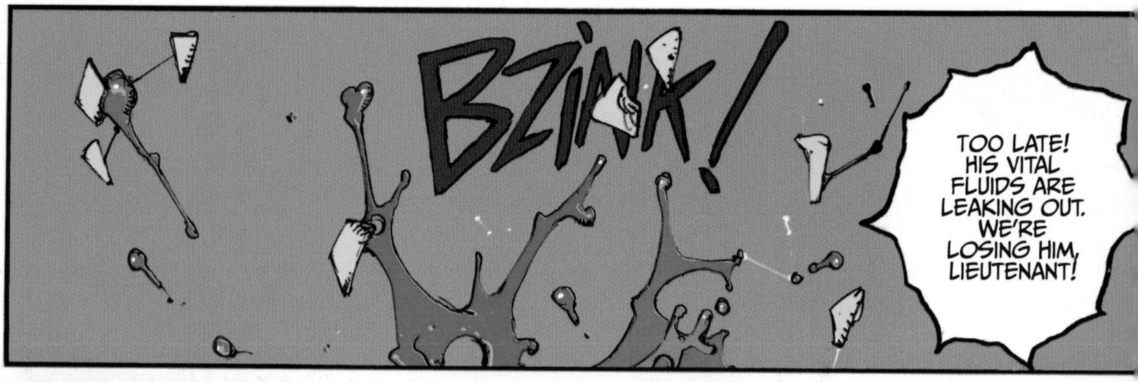
BZINK!
TOO LATE! HIS VITAL FLUIDS ARE LEAKING OUT. WE'RE LOSING HIM, LIEUTENANT!

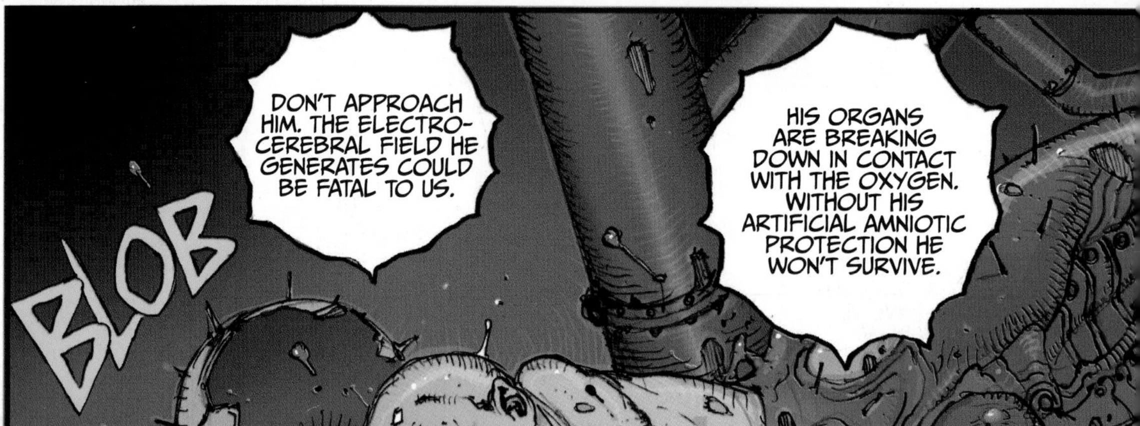
DON'T APPROACH HIM. THE ELECTRO-CEREBRAL FIELD HE GENERATES COULD BE FATAL TO US.
HIS ORGANS ARE BREAKING DOWN IN CONTACT WITH THE OXYGEN. WITHOUT HIS ARTIFICIAL AMNIOTIC PROTECTION HE WON'T SURVIVE.
BLOB

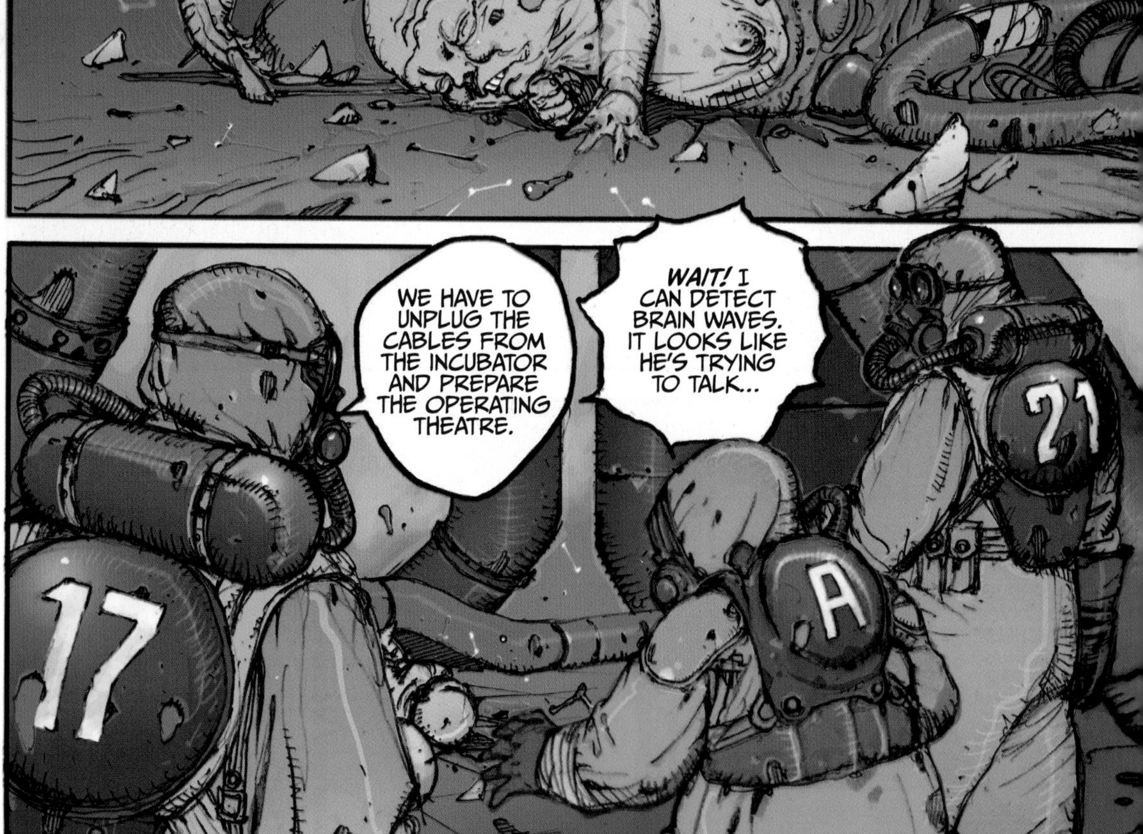
WE HAVE TO UNPLUG THE CABLES FROM THE INCUBATOR AND PREPARE THE OPERATING THEATRE.
WAIT! I CAN DETECT BRAIN WAVES. IT LOOKS LIKE HE'S TRYING TO TALK...
21
A
17

AAAAH! ANGER COME! VERY CLOSE! HHHHHHH!

RRREEEEEK! I... I FADE... I... I SEE... WEEEEEHHHHHHH THE MAN PIG. HE MUST... GAAARGL!

BLURBL

HE COMES! YOU MUST STOP HIM FROM... BEFORE...

DANGER! BLAAARG! QUIICK! THEY COME CLOSER.

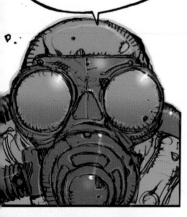

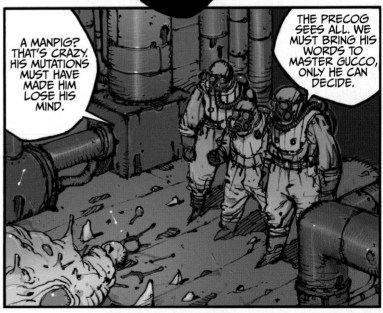

IT'S A DISASTER! HE'S DYING! THE PRECOG JUST GAVE HIS LAST VISION. WE HAVE TO WARN THE BARON AT ONCE.

A MANPIG? THAT'S CRAZY. HIS MUTATIONS MUST HAVE MADE HIM LOSE HIS MIND.

THE PRECOG SEES ALL. WE MUST BRING HIS WORDS TO MASTER GUCCO, ONLY HE CAN DECIDE.

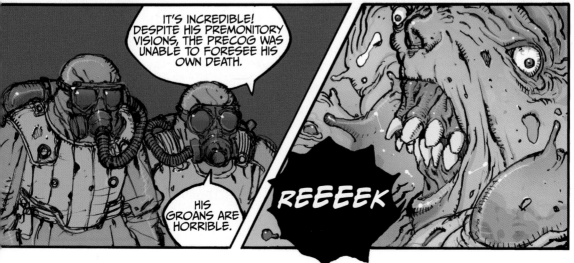

IT'S INCREDIBLE! DESPITE HIS PREMONITORY VISIONS, THE PRECOG WAS UNABLE TO FORESEE HIS OWN DEATH.

HIS GROANS ARE HORRIBLE.

REEEEK!

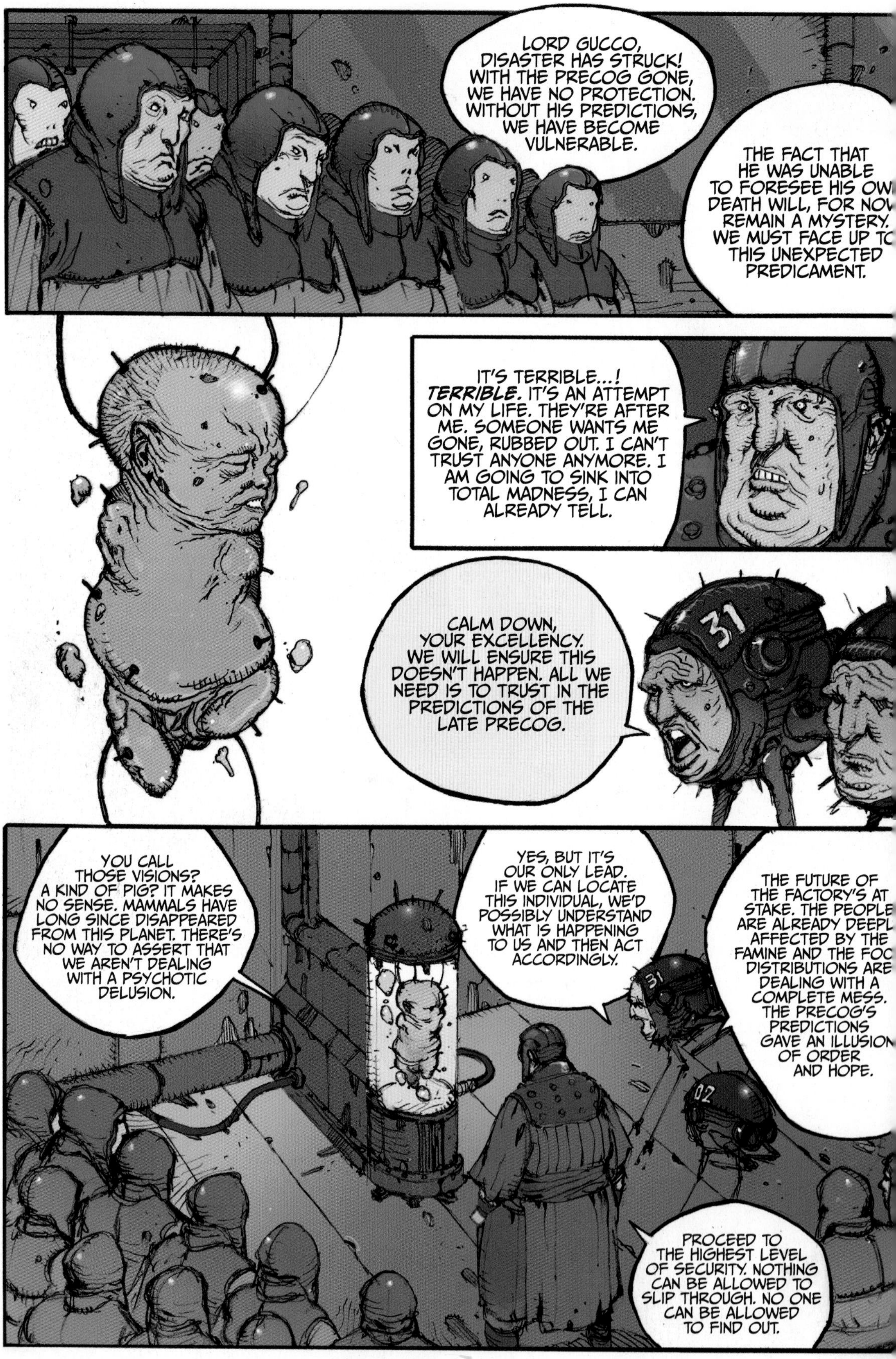
LORD GUCCO, DISASTER HAS STRUCK! WITH THE PRECOG GONE, WE HAVE NO PROTECTION. WITHOUT HIS PREDICTIONS, WE HAVE BECOME VULNERABLE.
THE FACT THAT HE WAS UNABLE TO FORESEE HIS OW DEATH WILL, FOR NOW REMAIN A MYSTERY. WE MUST FACE UP TO THIS UNEXPECTED PREDICAMENT.
IT'S TERRIBLE...! *TERRIBLE.* IT'S AN ATTEMPT ON MY LIFE. THEY'RE AFTER ME. SOMEONE WANTS ME GONE, RUBBED OUT. I CAN'T TRUST ANYONE ANYMORE. I AM GOING TO SINK INTO TOTAL MADNESS, I CAN ALREADY TELL.
CALM DOWN, YOUR EXCELLENCY. WE WILL ENSURE THIS DOESN'T HAPPEN. ALL WE NEED IS TO TRUST IN THE PREDICTIONS OF THE LATE PRECOG.
31
YOU CALL THOSE VISIONS? A KIND OF PIG? IT MAKES NO SENSE. MAMMALS HAVE LONG SINCE DISAPPEARED FROM THIS PLANET. THERE'S NO WAY TO ASSERT THAT WE AREN'T DEALING WITH A PSYCHOTIC DELUSION.
YES, BUT IT'S OUR ONLY LEAD. IF WE CAN LOCATE THIS INDIVIDUAL, WE'D POSSIBLY UNDERSTAND WHAT IS HAPPENING TO US AND THEN ACT ACCORDINGLY.
THE FUTURE OF THE FACTORY'S AT STAKE. THE PEOPLE ARE ALREADY DEEPL AFFECTED BY THE FAMINE AND THE FOO DISTRIBUTIONS ARE DEALING WITH A COMPLETE MESS. THE PRECOG'S PREDICTIONS GAVE AN ILLUSION OF ORDER AND HOPE.
02
PROCEED TO THE HIGHEST LEVEL OF SECURITY. NOTHING CAN BE ALLOWED TO SLIP THROUGH. NO ONE CAN BE ALLOWED TO FIND OUT.

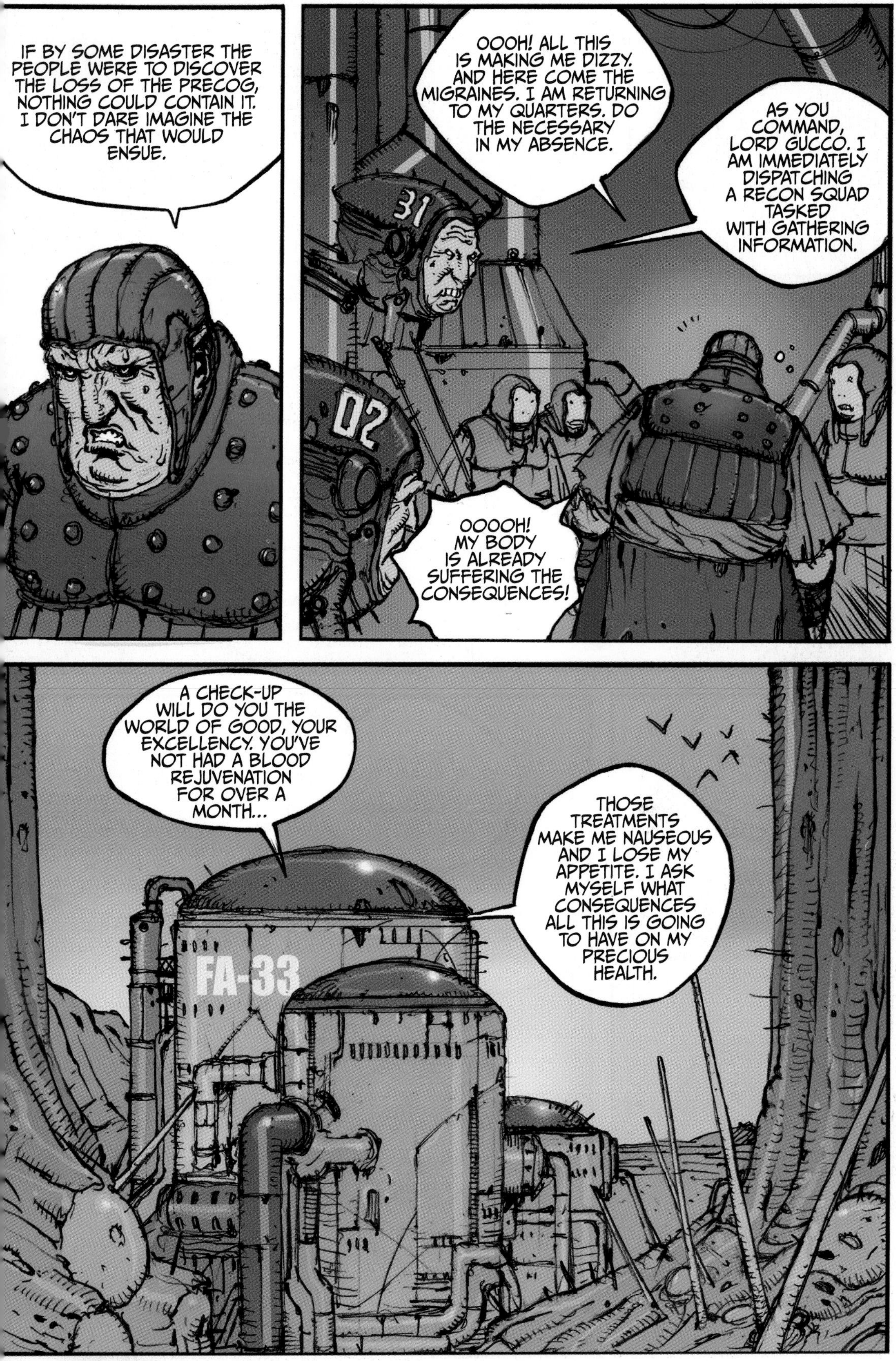
IF BY SOME DISASTER THE PEOPLE WERE TO DISCOVER THE LOSS OF THE PRECOG, NOTHING COULD CONTAIN IT. I DON'T DARE IMAGINE THE CHAOS THAT WOULD ENSUE.
OOOH! ALL THIS IS MAKING ME DIZZY. AND HERE COME THE MIGRAINES. I AM RETURNING TO MY QUARTERS. DO THE NECESSARY IN MY ABSENCE.
AS YOU COMMAND, LORD GUCCO. I AM IMMEDIATELY DISPATCHING A RECON SQUAD TASKED WITH GATHERING INFORMATION.
31
02
OOOOH! MY BODY IS ALREADY SUFFERING THE CONSEQUENCES!
A CHECK-UP WILL DO YOU THE WORLD OF GOOD, YOUR EXCELLENCY. YOU'VE NOT HAD A BLOOD REJUVENATION FOR OVER A MONTH...
THOSE TREATMENTS MAKE ME NAUSEOUS AND I LOSE MY APPETITE. I ASK MYSELF WHAT CONSEQUENCES ALL THIS IS GOING TO HAVE ON MY PRECIOUS HEALTH.
FA-33

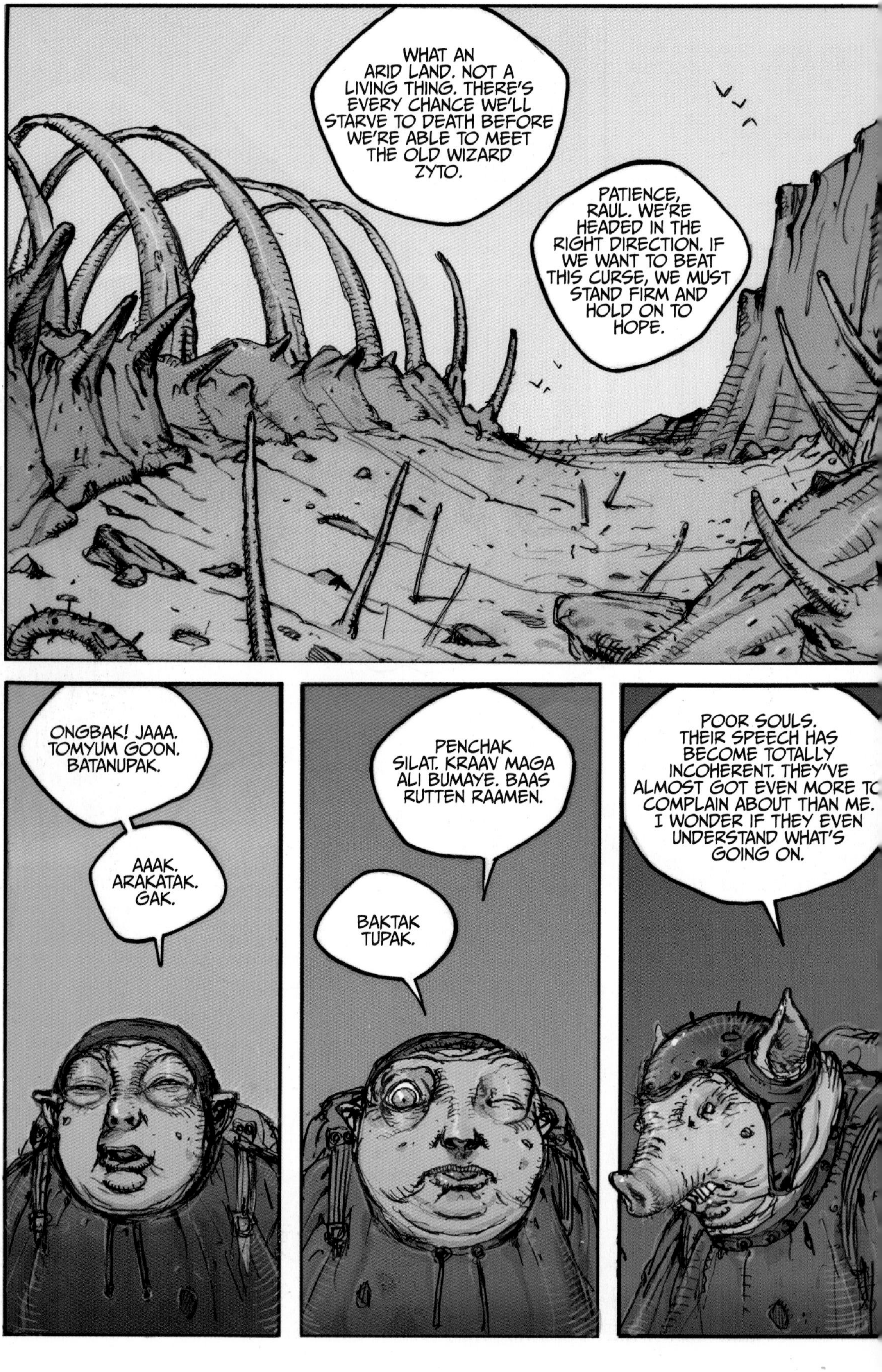
WHAT AN ARID LAND. NOT A LIVING THING. THERE'S EVERY CHANCE WE'LL STARVE TO DEATH BEFORE WE'RE ABLE TO MEET THE OLD WIZARD ZYTO.
PATIENCE, RAUL. WE'RE HEADED IN THE RIGHT DIRECTION. IF WE WANT TO BEAT THIS CURSE, WE MUST STAND FIRM AND HOLD ON TO HOPE.
ONGBAK! JAAA. TOMYUM GOON. BATANUPAK.
AAAK. ARAKATAK. GAK.
PENCHAK SILAT. KRAAV MAGA ALI BUMAYE. BAAS RUTTEN RAAMEN.
BAKTAK TUPAK.
POOR SOULS. THEIR SPEECH HAS BECOME TOTALLY INCOHERENT. THEY'VE ALMOST GOT EVEN MORE TO COMPLAIN ABOUT THAN ME. I WONDER IF THEY EVEN UNDERSTAND WHAT'S GOING ON.

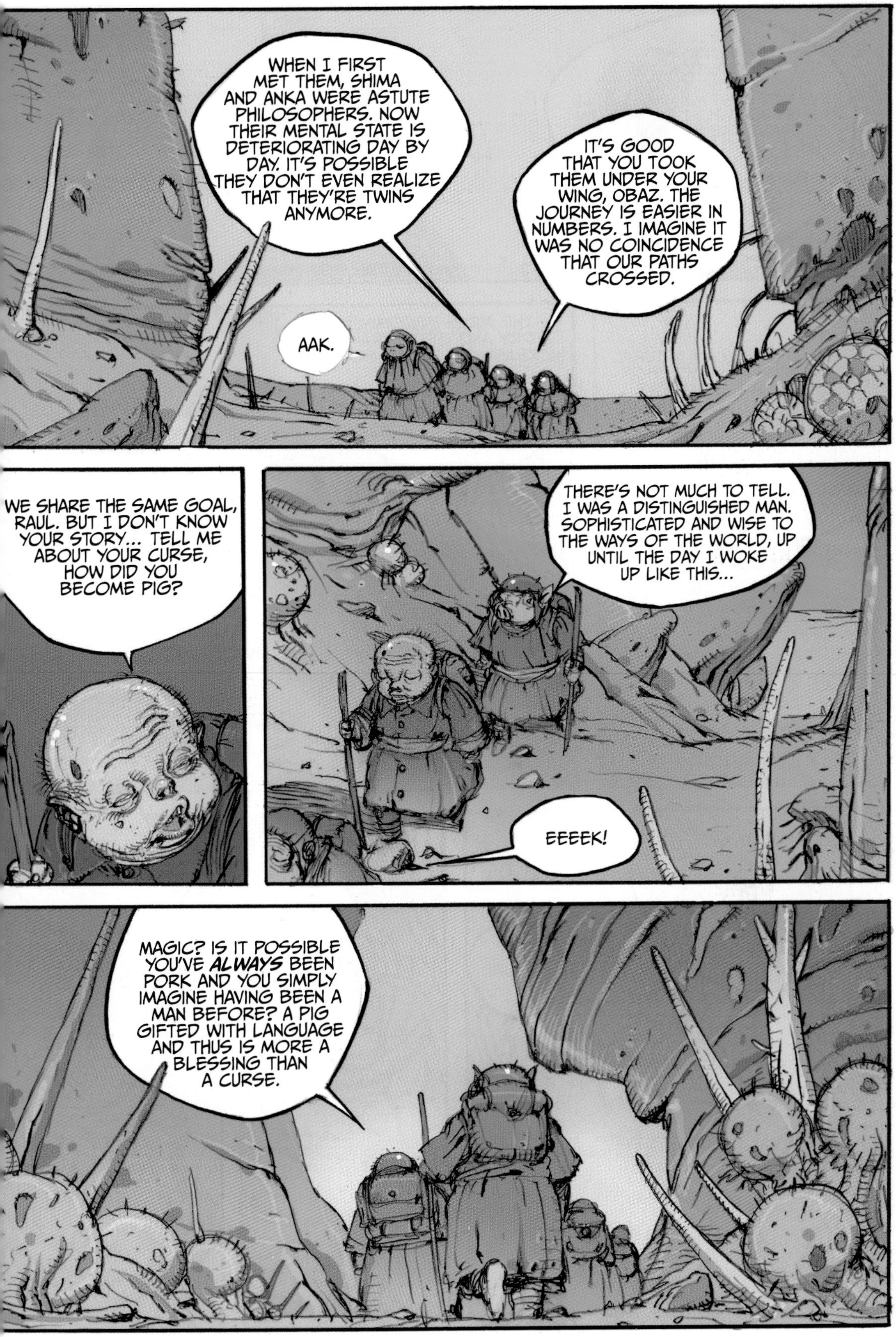
WHEN I FIRST MET THEM, SHIMA AND ANKA WERE ASTUTE PHILOSOPHERS. NOW THEIR MENTAL STATE IS DETERIORATING DAY BY DAY. IT'S POSSIBLE THEY DON'T EVEN REALIZE THAT THEY'RE TWINS ANYMORE.
AAK.
IT'S GOOD THAT YOU TOOK THEM UNDER YOUR WING, OBAZ. THE JOURNEY IS EASIER IN NUMBERS. I IMAGINE IT WAS NO COINCIDENCE THAT OUR PATHS CROSSED.
WE SHARE THE SAME GOAL, RAUL. BUT I DON'T KNOW YOUR STORY... TELL ME ABOUT YOUR CURSE, HOW DID YOU BECOME PIG?
THERE'S NOT MUCH TO TELL. I WAS A DISTINGUISHED MAN. SOPHISTICATED AND WISE TO THE WAYS OF THE WORLD, UP UNTIL THE DAY I WOKE UP LIKE THIS...
EEEEK!
MAGIC? IS IT POSSIBLE YOU'VE *ALWAYS* BEEN PORK AND YOU SIMPLY IMAGINE HAVING BEEN A MAN BEFORE? A PIG GIFTED WITH LANGUAGE AND THUS IS MORE A BLESSING THAN A CURSE.

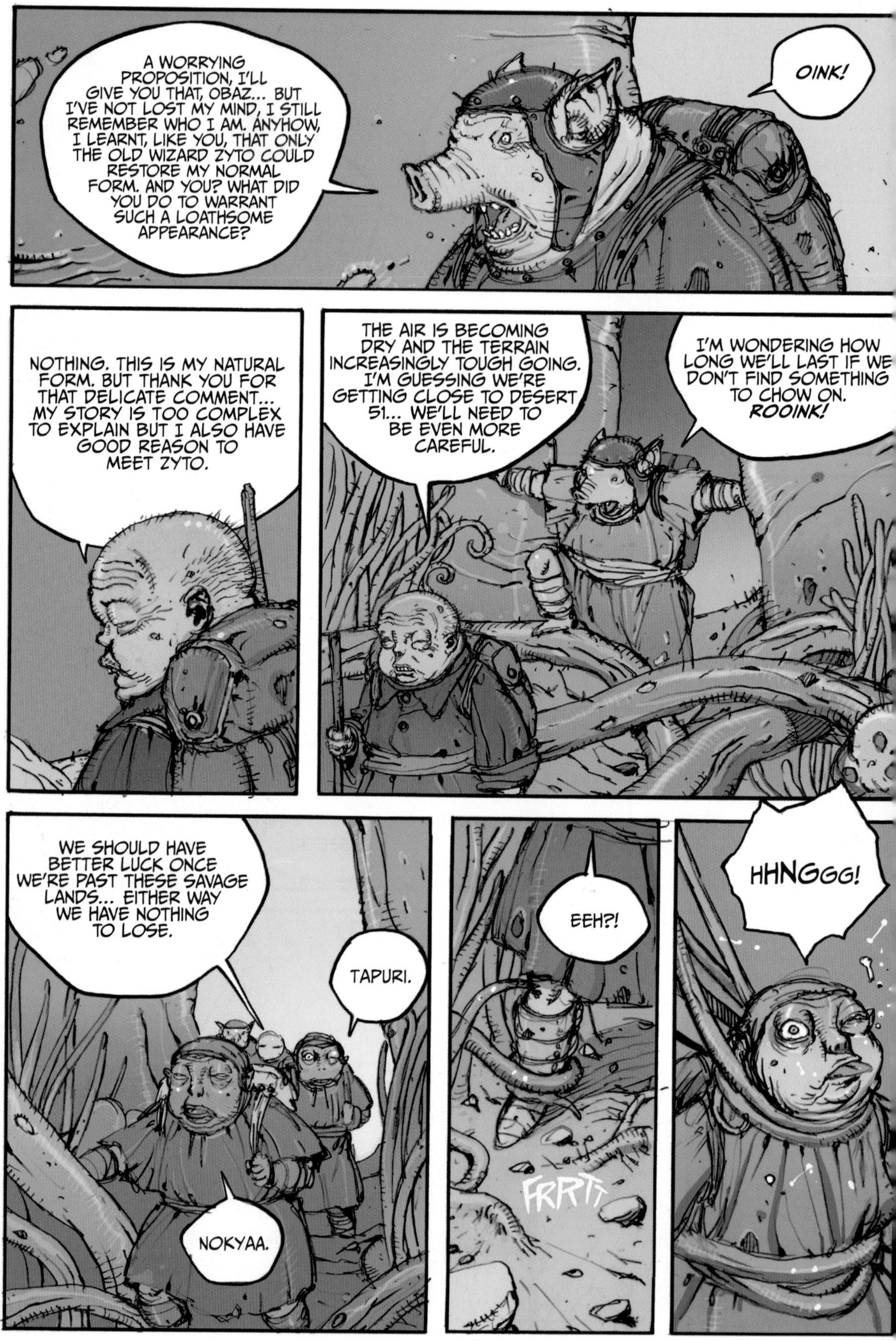
A WORRYING PROPOSITION, I'LL GIVE YOU THAT, OBAZ... BUT I'VE NOT LOST MY MIND, I STILL REMEMBER WHO I AM. ANYHOW, I LEARNT, LIKE YOU, THAT ONLY THE OLD WIZARD ZYTO COULD RESTORE MY NORMAL FORM. AND YOU? WHAT DID YOU DO TO WARRANT SUCH A LOATHSOME APPEARANCE?
OINK!
NOTHING. THIS IS MY NATURAL FORM. BUT THANK YOU FOR THAT DELICATE COMMENT... MY STORY IS TOO COMPLEX TO EXPLAIN BUT I ALSO HAVE GOOD REASON TO MEET ZYTO.
THE AIR IS BECOMING DRY AND THE TERRAIN INCREASINGLY TOUGH GOING. I'M GUESSING WE'RE GETTING CLOSE TO DESERT 51... WE'LL NEED TO BE EVEN MORE CAREFUL.
I'M WONDERING HOW LONG WE'LL LAST IF WE DON'T FIND SOMETHING TO CHOW ON. *ROOINK!*
WE SHOULD HAVE BETTER LUCK ONCE WE'RE PAST THESE SAVAGE LANDS... EITHER WAY WE HAVE NOTHING TO LOSE.
TAPURI.
NOKYAA.
EEH?!
FRRTT
HHNGGG!

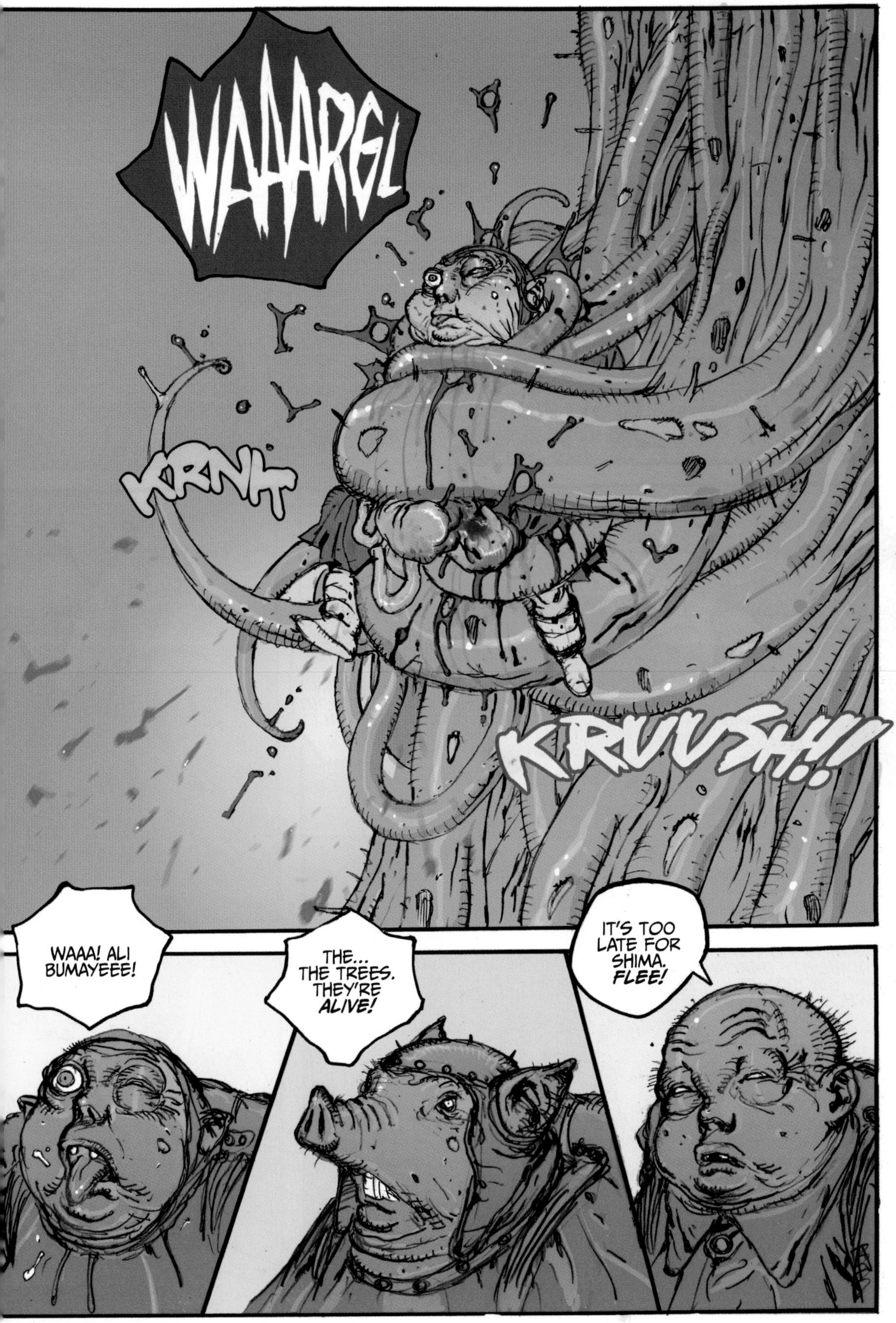
WAAARGL
KRNK
KRUUSH!!
WAAA! ALI BUMAYEEE!
THE... THE TREES. THEY'RE *ALIVE!*
IT'S TOO LATE FOR SHIMA. *FLEE!*

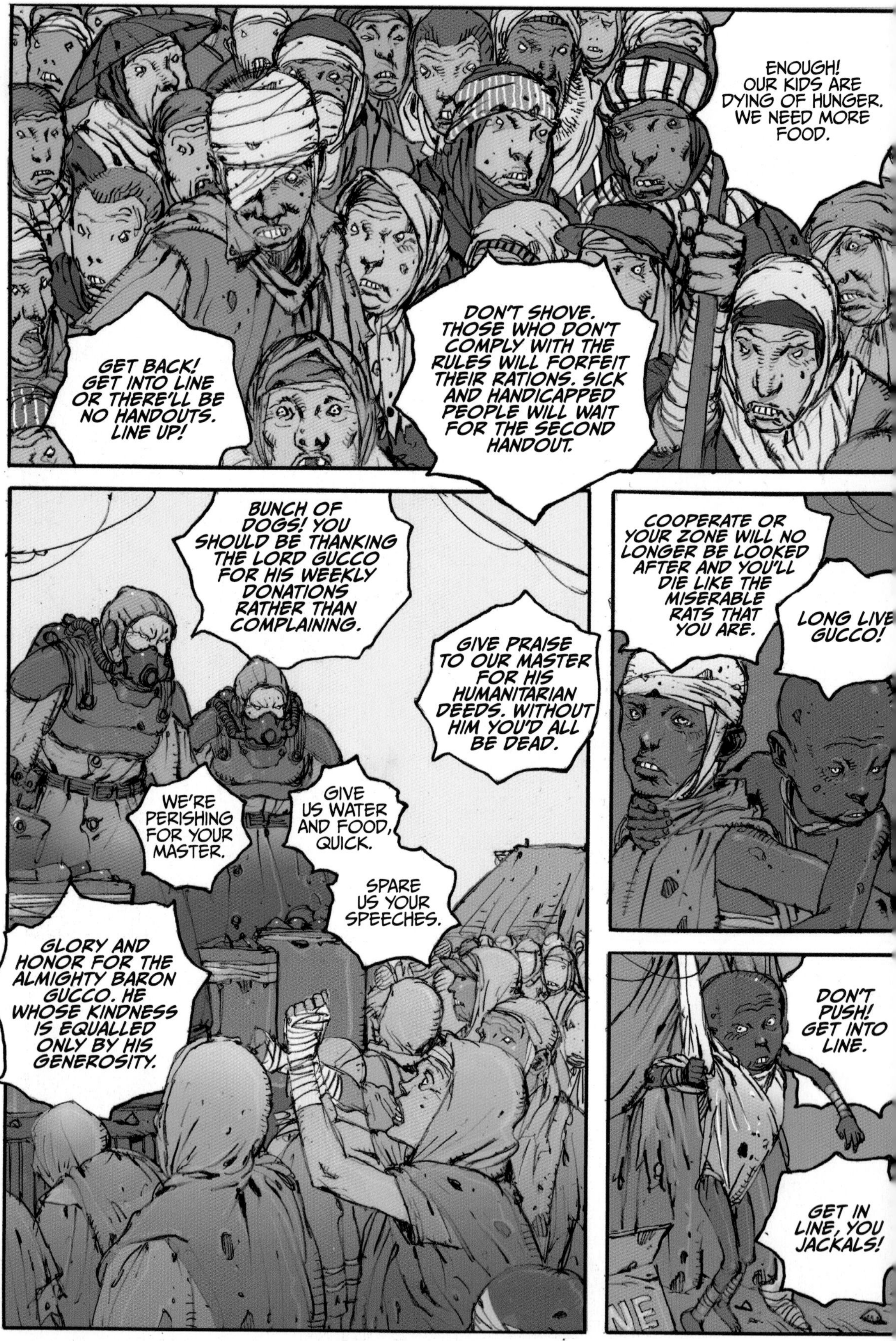
ENOUGH! OUR KIDS ARE DYING OF HUNGER. WE NEED MORE FOOD.
GET BACK! GET INTO LINE OR THERE'LL BE NO HANDOUTS. LINE UP!
DON'T SHOVE. THOSE WHO DON'T COMPLY WITH THE RULES WILL FORFEIT THEIR RATIONS. SICK AND HANDICAPPED PEOPLE WILL WAIT FOR THE SECOND HANDOUT.
BUNCH OF DOGS! YOU SHOULD BE THANKING THE LORD GUCCO FOR HIS WEEKLY DONATIONS RATHER THAN COMPLAINING.
GIVE PRAISE TO OUR MASTER FOR HIS HUMANITARIAN DEEDS. WITHOUT HIM YOU'D ALL BE DEAD.
WE'RE PERISHING FOR YOUR MASTER.
GIVE US WATER AND FOOD, QUICK.
SPARE US YOUR SPEECHES.
GLORY AND HONOR FOR THE ALMIGHTY BARON GUCCO. HE WHOSE KINDNESS IS EQUALLED ONLY BY HIS GENEROSITY.
COOPERATE OR YOUR ZONE WILL NO LONGER BE LOOKED AFTER AND YOU'LL DIE LIKE THE MISERABLE RATS THAT YOU ARE.
LONG LIVE GUCCO!
DON'T PUSH! GET INTO LINE.
GET IN LINE, YOU JACKALS!

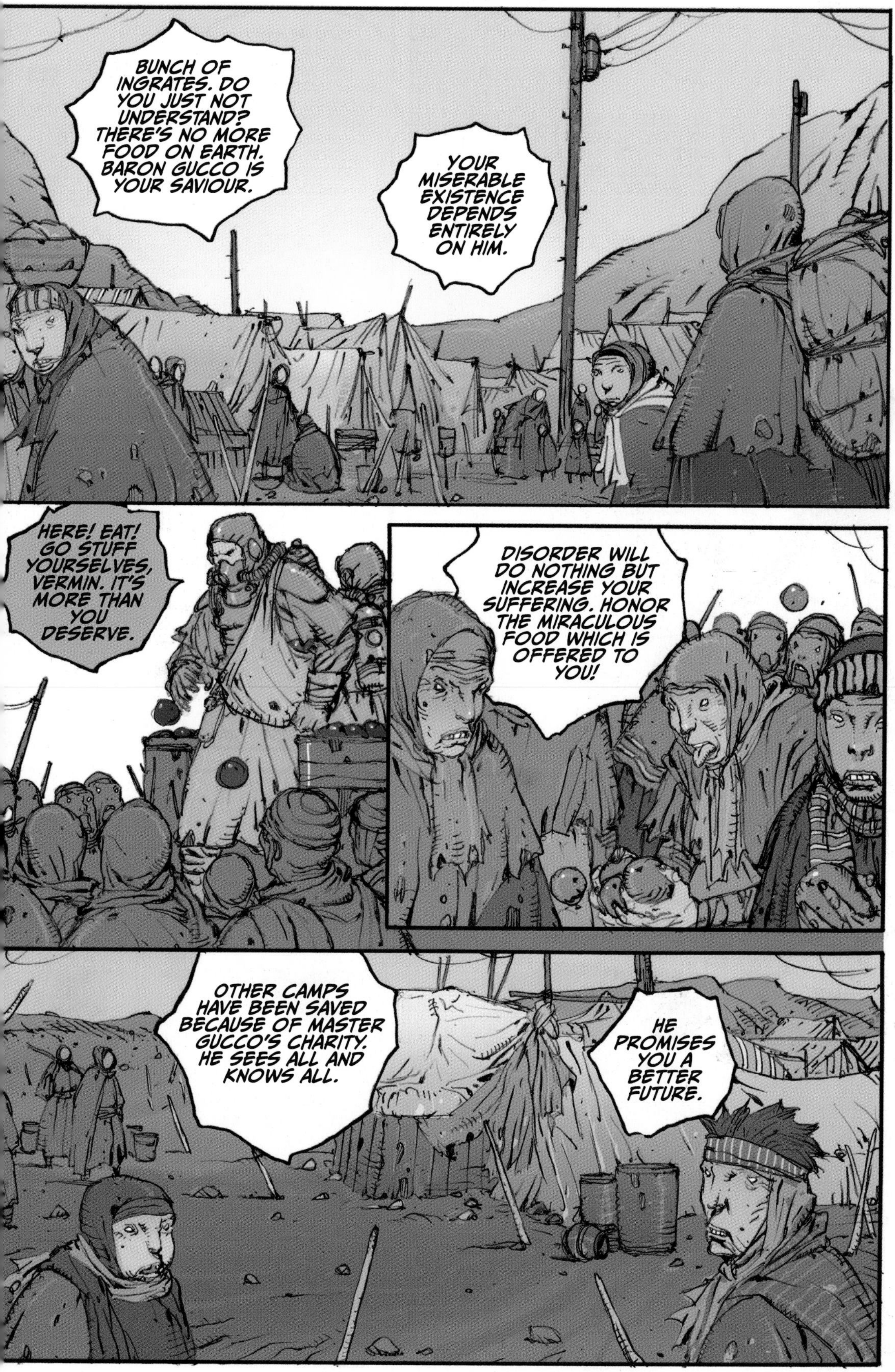
BUNCH OF INGRATES. DO YOU JUST NOT UNDERSTAND? THERE'S NO MORE FOOD ON EARTH. BARON GUCCO IS YOUR SAVIOUR.
YOUR MISERABLE EXISTENCE DEPENDS ENTIRELY ON HIM.
HERE! EAT! GO STUFF YOURSELVES, VERMIN. IT'S MORE THAN YOU DESERVE.
DISORDER WILL DO NOTHING BUT INCREASE YOUR SUFFERING. HONOR THE MIRACULOUS FOOD WHICH IS OFFERED TO YOU!
OTHER CAMPS HAVE BEEN SAVED BECAUSE OF MASTER GUCCO'S CHARITY. HE SEES ALL AND KNOWS ALL.
HE PROMISES YOU A BETTER FUTURE.

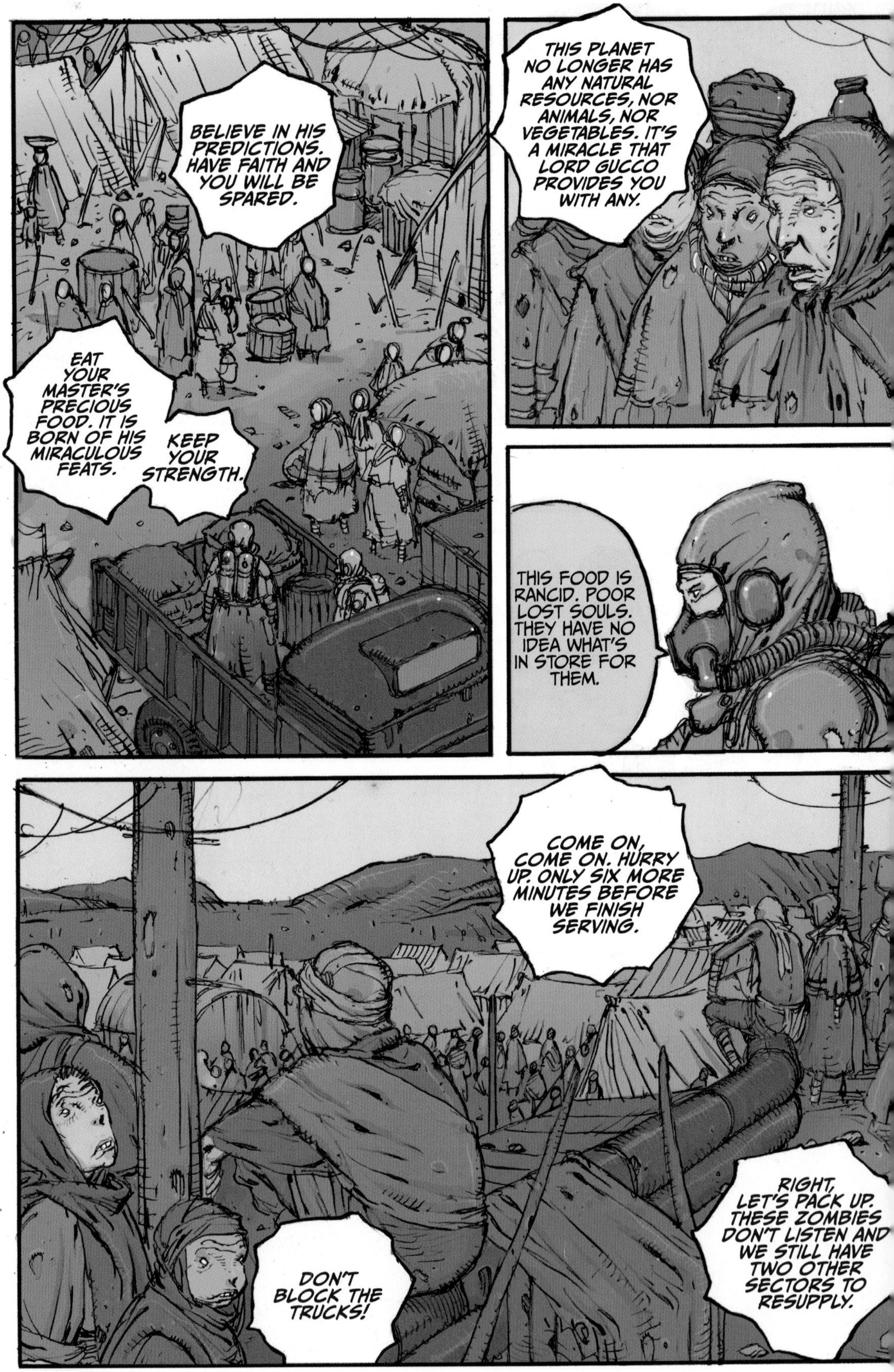

BELIEVE IN HIS PREDICTIONS. HAVE FAITH AND YOU WILL BE SPARED.
EAT YOUR MASTER'S PRECIOUS FOOD. IT IS BORN OF HIS MIRACULOUS FEATS.
KEEP YOUR STRENGTH.
THIS PLANET NO LONGER HAS ANY NATURAL RESOURCES, NOR ANIMALS, NOR VEGETABLES. IT'S A MIRACLE THAT LORD GUCCO PROVIDES YOU WITH ANY.
THIS FOOD IS RANCID. POOR LOST SOULS. THEY HAVE NO IDEA WHAT'S IN STORE FOR THEM.
COME ON, COME ON. HURRY UP. ONLY SIX MORE MINUTES BEFORE WE FINISH SERVING.
DON'T BLOCK THE TRUCKS!
RIGHT, LET'S PACK UP. THESE ZOMBIES DON'T LISTEN AND WE STILL HAVE TWO OTHER SECTORS TO RESUPPLY.

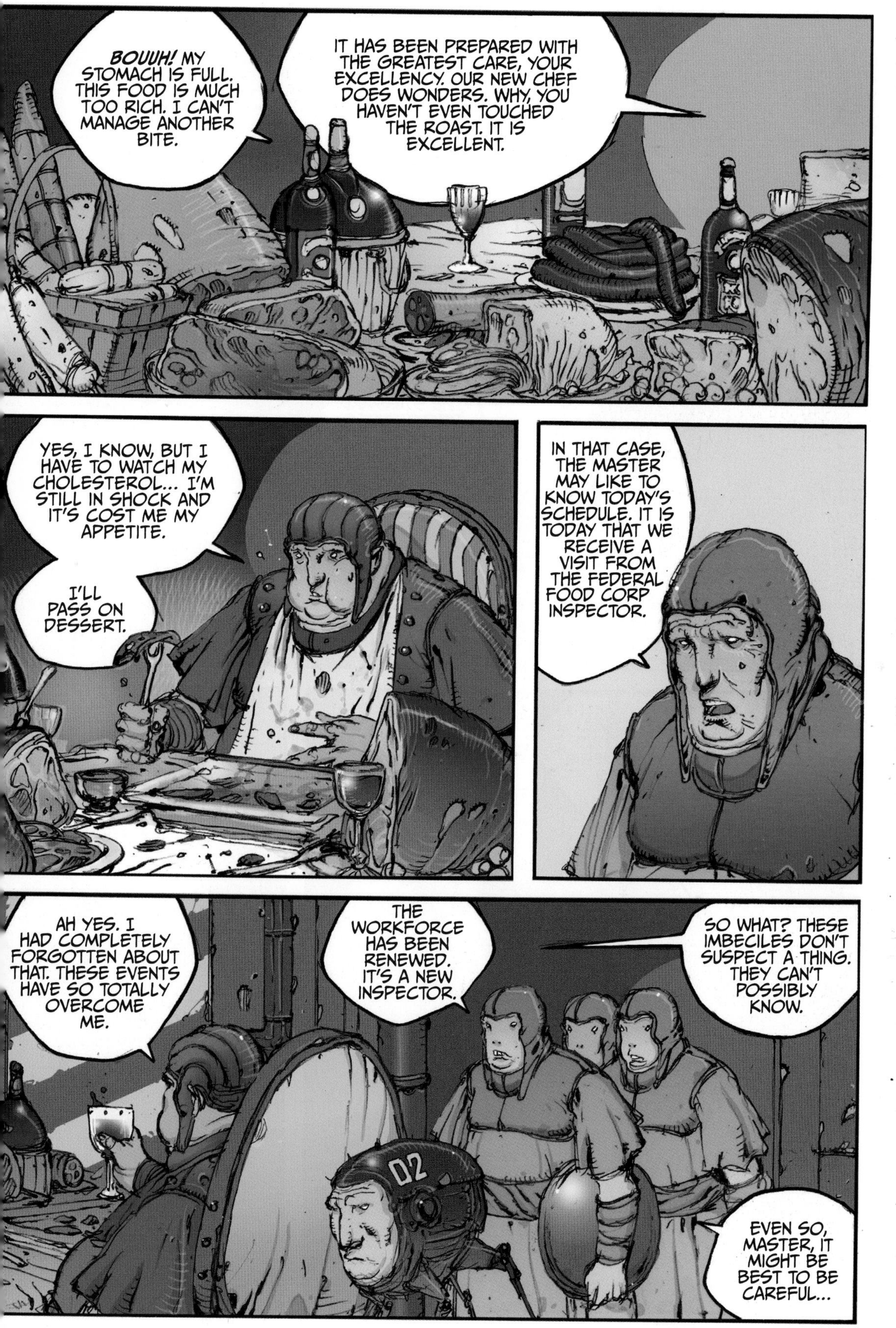
BOUUH! MY STOMACH IS FULL. THIS FOOD IS MUCH TOO RICH. I CAN'T MANAGE ANOTHER BITE.
IT HAS BEEN PREPARED WITH THE GREATEST CARE, YOUR EXCELLENCY. OUR NEW CHEF DOES WONDERS. WHY, YOU HAVEN'T EVEN TOUCHED THE ROAST. IT IS EXCELLENT.
YES, I KNOW, BUT I HAVE TO WATCH MY CHOLESTEROL... I'M STILL IN SHOCK AND IT'S COST ME MY APPETITE.
I'LL PASS ON DESSERT.
IN THAT CASE, THE MASTER MAY LIKE TO KNOW TODAY'S SCHEDULE. IT IS TODAY THAT WE RECEIVE A VISIT FROM THE FEDERAL FOOD CORP INSPECTOR.
AH YES. I HAD COMPLETELY FORGOTTEN ABOUT THAT. THESE EVENTS HAVE SO TOTALLY OVERCOME ME.
THE WORKFORCE HAS BEEN RENEWED. IT'S A NEW INSPECTOR.
SO WHAT? THESE IMBECILES DON'T SUSPECT A THING. THEY CAN'T POSSIBLY KNOW.
02
EVEN SO, MASTER, IT MIGHT BE BEST TO BE CAREFUL...

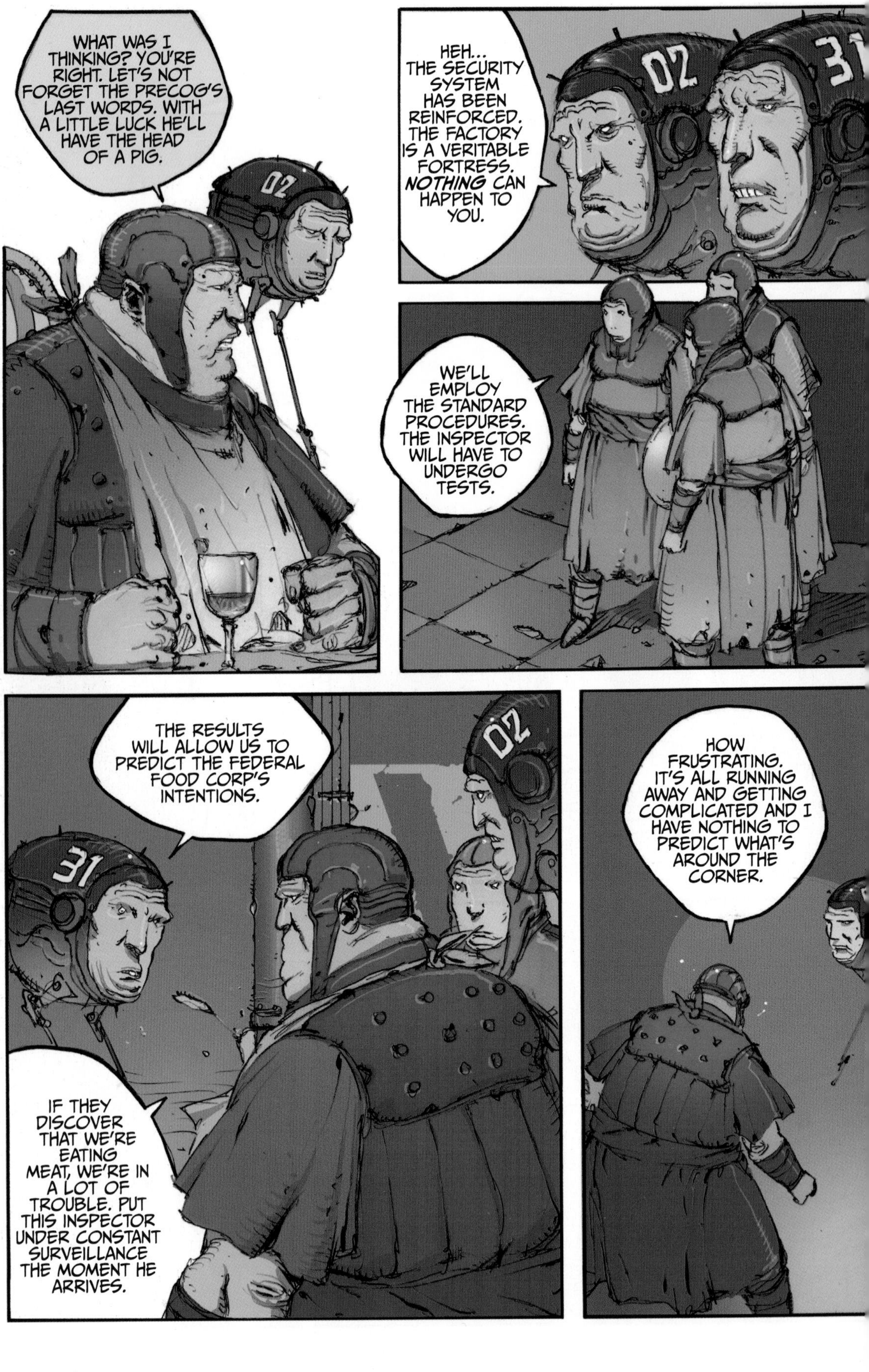

WHAT WAS I THINKING? YOU'RE RIGHT. LET'S NOT FORGET THE PRECOG'S LAST WORDS. WITH A LITTLE LUCK HE'LL HAVE THE HEAD OF A PIG.
HEH... THE SECURITY SYSTEM HAS BEEN REINFORCED. THE FACTORY IS A VERITABLE FORTRESS. *NOTHING* CAN HAPPEN TO YOU.
02
31
WE'LL EMPLOY THE STANDARD PROCEDURES. THE INSPECTOR WILL HAVE TO UNDERGO TESTS.
THE RESULTS WILL ALLOW US TO PREDICT THE FEDERAL FOOD CORP'S INTENTIONS.
IF THEY DISCOVER THAT WE'RE EATING MEAT, WE'RE IN A LOT OF TROUBLE. PUT THIS INSPECTOR UNDER CONSTANT SURVEILLANCE THE MOMENT HE ARRIVES.
HOW FRUSTRATING. IT'S ALL RUNNING AWAY AND GETTING COMPLICATED AND I HAVE NOTHING TO PREDICT WHAT'S AROUND THE CORNER.

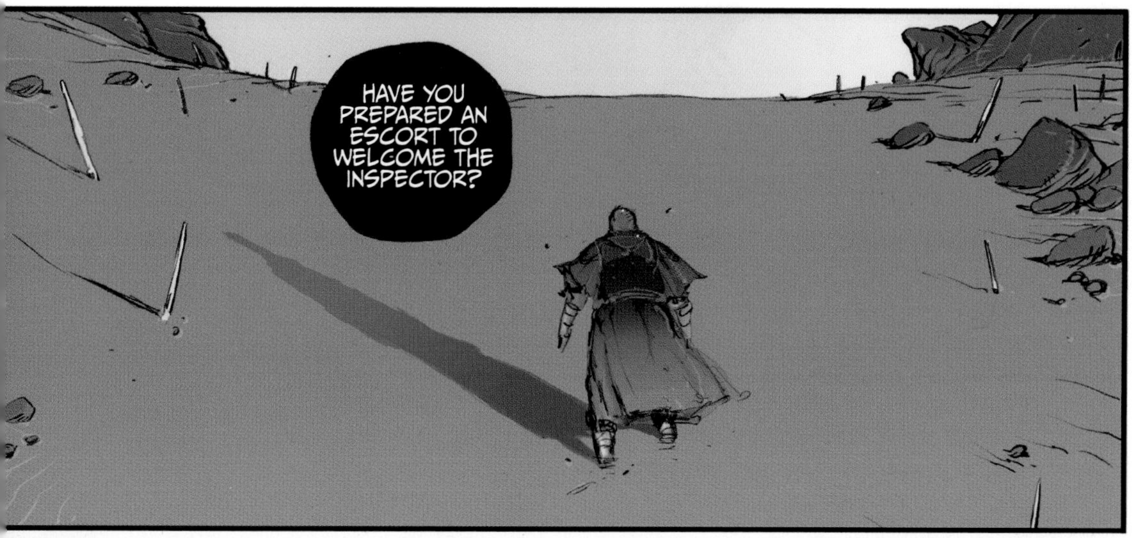
HAVE YOU PREPARED AN ESCORT TO WELCOME THE INSPECTOR?

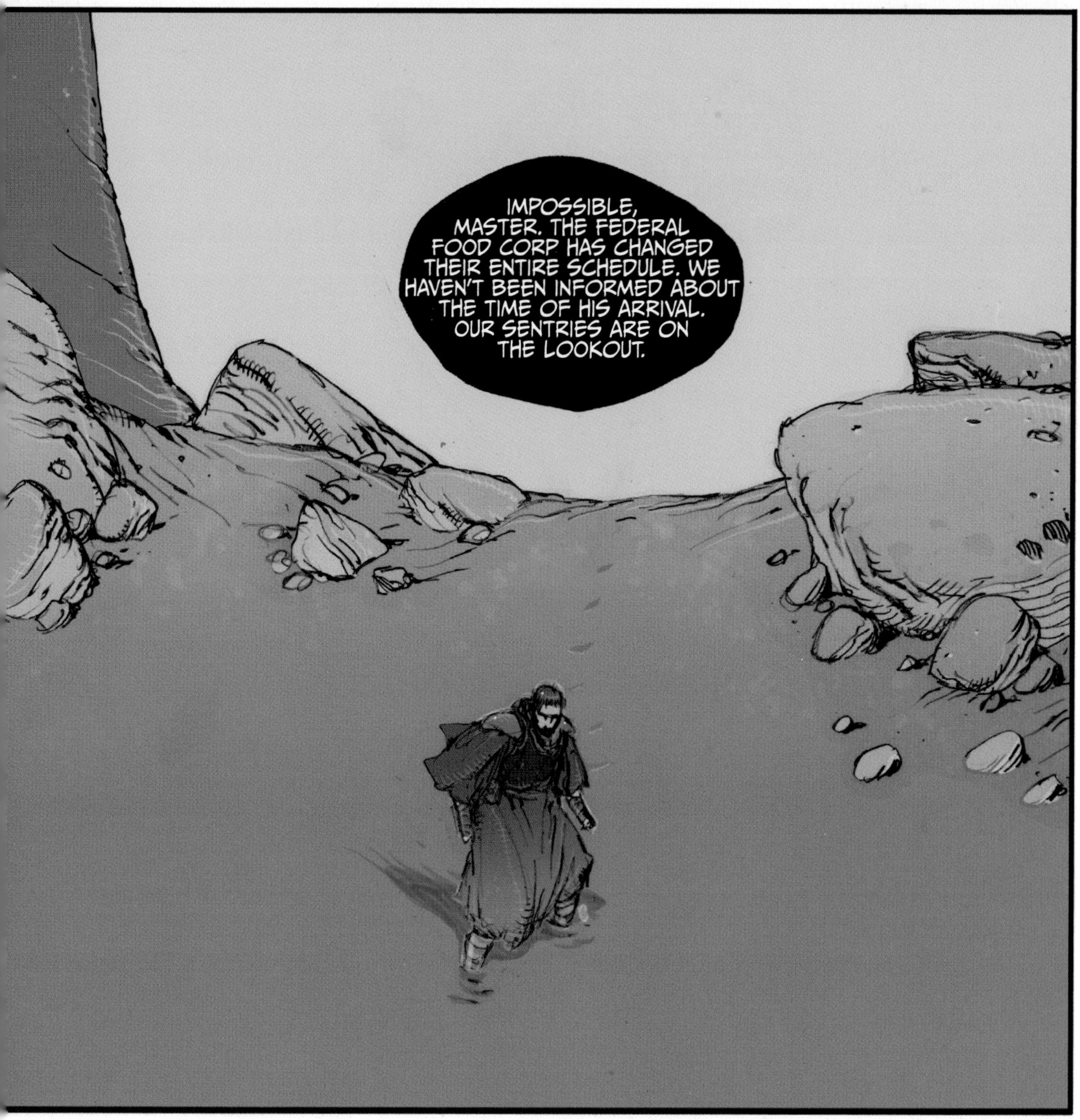
IMPOSSIBLE, MASTER. THE FEDERAL FOOD CORP HAS CHANGED THEIR ENTIRE SCHEDULE. WE HAVEN'T BEEN INFORMED ABOUT THE TIME OF HIS ARRIVAL. OUR SENTRIES ARE ON THE LOOKOUT.

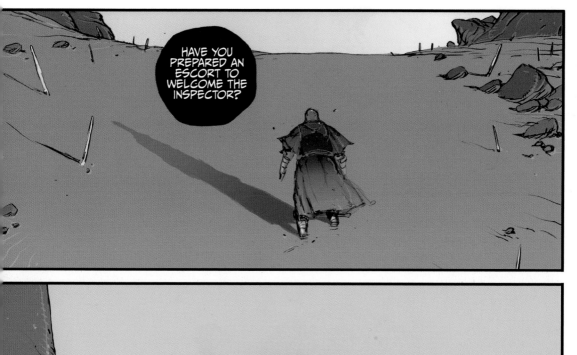

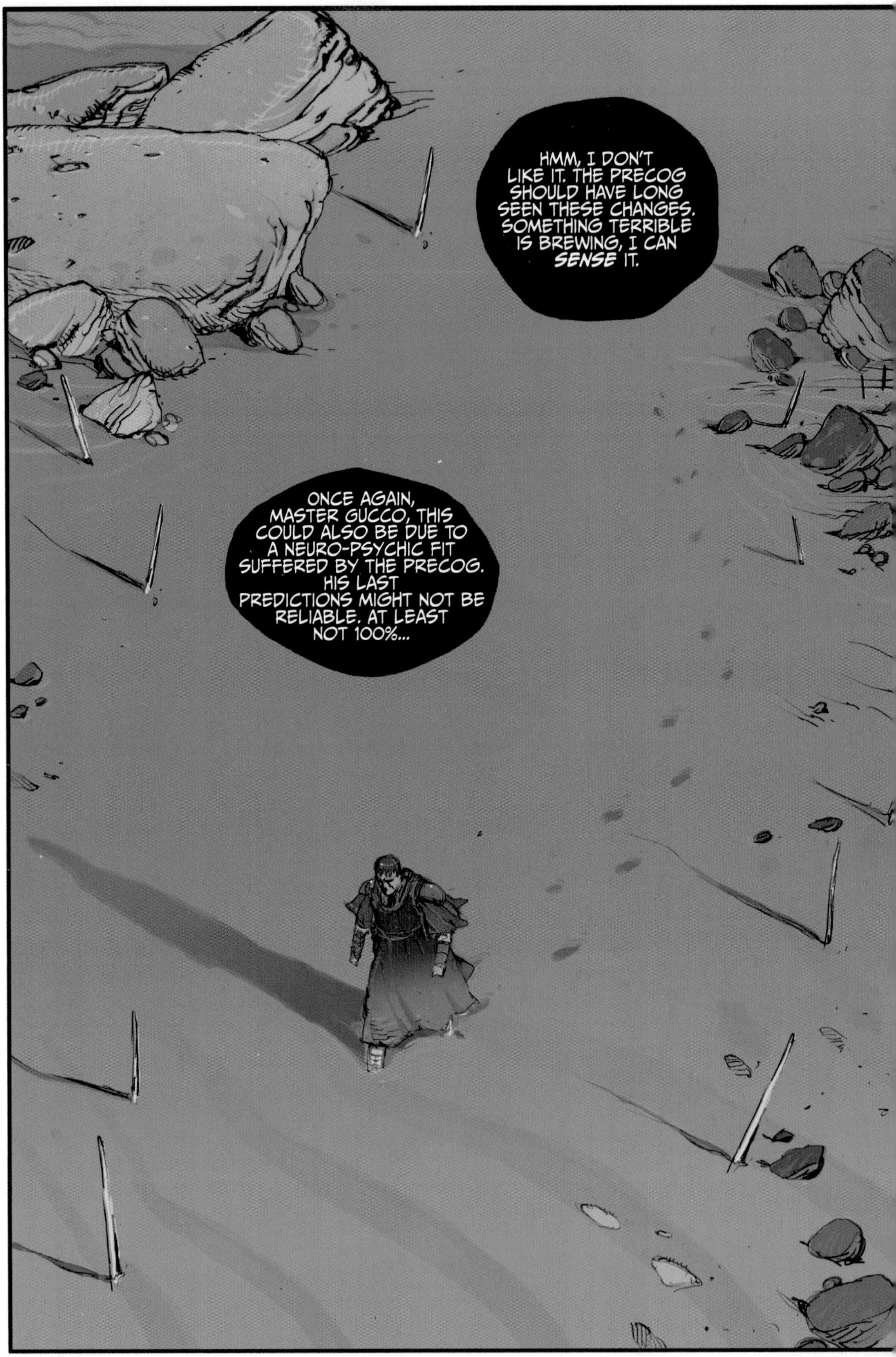
HMM, I DON'T LIKE IT. THE PRECOG SHOULD HAVE LONG SEEN THESE CHANGES. SOMETHING TERRIBLE IS BREWING, I CAN SENSE IT.
ONCE AGAIN, MASTER GUCCO, THIS COULD ALSO BE DUE TO A NEURO-PSYCHIC FIT SUFFERED BY THE PRECOG. HIS LAST PREDICTIONS MIGHT NOT BE RELIABLE. AT LEAST NOT 100%...

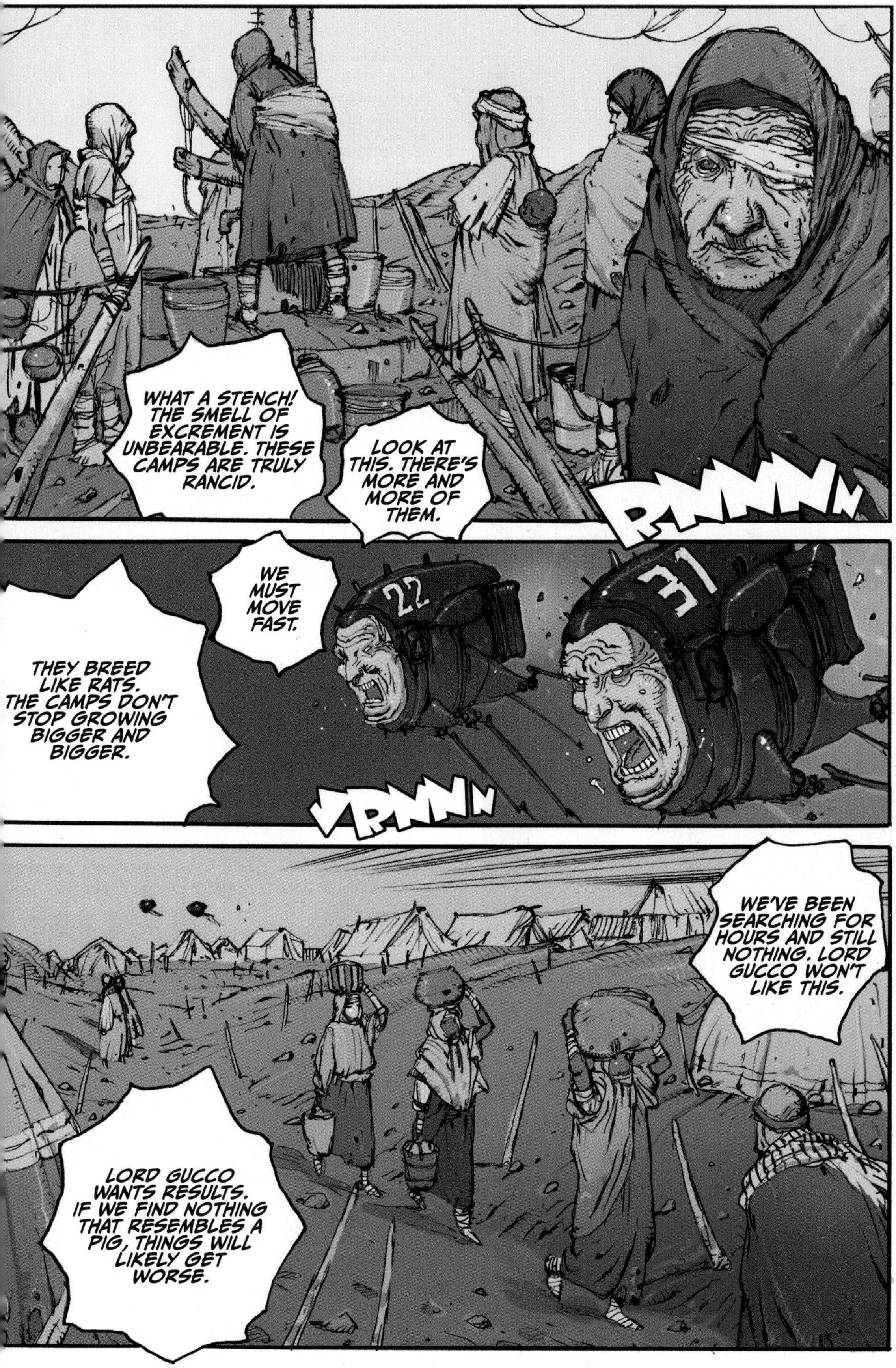
WHAT A STENCH! THE SMELL OF EXCREMENT IS UNBEARABLE. THESE CAMPS ARE TRULY RANCID.
LOOK AT THIS. THERE'S MORE AND MORE OF THEM.
RMMMN
WE MUST MOVE FAST.
THEY BREED LIKE RATS. THE CAMPS DON'T STOP GROWING BIGGER AND BIGGER.
22
31
VRMMN
WE'VE BEEN SEARCHING FOR HOURS AND STILL NOTHING. LORD GUCCO WON'T LIKE THIS.
LORD GUCCO WANTS RESULTS. IF WE FIND NOTHING THAT RESEMBLES A PIG, THINGS WILL LIKELY GET WORSE.

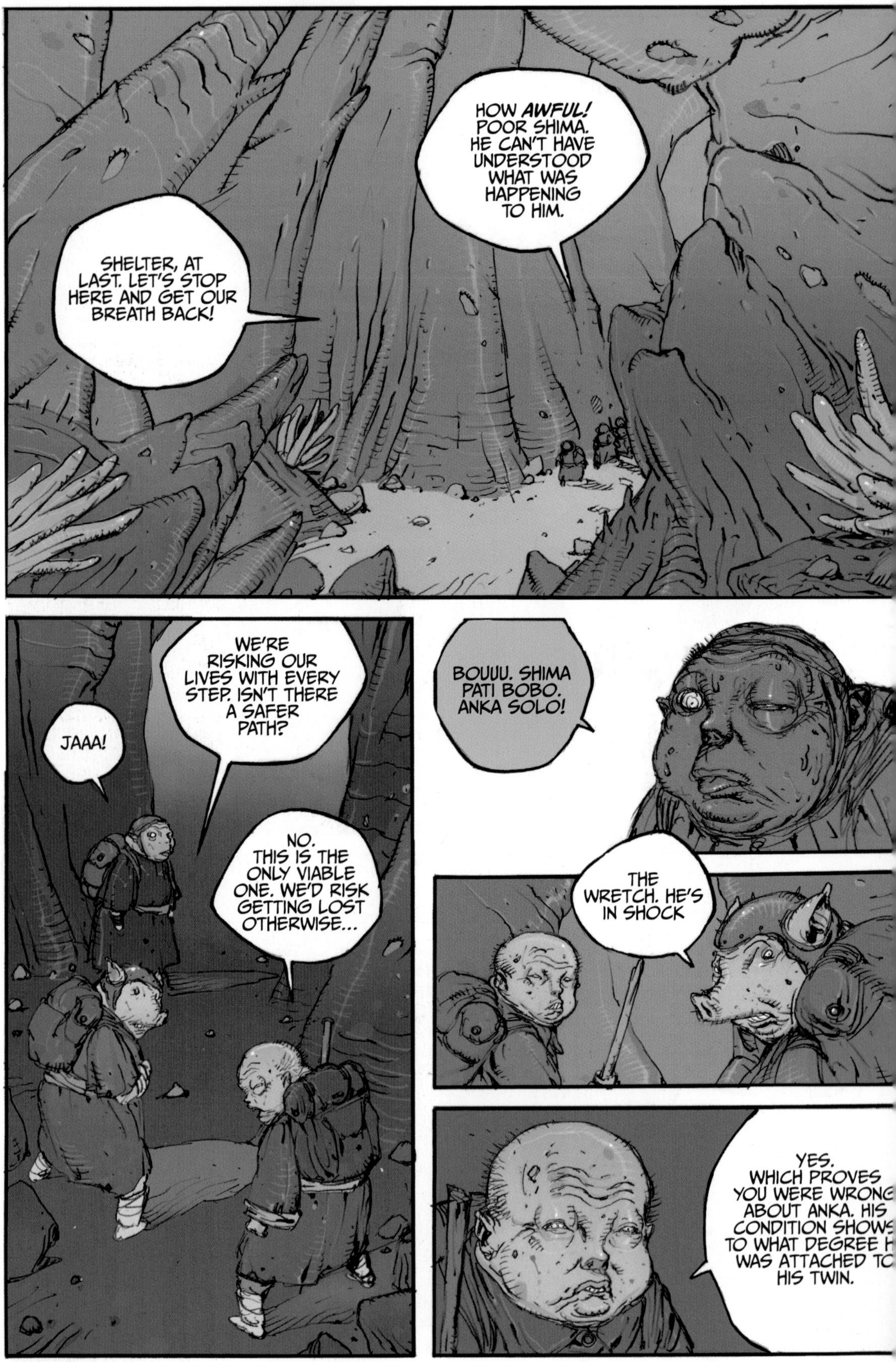
SHELTER, AT LAST. LET'S STOP HERE AND GET OUR BREATH BACK!
HOW AWFUL! POOR SHIMA. HE CAN'T HAVE UNDERSTOOD WHAT WAS HAPPENING TO HIM.
JAAA!
WE'RE RISKING OUR LIVES WITH EVERY STEP. ISN'T THERE A SAFER PATH?
NO. THIS IS THE ONLY VIABLE ONE. WE'D RISK GETTING LOST OTHERWISE...
BOUUU. SHIMA PATI BOBO. ANKA SOLO!
THE WRETCH. HE'S IN SHOCK
YES. WHICH PROVES YOU WERE WRONG ABOUT ANKA. HIS CONDITION SHOWS TO WHAT DEGREE H WAS ATTACHED TO HIS TWIN.

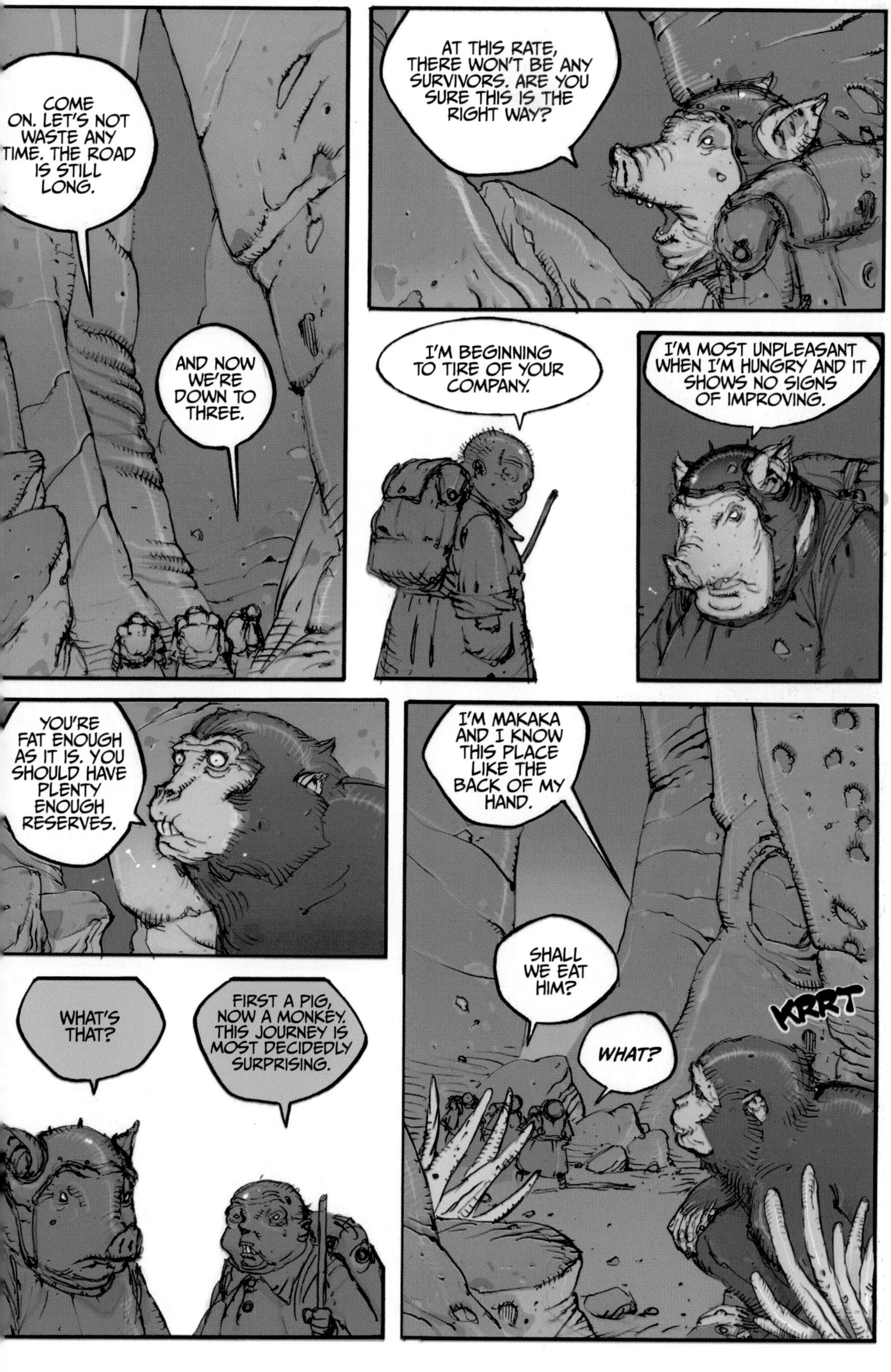
COME ON. LET'S NOT WASTE ANY TIME. THE ROAD IS STILL LONG.
AT THIS RATE, THERE WON'T BE ANY SURVIVORS. ARE YOU SURE THIS IS THE RIGHT WAY?
AND NOW WE'RE DOWN TO THREE.
I'M BEGINNING TO TIRE OF YOUR COMPANY.
I'M MOST UNPLEASANT WHEN I'M HUNGRY AND IT SHOWS NO SIGNS OF IMPROVING.
YOU'RE FAT ENOUGH AS IT IS. YOU SHOULD HAVE PLENTY ENOUGH RESERVES.
I'M MAKAKA AND I KNOW THIS PLACE LIKE THE BACK OF MY HAND.
WHAT'S THAT?
FIRST A PIG, NOW A MONKEY. THIS JOURNEY IS MOST DECIDEDLY SURPRISING.
SHALL WE EAT HIM?
WHAT?
KRRT

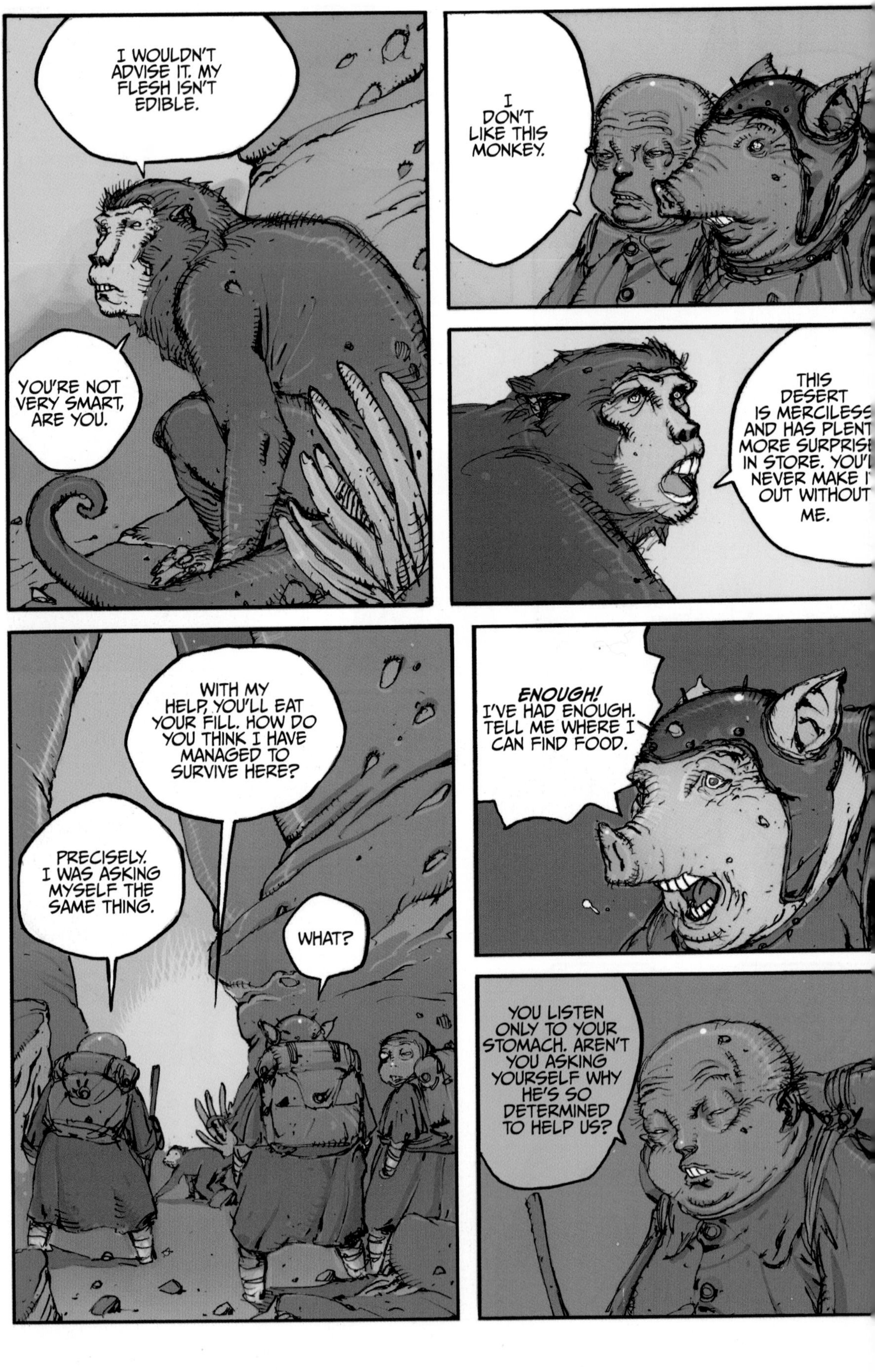
I WOULDN'T ADVISE IT. MY FLESH ISN'T EDIBLE.
YOU'RE NOT VERY SMART, ARE YOU.
I DON'T LIKE THIS MONKEY.
THIS DESERT IS MERCILESS AND HAS PLENT MORE SURPRIS IN STORE. YOU'L NEVER MAKE I OUT WITHOUT ME.
WITH MY HELP, YOU'LL EAT YOUR FILL. HOW DO YOU THINK I HAVE MANAGED TO SURVIVE HERE?
PRECISELY. I WAS ASKING MYSELF THE SAME THING.
WHAT?
ENOUGH! I'VE HAD ENOUGH. TELL ME WHERE I CAN FIND FOOD.
YOU LISTEN ONLY TO YOUR STOMACH. AREN'T YOU ASKING YOURSELF WHY HE'S SO DETERMINED TO HELP US?

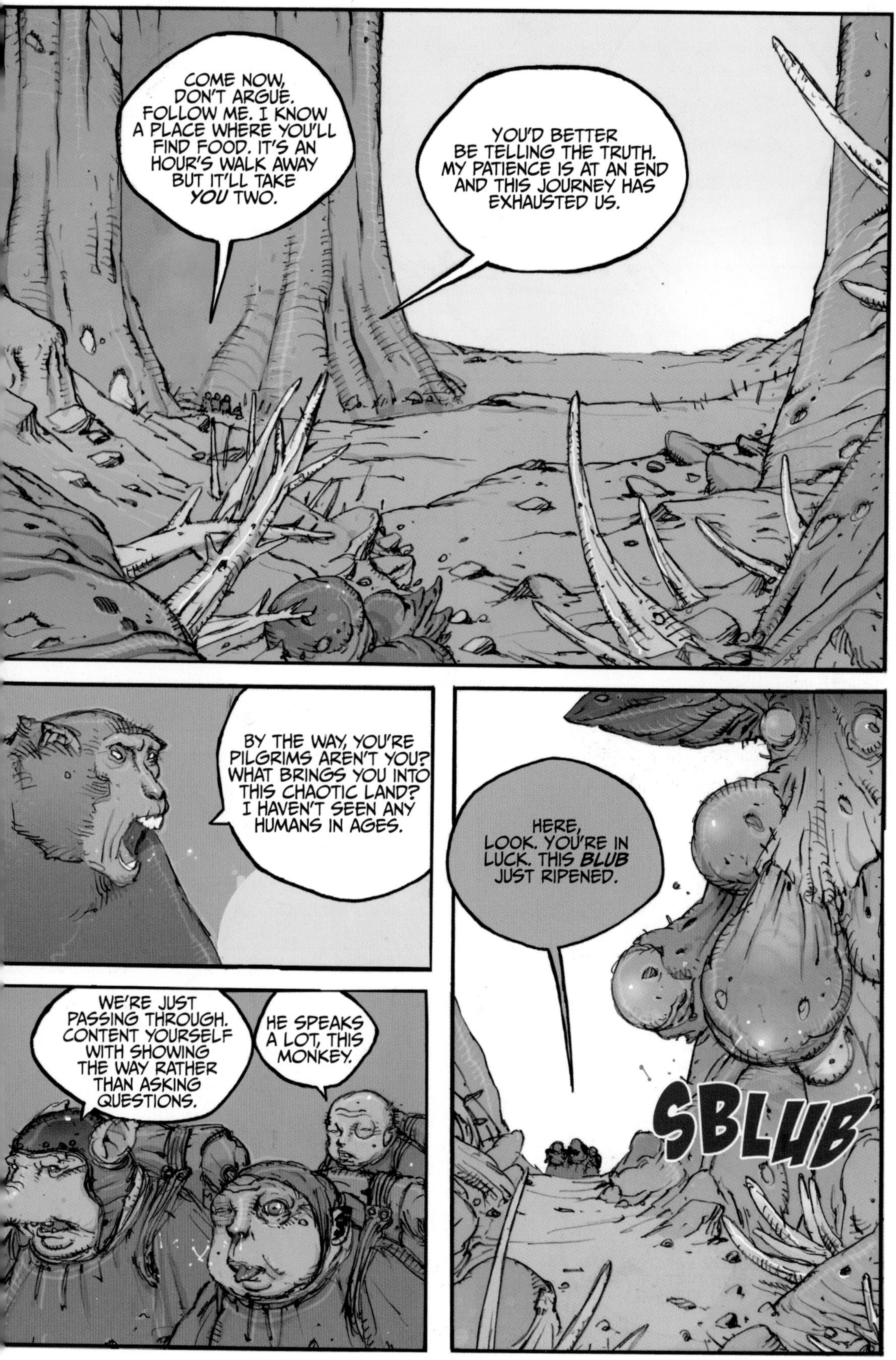
COME NOW, DON'T ARGUE. FOLLOW ME. I KNOW A PLACE WHERE YOU'LL FIND FOOD. IT'S AN HOUR'S WALK AWAY BUT IT'LL TAKE *YOU* TWO.
YOU'D BETTER BE TELLING THE TRUTH. MY PATIENCE IS AT AN END AND THIS JOURNEY HAS EXHAUSTED US.
BY THE WAY, YOU'RE PILGRIMS AREN'T YOU? WHAT BRINGS YOU INTO THIS CHAOTIC LAND? I HAVEN'T SEEN ANY HUMANS IN AGES.
WE'RE JUST PASSING THROUGH. CONTENT YOURSELF WITH SHOWING THE WAY RATHER THAN ASKING QUESTIONS.
HE SPEAKS A LOT, THIS MONKEY.
HERE, LOOK. YOU'RE IN LUCK. THIS *BLUB* JUST RIPENED.
SBLUB

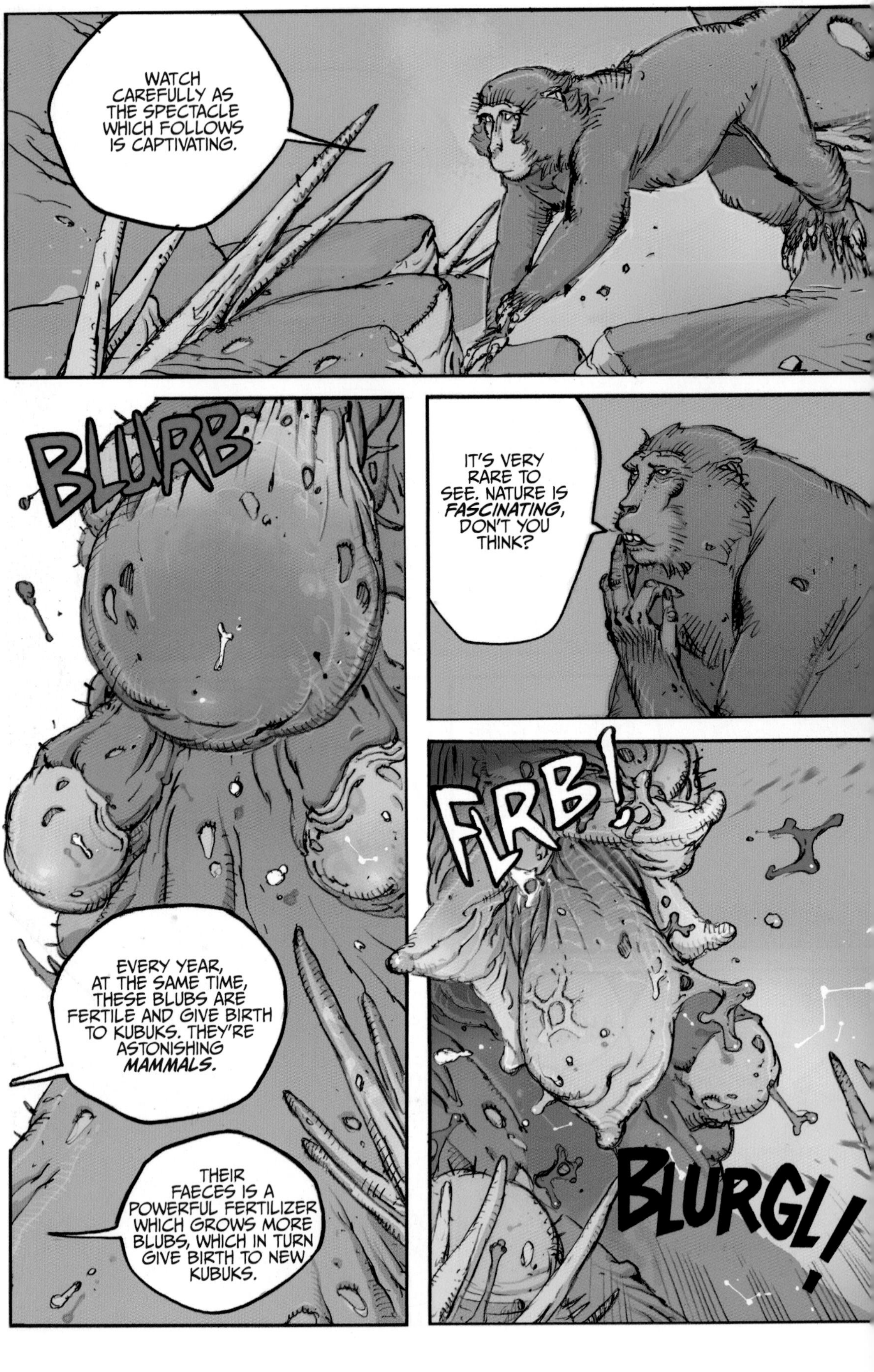
WATCH CAREFULLY AS THE SPECTACLE WHICH FOLLOWS IS CAPTIVATING.
BLURB
IT'S VERY RARE TO SEE. NATURE IS *FASCINATING*, DON'T YOU THINK?
EVERY YEAR, AT THE SAME TIME, THESE BLUBS ARE FERTILE AND GIVE BIRTH TO KUBUKS. THEY'RE ASTONISHING *MAMMALS.*
THEIR FAECES IS A POWERFUL FERTILIZER WHICH GROWS MORE BLUBS, WHICH IN TURN GIVE BIRTH TO NEW KUBUKS.
FLRB!
BLURGL!

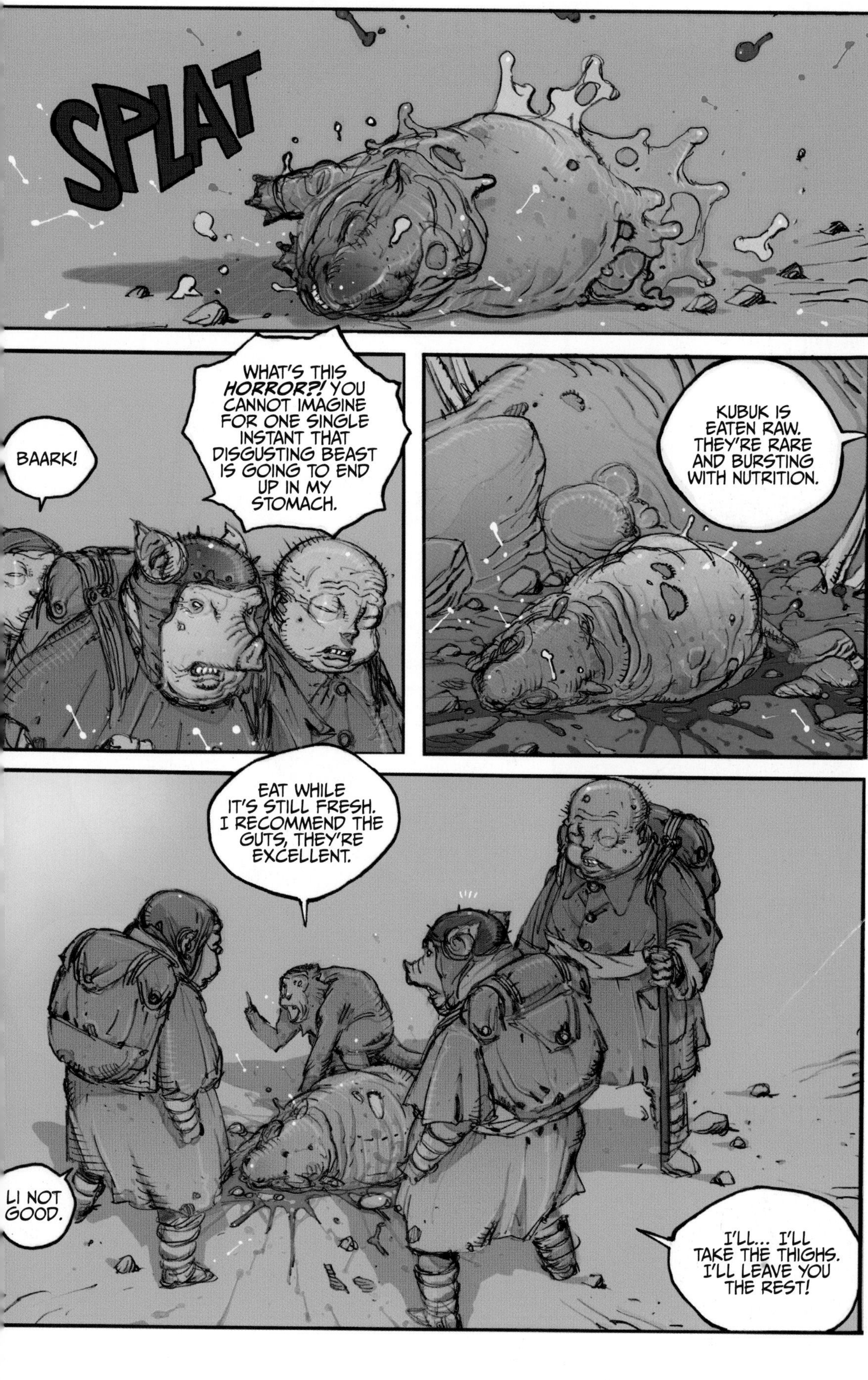
SPLAT
BAARK!
WHAT'S THIS *HORROR?!* YOU CANNOT IMAGINE FOR ONE SINGLE INSTANT THAT DISGUSTING BEAST IS GOING TO END UP IN MY STOMACH.
KUBUK IS EATEN RAW. THEY'RE RARE AND BURSTING WITH NUTRITION.
EAT WHILE IT'S STILL FRESH. I RECOMMEND THE GUTS, THEY'RE EXCELLENT.
LI NOT GOOD.
I'LL... I'LL TAKE THE THIGHS. I'LL LEAVE YOU THE REST!

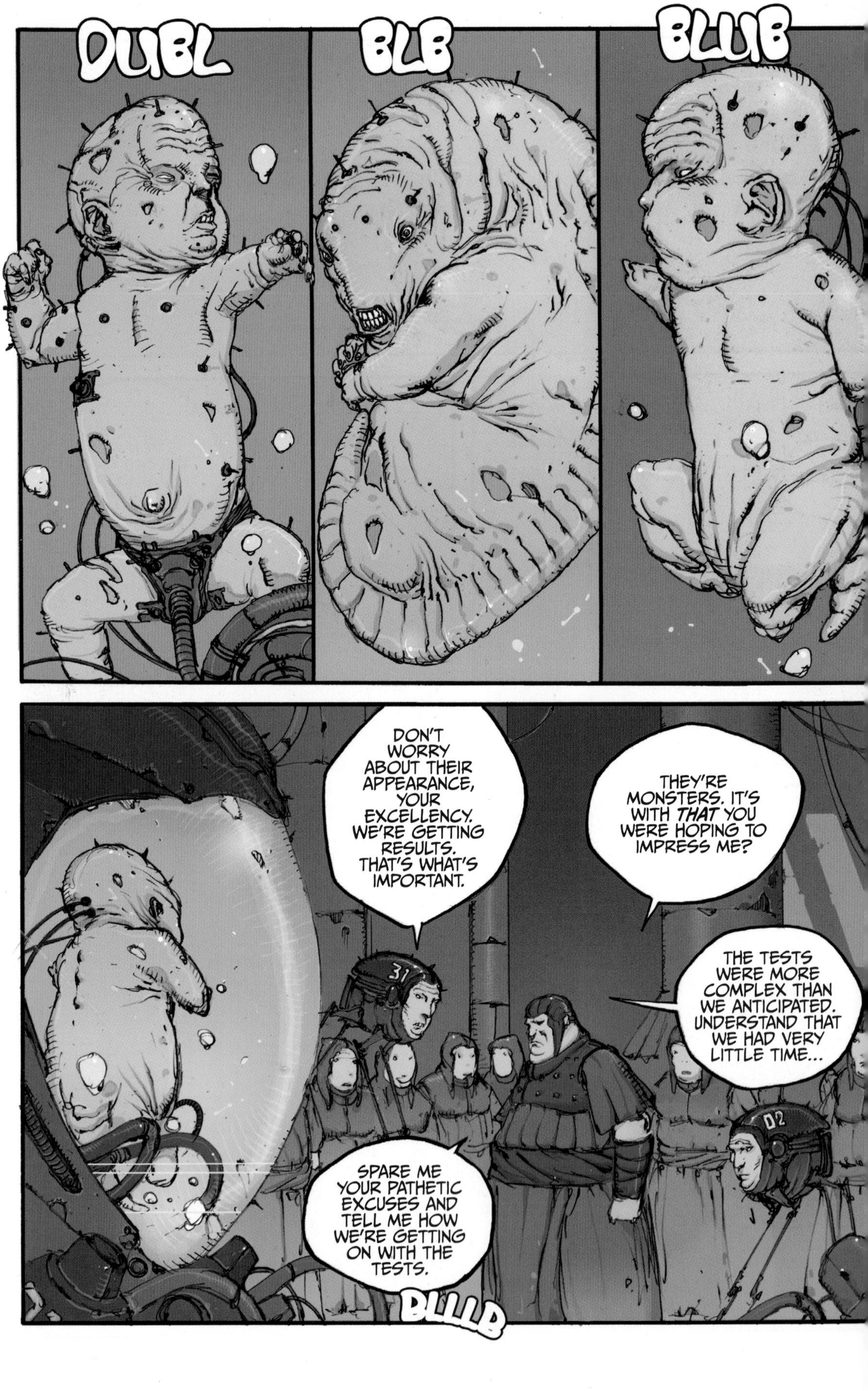
DUBL
BLB
BLUB
DON'T WORRY ABOUT THEIR APPEARANCE, YOUR EXCELLENCY. WE'RE GETTING RESULTS. THAT'S WHAT'S IMPORTANT.
THEY'RE MONSTERS. IT'S WITH *THAT* YOU WERE HOPING TO IMPRESS ME?
THE TESTS WERE MORE COMPLEX THAN WE ANTICIPATED. UNDERSTAND THAT WE HAD VERY LITTLE TIME...
SPARE ME YOUR PATHETIC EXCUSES AND TELL ME HOW WE'RE GETTING ON WITH THE TESTS.
BLLLB

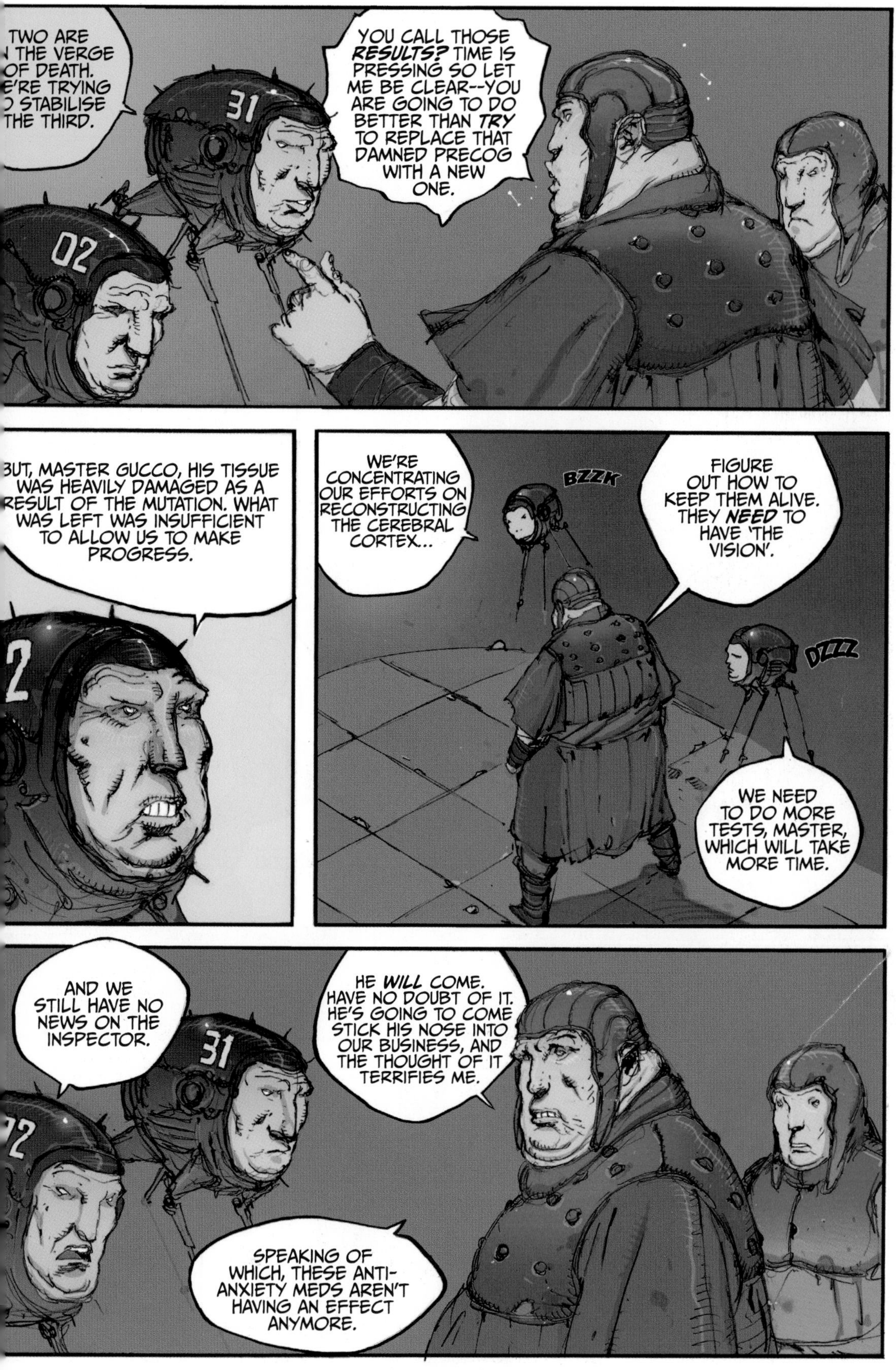

TWO ARE
N THE VERGE
OF DEATH.
E'RE TRYING
O STABILISE
THE THIRD.
YOU CALL THOSE RESULTS? TIME IS PRESSING SO LET ME BE CLEAR--YOU ARE GOING TO DO BETTER THAN TRY TO REPLACE THAT DAMNED PRECOG WITH A NEW ONE.
BUT, MASTER GUCCO, HIS TISSUE WAS HEAVILY DAMAGED AS A RESULT OF THE MUTATION. WHAT WAS LEFT WAS INSUFFICIENT TO ALLOW US TO MAKE PROGRESS.
WE'RE CONCENTRATING OUR EFFORTS ON RECONSTRUCTING THE CEREBRAL CORTEX...
BZZK
FIGURE OUT HOW TO KEEP THEM ALIVE. THEY NEED TO HAVE 'THE VISION'.
DZZZ
WE NEED TO DO MORE TESTS, MASTER, WHICH WILL TAKE MORE TIME.
AND WE STILL HAVE NO NEWS ON THE INSPECTOR.
HE WILL COME. HAVE NO DOUBT OF IT. HE'S GOING TO COME STICK HIS NOSE INTO OUR BUSINESS, AND THE THOUGHT OF IT TERRIFIES ME.
SPEAKING OF WHICH, THESE ANTI-ANXIETY MEDS AREN'T HAVING AN EFFECT ANYMORE.

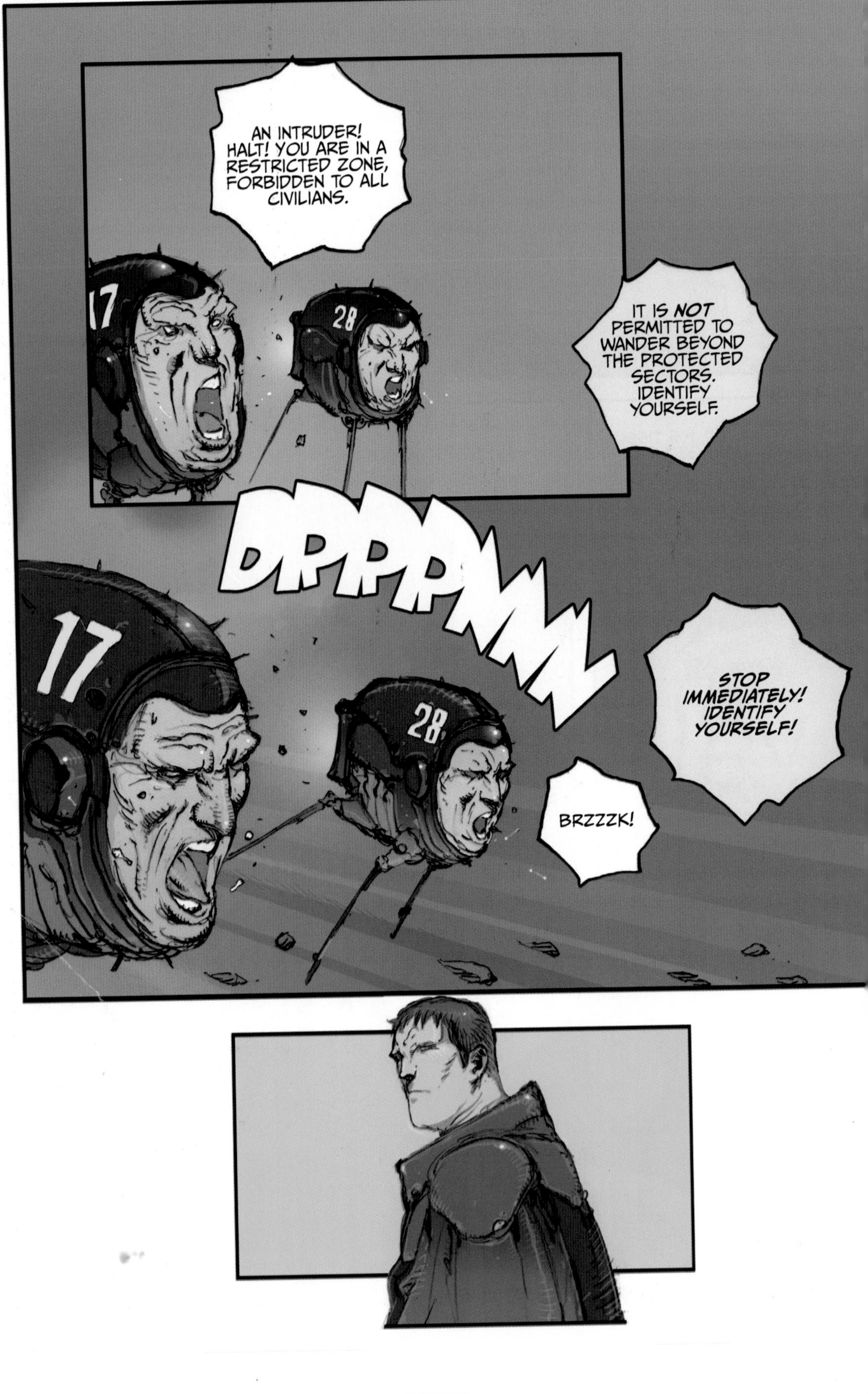
AN INTRUDER! HALT! YOU ARE IN A RESTRICTED ZONE, FORBIDDEN TO ALL CIVILIANS.
IT IS *NOT* PERMITTED TO WANDER BEYOND THE PROTECTED SECTORS. IDENTIFY YOURSELF.
17
28
DRRRWWW
17
28
STOP IMMEDIATELY! IDENTIFY YOURSELF!
BRZZZK!

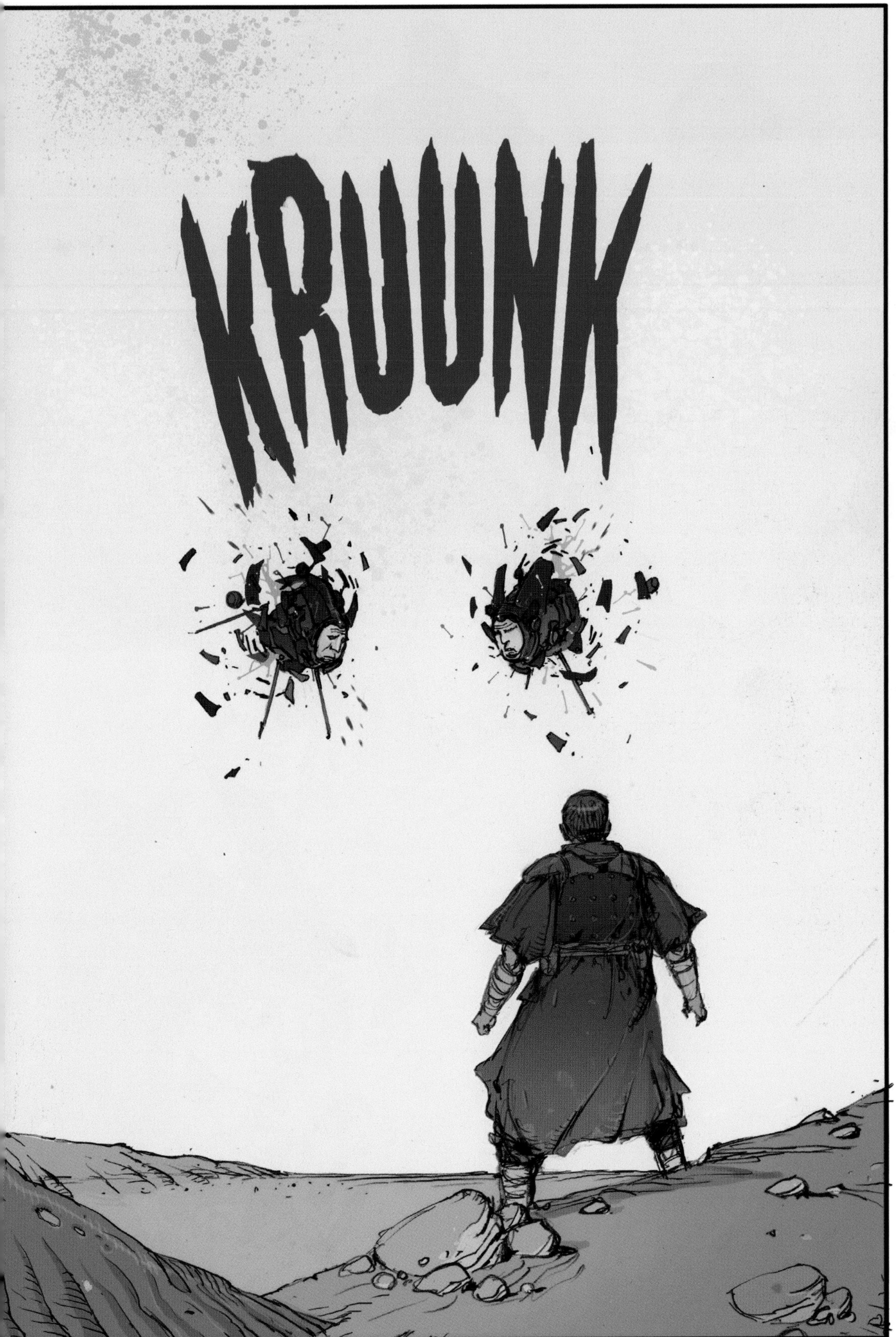
KRUUNK

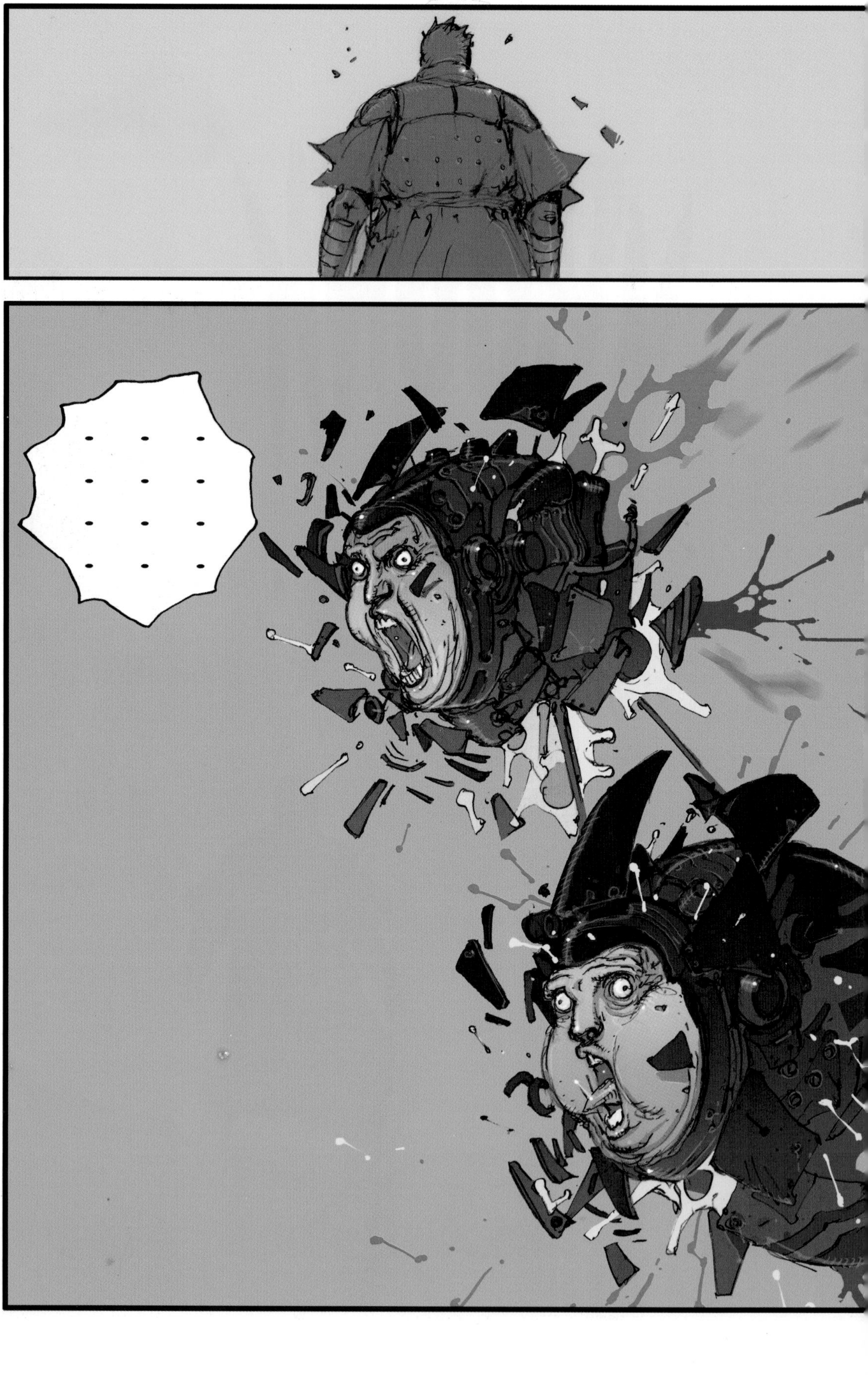

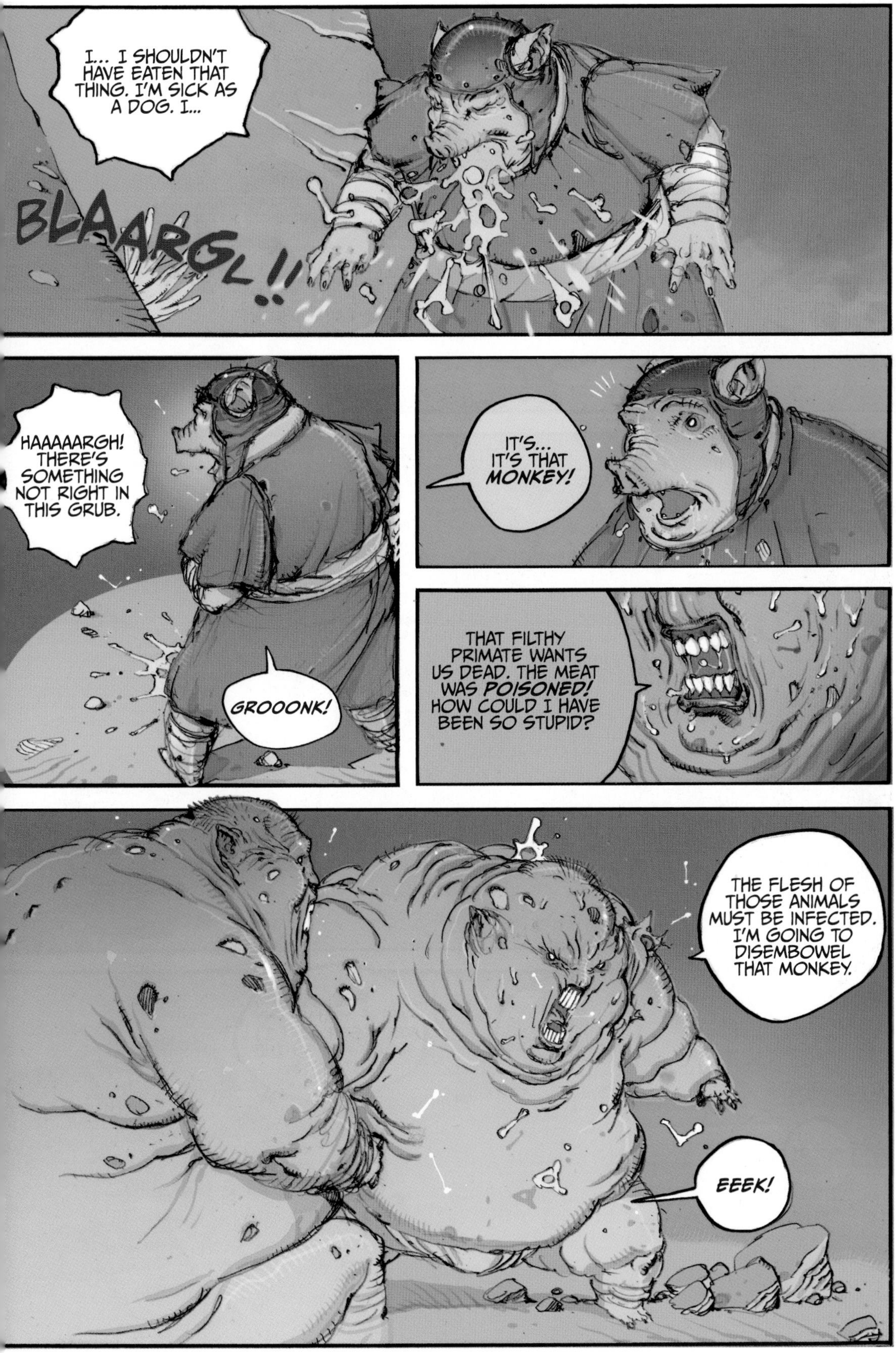
I... I SHOULDN'T HAVE EATEN THAT THING. I'M SICK AS A DOG. I...
BLAARGL!!
HAAAAARGH! THERE'S SOMETHING NOT RIGHT IN THIS GRUB.
GROOONK!
IT'S... IT'S THAT MONKEY!
THAT FILTHY PRIMATE WANTS US DEAD. THE MEAT WAS POISONED! HOW COULD I HAVE BEEN SO STUPID?
THE FLESH OF THOSE ANIMALS MUST BE INFECTED. I'M GOING TO DISEMBOWEL THAT MONKEY.
EEEK!

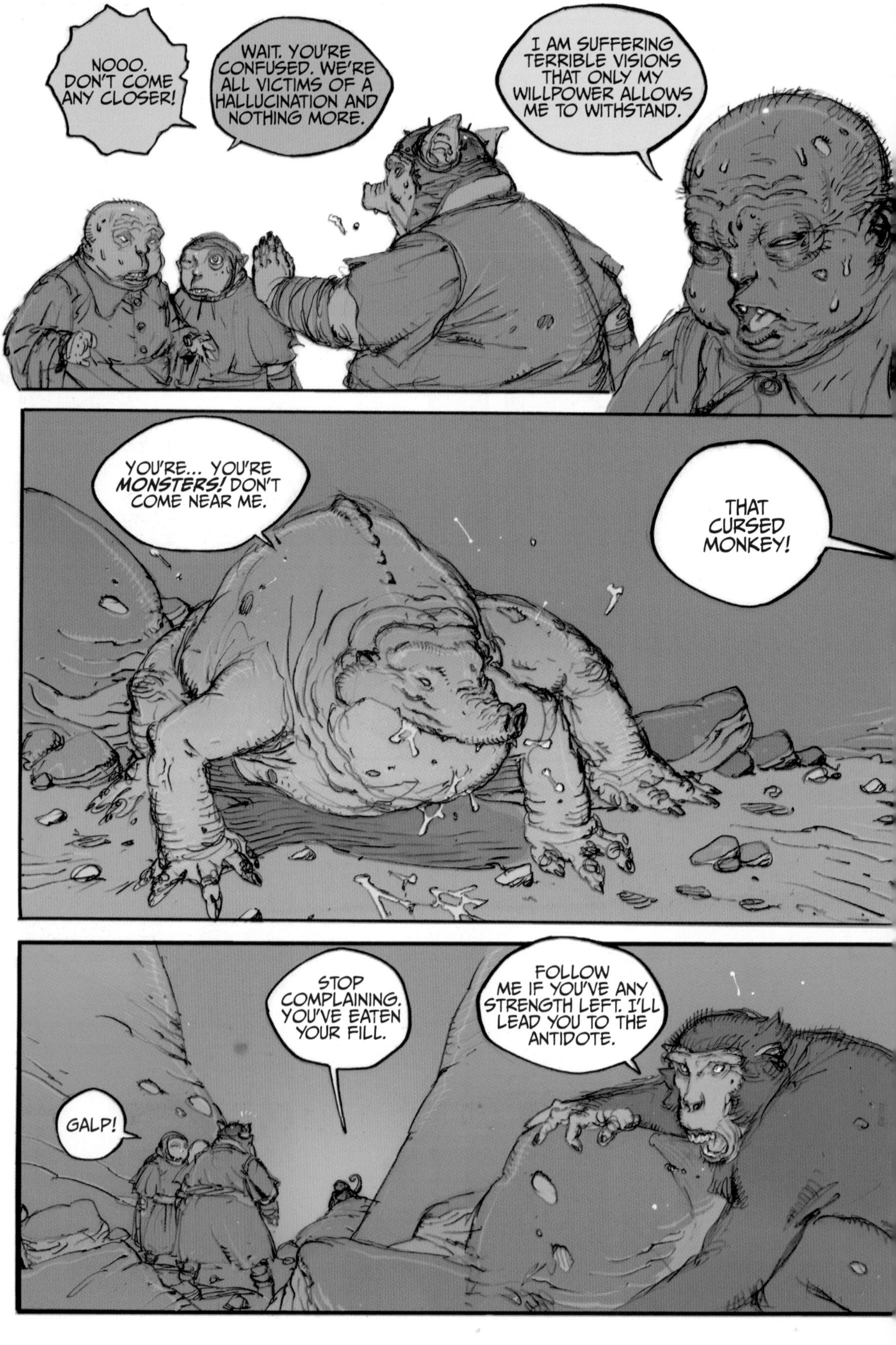
NOOO. DON'T COME ANY CLOSER!
WAIT. YOU'RE CONFUSED. WE'RE ALL VICTIMS OF A HALLUCINATION AND NOTHING MORE.
I AM SUFFERING TERRIBLE VISIONS THAT ONLY MY WILLPOWER ALLOWS ME TO WITHSTAND.
YOU'RE... YOU'RE MONSTERS! DON'T COME NEAR ME.
THAT CURSED MONKEY!
GALP!
STOP COMPLAINING. YOU'VE EATEN YOUR FILL.
FOLLOW ME IF YOU'VE ANY STRENGTH LEFT. I'LL LEAD YOU TO THE ANTIDOTE.

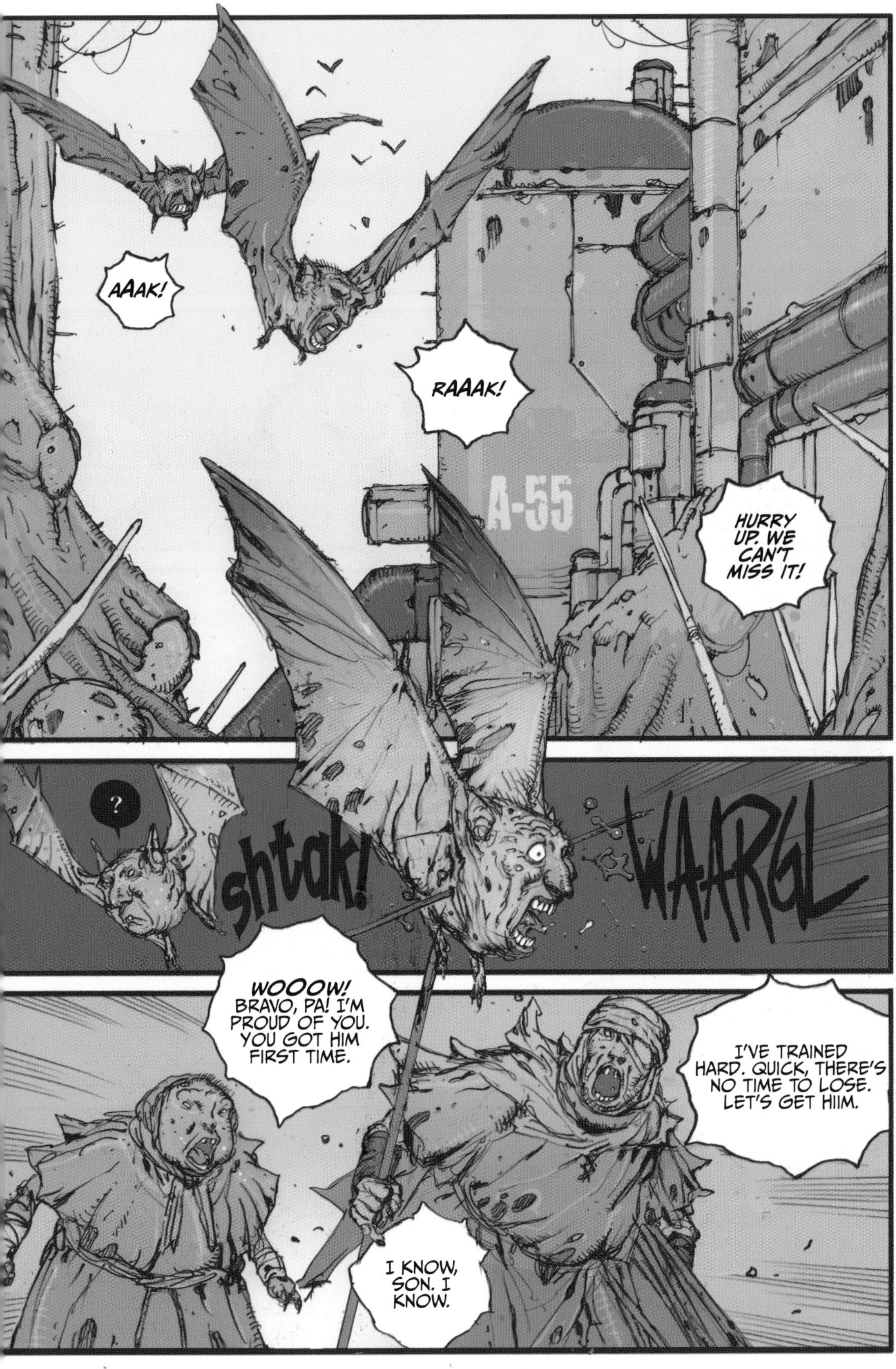
AAAK!
RAAAK!
A-55
HURRY UP. WE CAN'T MISS IT!
?
shtak!
WAARGL
WOOOW! BRAVO, PA! I'M PROUD OF YOU. YOU GOT HIM FIRST TIME.
I'VE TRAINED HARD. QUICK, THERE'S NO TIME TO LOSE. LET'S GET HIIM.
I KNOW, SON. I KNOW.

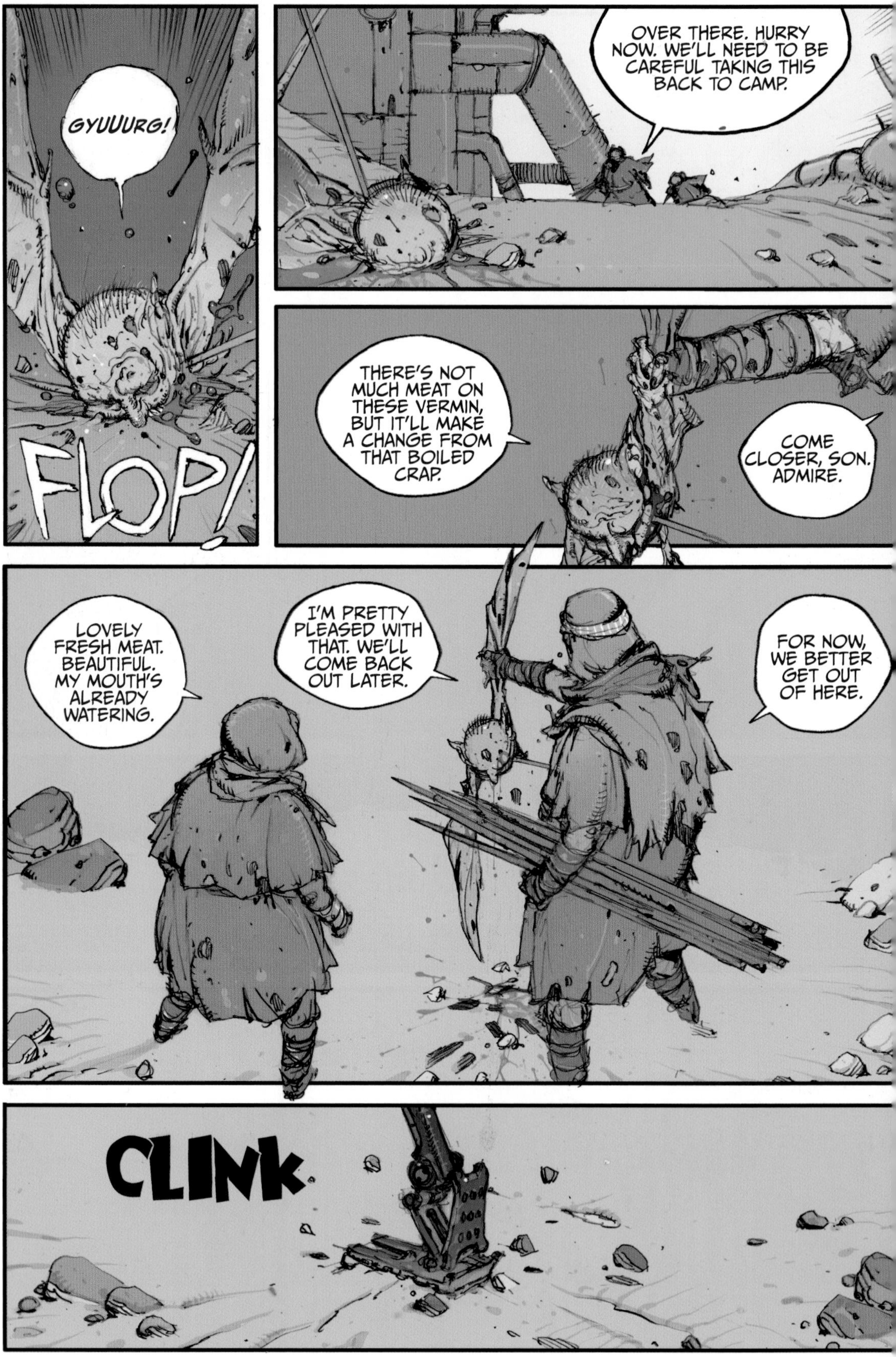
GYUUURG!
FLOP!
OVER THERE. HURRY NOW. WE'LL NEED TO BE CAREFUL TAKING THIS BACK TO CAMP.
THERE'S NOT MUCH MEAT ON THESE VERMIN, BUT IT'LL MAKE A CHANGE FROM THAT BOILED CRAP.
COME CLOSER, SON. ADMIRE.
LOVELY FRESH MEAT. BEAUTIFUL. MY MOUTH'S ALREADY WATERING.
I'M PRETTY PLEASED WITH THAT. WE'LL COME BACK OUT LATER.
FOR NOW, WE BETTER GET OUT OF HERE.
CLINK.

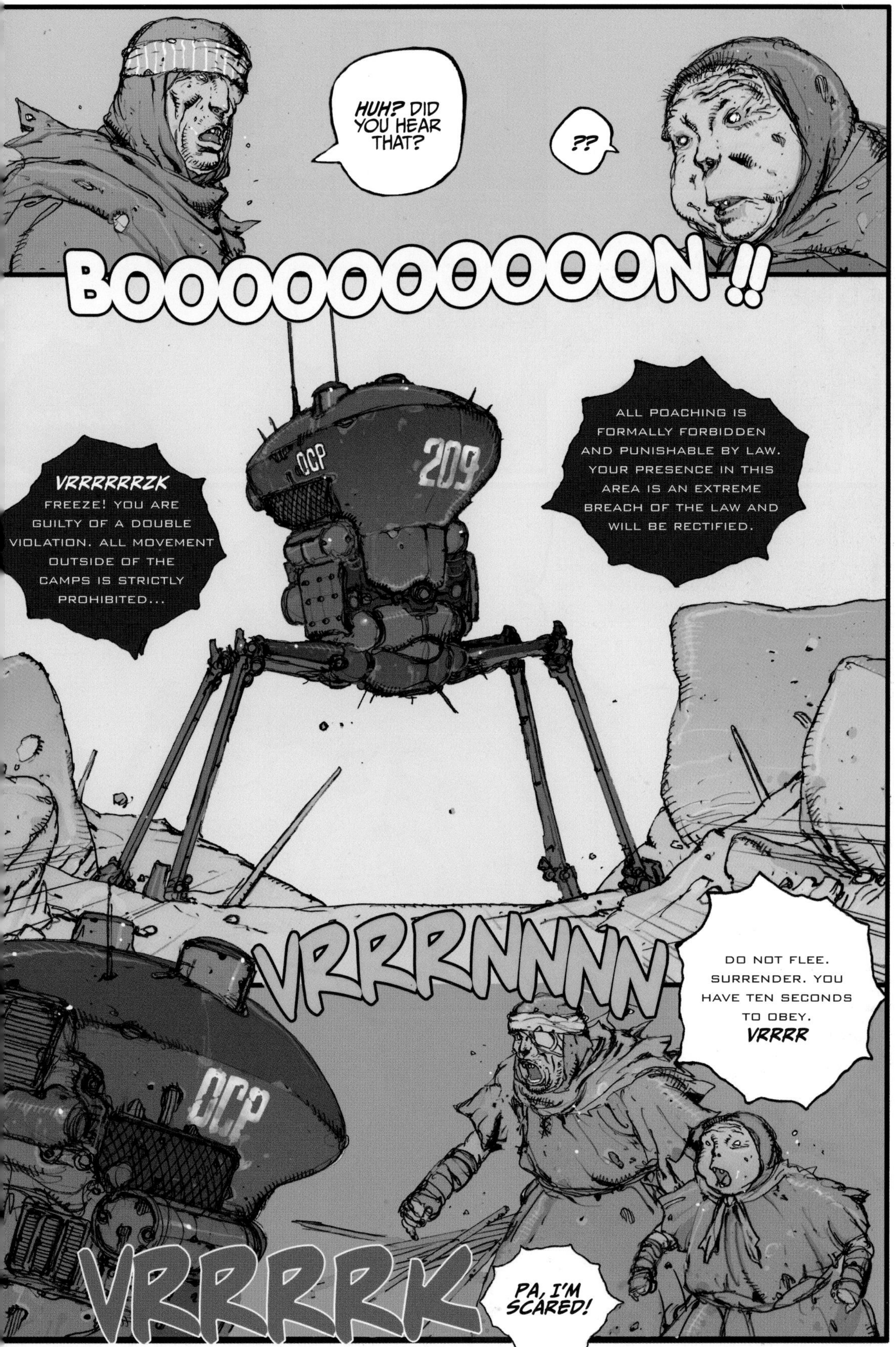
HUH? DID YOU HEAR THAT?
??
BOOOOOOOOON !!
VRRRRRRZK FREEZE! YOU ARE GUILTY OF A DOUBLE VIOLATION. ALL MOVEMENT OUTSIDE OF THE CAMPS IS STRICTLY PROHIBITED...
OCP
209
ALL POACHING IS FORMALLY FORBIDDEN AND PUNISHABLE BY LAW. YOUR PRESENCE IN THIS AREA IS AN EXTREME BREACH OF THE LAW AND WILL BE RECTIFIED.
VRRRNNNNN
DO NOT FLEE. SURRENDER. YOU HAVE TEN SECONDS TO OBEY. VRRRR
OCP
VRRRRK
PA, I'M SCARED!

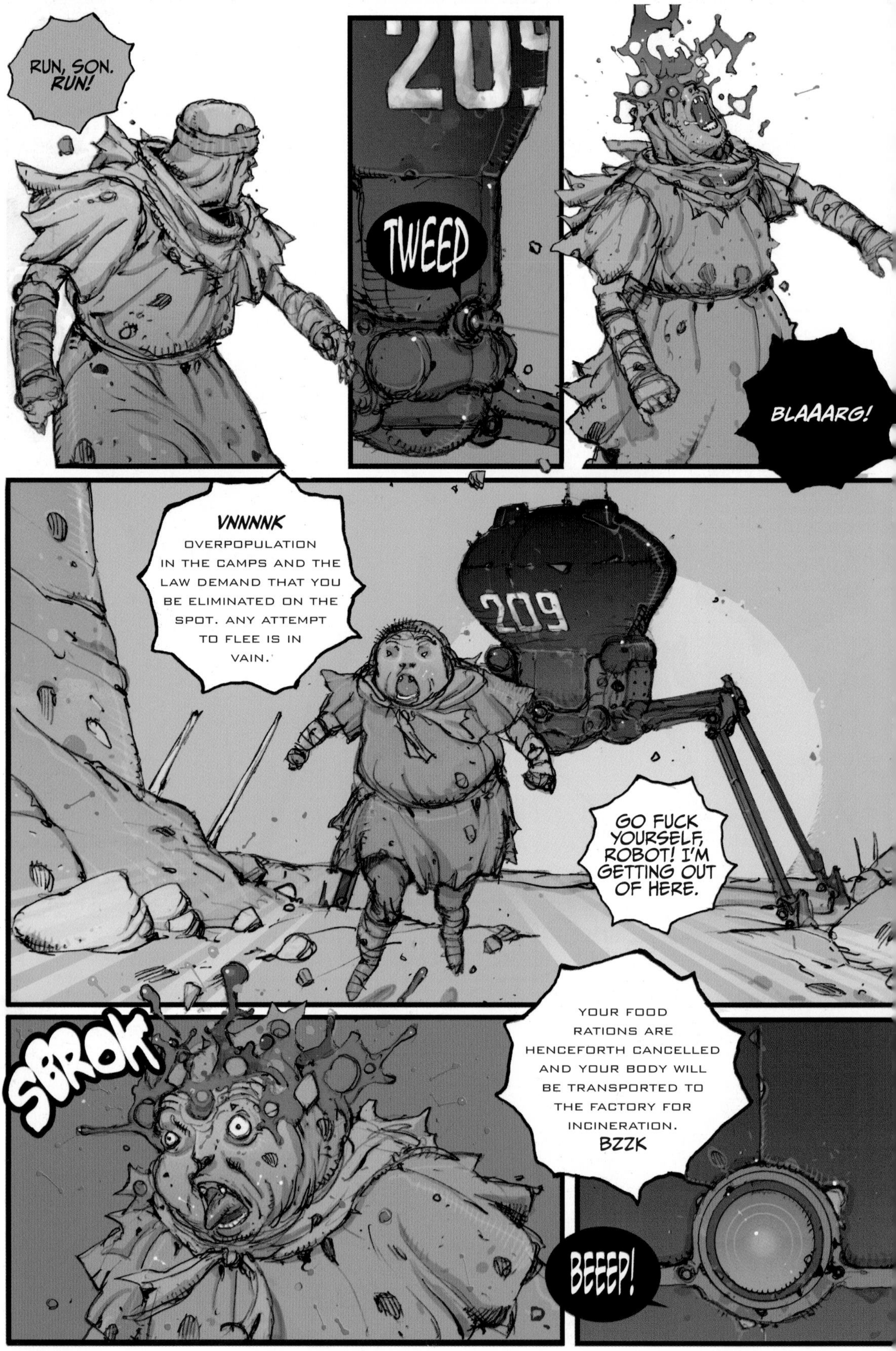
RUN, SON. *RUN!*
209
TWEEP
BLAAARG!
VNNNNK OVERPOPULATION IN THE CAMPS AND THE LAW DEMAND THAT YOU BE ELIMINATED ON THE SPOT. ANY ATTEMPT TO FLEE IS IN VAIN.
209
GO FUCK YOURSELF, ROBOT! I'M GETTING OUT OF HERE.
SBROK
YOUR FOOD RATIONS ARE HENCEFORTH CANCELLED AND YOUR BODY WILL BE TRANSPORTED TO THE FACTORY FOR INCINERATION. BZZK
BEEEP!

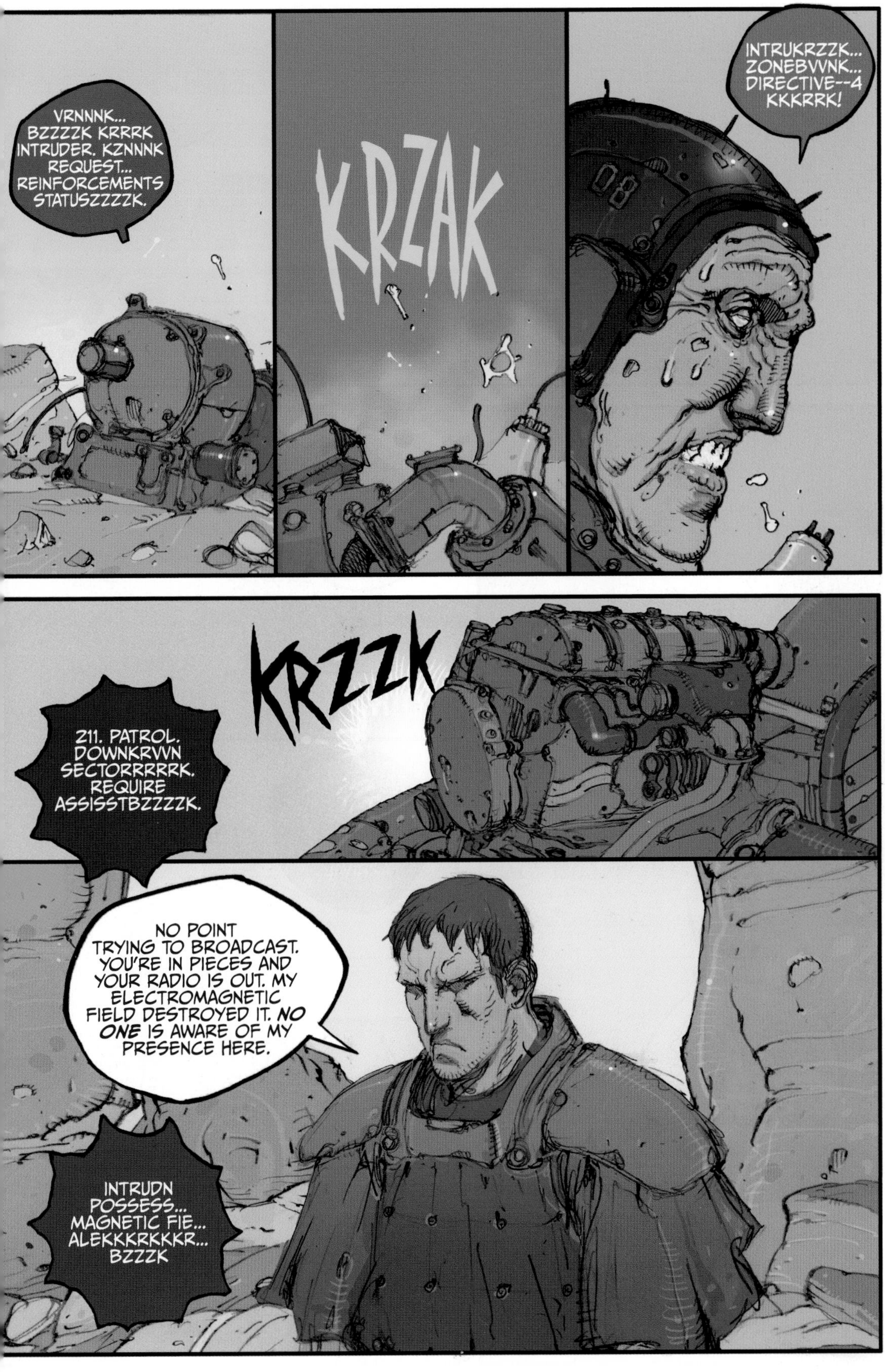

VRNNNK... BZZZZK KRRRK INTRUDER. KZNNNK REQUEST... REINFORCEMENTS STATUSZZZZK.
KRZAK
INTRUKRZZK... ZONEBVVNK... DIRECTIVE--4 KKKRRK!
KRZZK
211. PATROL. DOWNKRVVN SECTORRRRRK. REQUIRE ASSISSTBZZZZK.
NO POINT TRYING TO BROADCAST. YOU'RE IN PIECES AND YOUR RADIO IS OUT. MY ELECTROMAGNETIC FIELD DESTROYED IT. NO ONE IS AWARE OF MY PRESENCE HERE.
INTRUDN POSSESS... MAGNETIC FIE... ALEKKKRKKKR... BZZZK

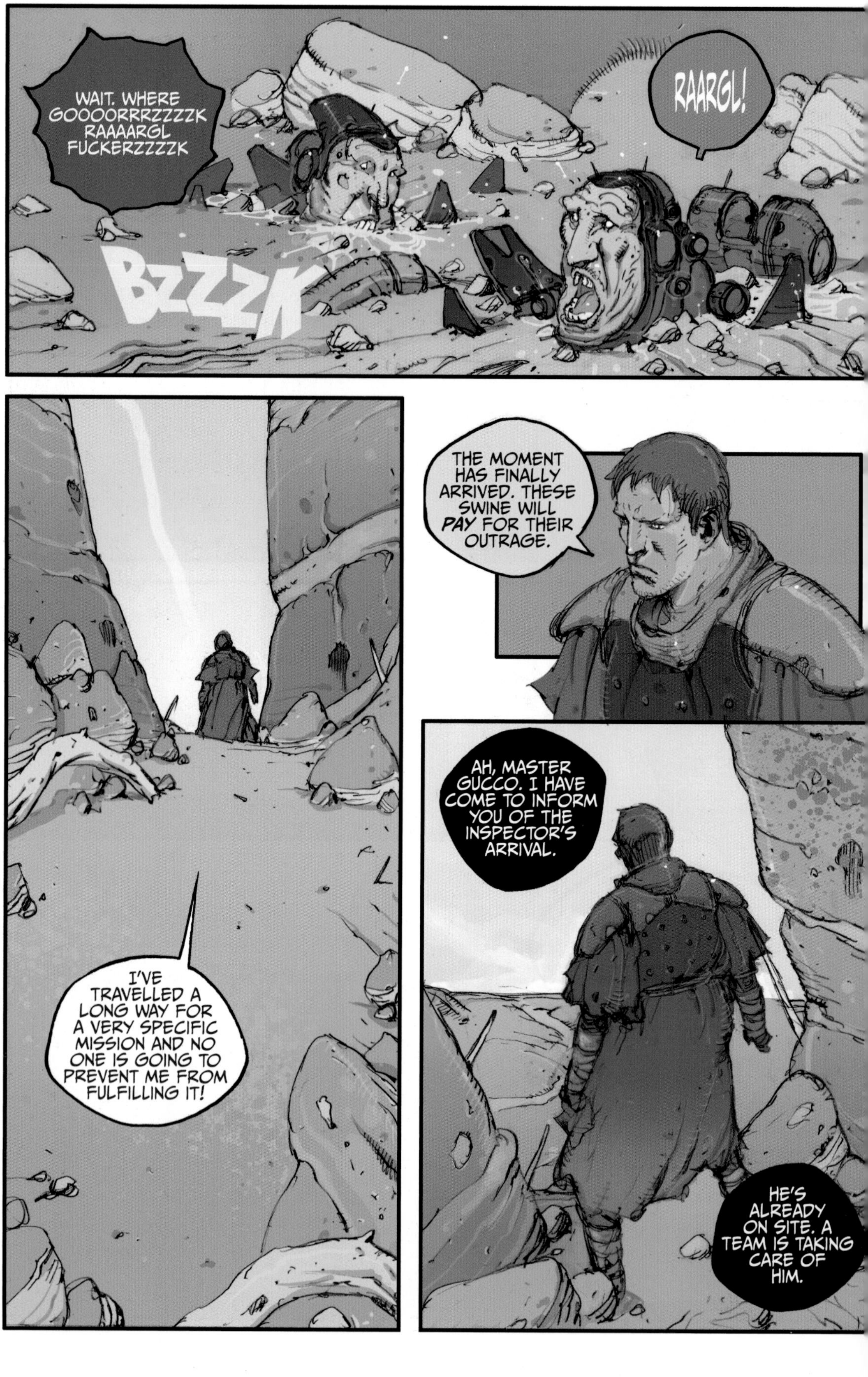

WAIT. WHERE GOOOORRRZZZZZK RAAAARGL FUCKERZZZZZK
RAARGL!
BZZZK
I'VE TRAVELLED A LONG WAY FOR A VERY SPECIFIC MISSION AND NO ONE IS GOING TO PREVENT ME FROM FULFILLING IT!
THE MOMENT HAS FINALLY ARRIVED. THESE SWINE WILL PAY FOR THEIR OUTRAGE.
AH, MASTER GUCCO. I HAVE COME TO INFORM YOU OF THE INSPECTOR'S ARRIVAL.
HE'S ALREADY ON SITE. A TEAM IS TAKING CARE OF HIM.

INSPECTOR ROBS OF THE FEDERAL FOOD CORP, WHAT A PLEASURE TO RECEIVE YOU IN GOOD HEALTH. WE WERE EAGERLY AWAITING YOU. DID YOU HAVE A PLEASANT JOURNEY? THIS DESERT IS SO UNPREDICTABLE.

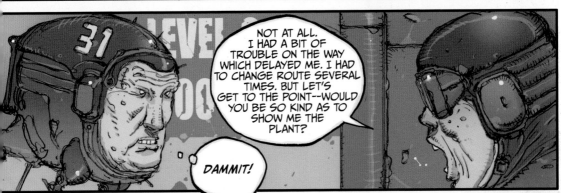

NOT AT ALL. I HAD A BIT OF TROUBLE ON THE WAY WHICH DELAYED ME. I HAD TO CHANGE ROUTE SEVERAL TIMES. BUT LET'S GET TO THE POINT--WOULD YOU BE SO KIND AS TO SHOW ME THE PLANT?

DAMMIT!

OF COURSE. FIRST WE'LL TAKE YOU TO YOUR APARTMENTS. YOUR JOURNEY WAS LONG AND YOU'LL NO DOUBT WISH TO FRESHEN UP. I HOPE YOU'LL FEEL AT HOME.

I DOUBT THAT! THIS FACTORY IS A *DISGRACE!* IT'S NOT BEEN INSPECTED FOR SOME TIME DUE TO A LACK OF STAFF. BUT I WILL BE CORRECTING ALL THAT.

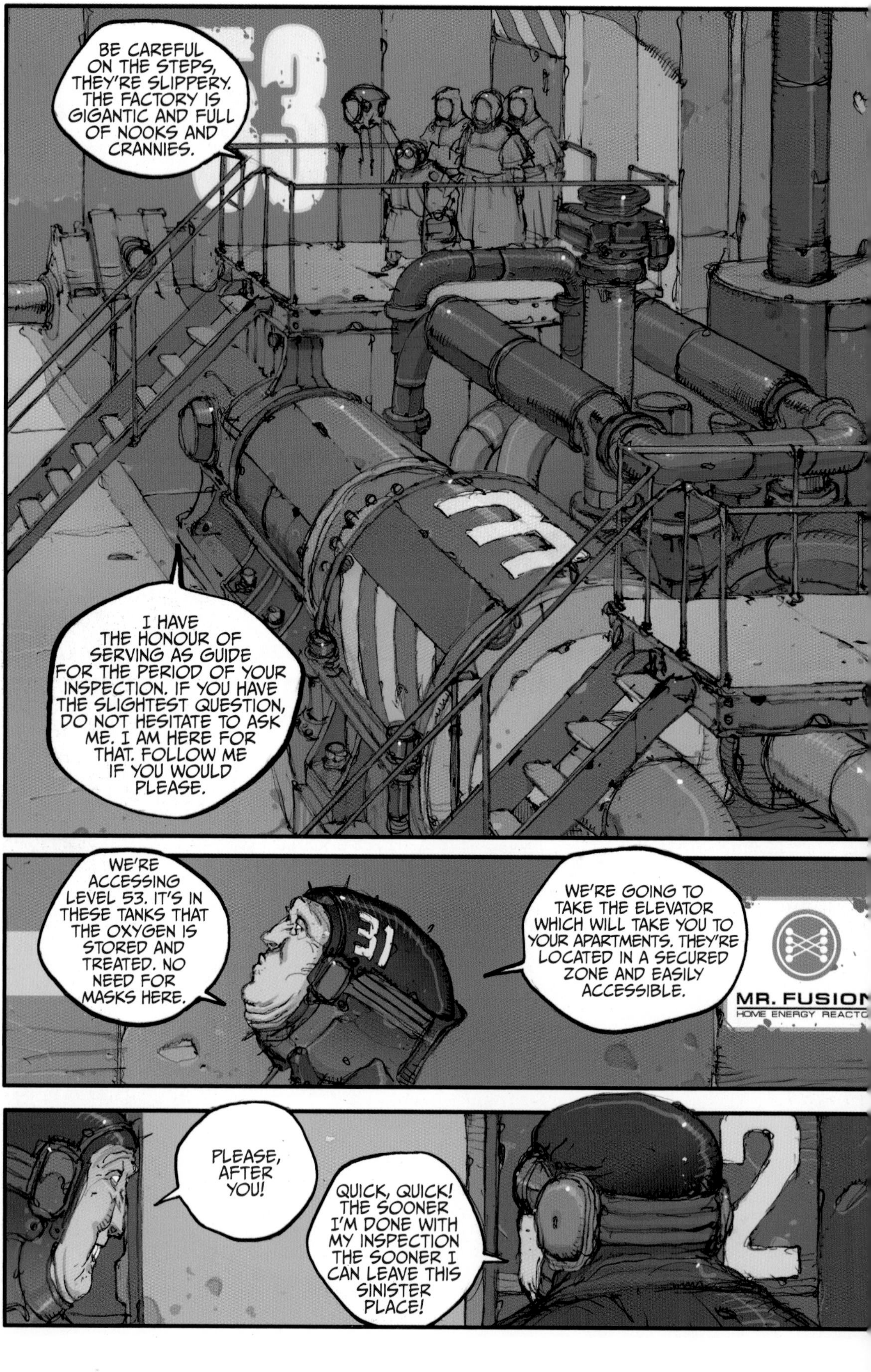

53
BE CAREFUL ON THE STEPS, THEY'RE SLIPPERY. THE FACTORY IS GIGANTIC AND FULL OF NOOKS AND CRANNIES.
I HAVE THE HONOUR OF SERVING AS GUIDE FOR THE PERIOD OF YOUR INSPECTION. IF YOU HAVE THE SLIGHTEST QUESTION, DO NOT HESITATE TO ASK ME. I AM HERE FOR THAT. FOLLOW ME IF YOU WOULD PLEASE.
WE'RE ACCESSING LEVEL 53. IT'S IN THESE TANKS THAT THE OXYGEN IS STORED AND TREATED. NO NEED FOR MASKS HERE.
31
WE'RE GOING TO TAKE THE ELEVATOR WHICH WILL TAKE YOU TO YOUR APARTMENTS. THEY'RE LOCATED IN A SECURED ZONE AND EASILY ACCESSIBLE.
MR. FUSION
HOME ENERGY REACTO
PLEASE, AFTER YOU!
QUICK, QUICK! THE SOONER I'M DONE WITH MY INSPECTION THE SOONER I CAN LEAVE THIS SINISTER PLACE!

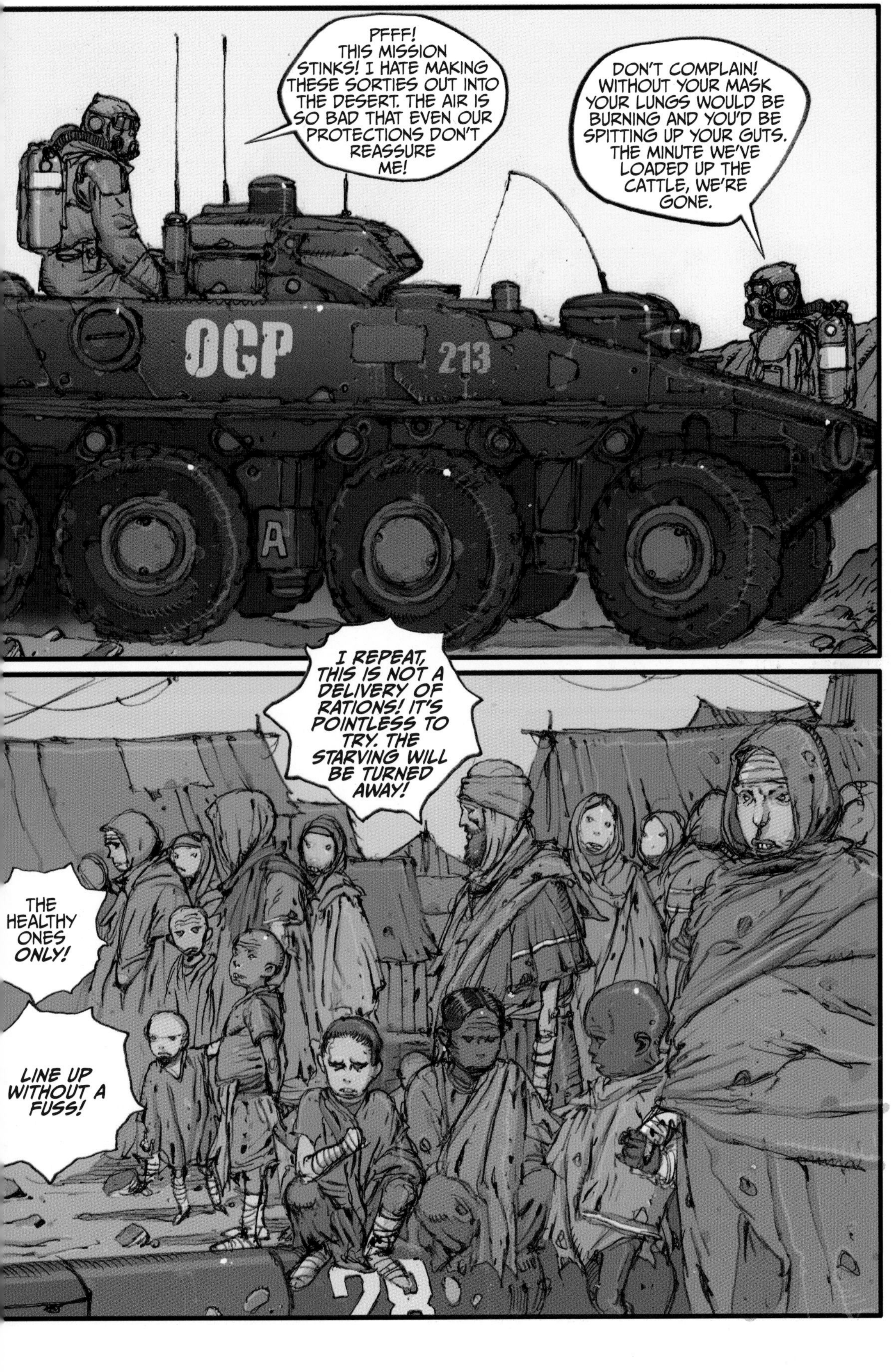
PFFF! THIS MISSION STINKS! I HATE MAKING THESE SORTIES OUT INTO THE DESERT. THE AIR IS SO BAD THAT EVEN OUR PROTECTIONS DON'T REASSURE ME!
DON'T COMPLAIN! WITHOUT YOUR MASK YOUR LUNGS WOULD BE BURNING AND YOU'D BE SPITTING UP YOUR GUTS. THE MINUTE WE'VE LOADED UP THE CATTLE, WE'RE GONE.
OCP
213
A
I REPEAT, THIS IS NOT A DELIVERY OF RATIONS! IT'S POINTLESS TO TRY. THE STARVING WILL BE TURNED AWAY!
THE HEALTHY ONES ONLY!
LINE UP WITHOUT A FUSS!
28

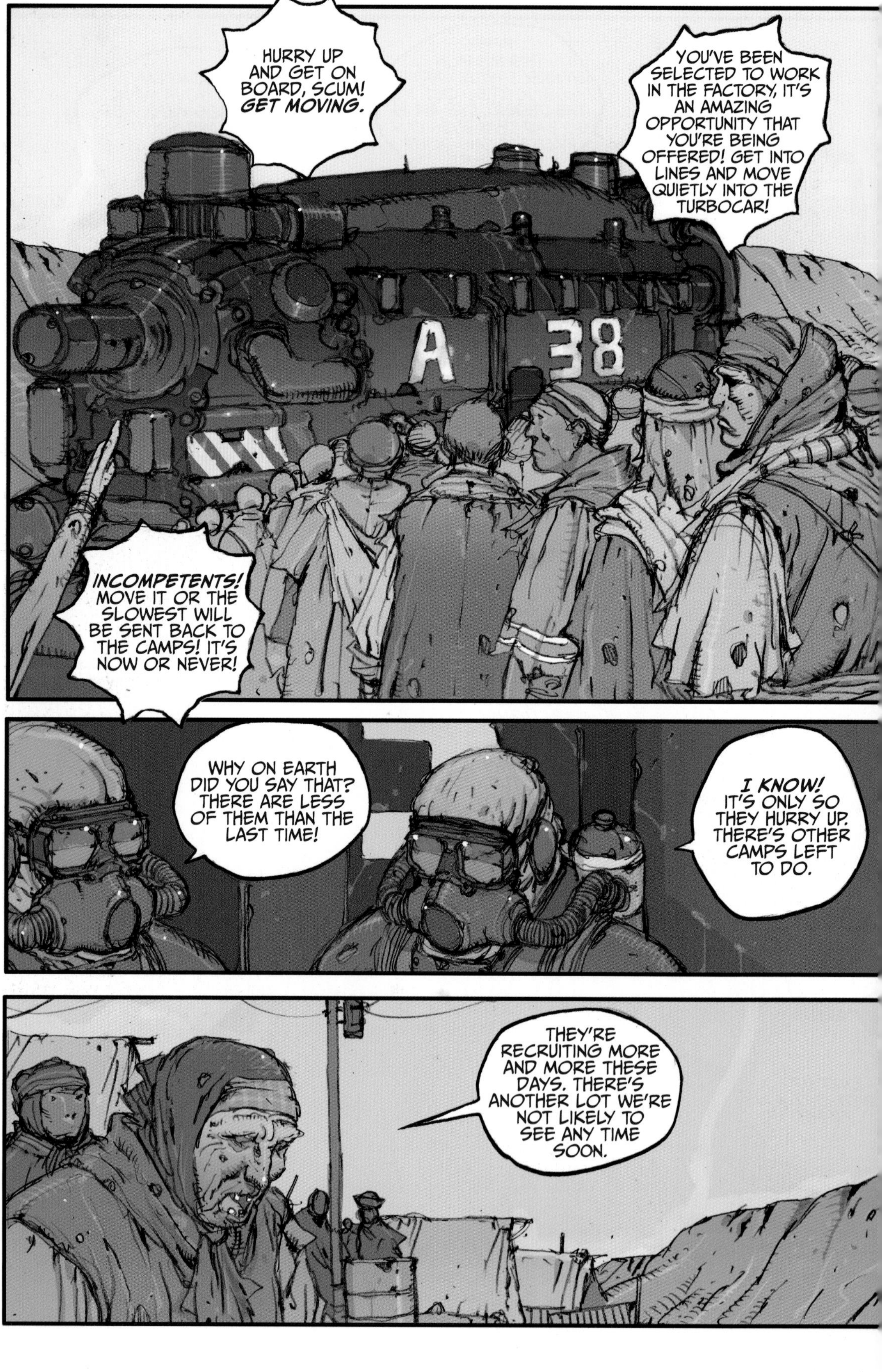

HURRY UP AND GET ON BOARD, SCUM! *GET MOVING.*
YOU'VE BEEN SELECTED TO WORK IN THE FACTORY, IT'S AN AMAZING OPPORTUNITY THAT YOU'RE BEING OFFERED! GET INTO LINES AND MOVE QUIETLY INTO THE TURBOCAR!
A 38
INCOMPETENTS! MOVE IT OR THE SLOWEST WILL BE SENT BACK TO THE CAMPS! IT'S NOW OR NEVER!
WHY ON EARTH DID YOU SAY THAT? THERE ARE LESS OF THEM THAN THE LAST TIME!
I KNOW! IT'S ONLY SO THEY HURRY UP. THERE'S OTHER CAMPS LEFT TO DO.
THEY'RE RECRUITING MORE AND MORE THESE DAYS. THERE'S ANOTHER LOT WE'RE NOT LIKELY TO SEE ANY TIME SOON.

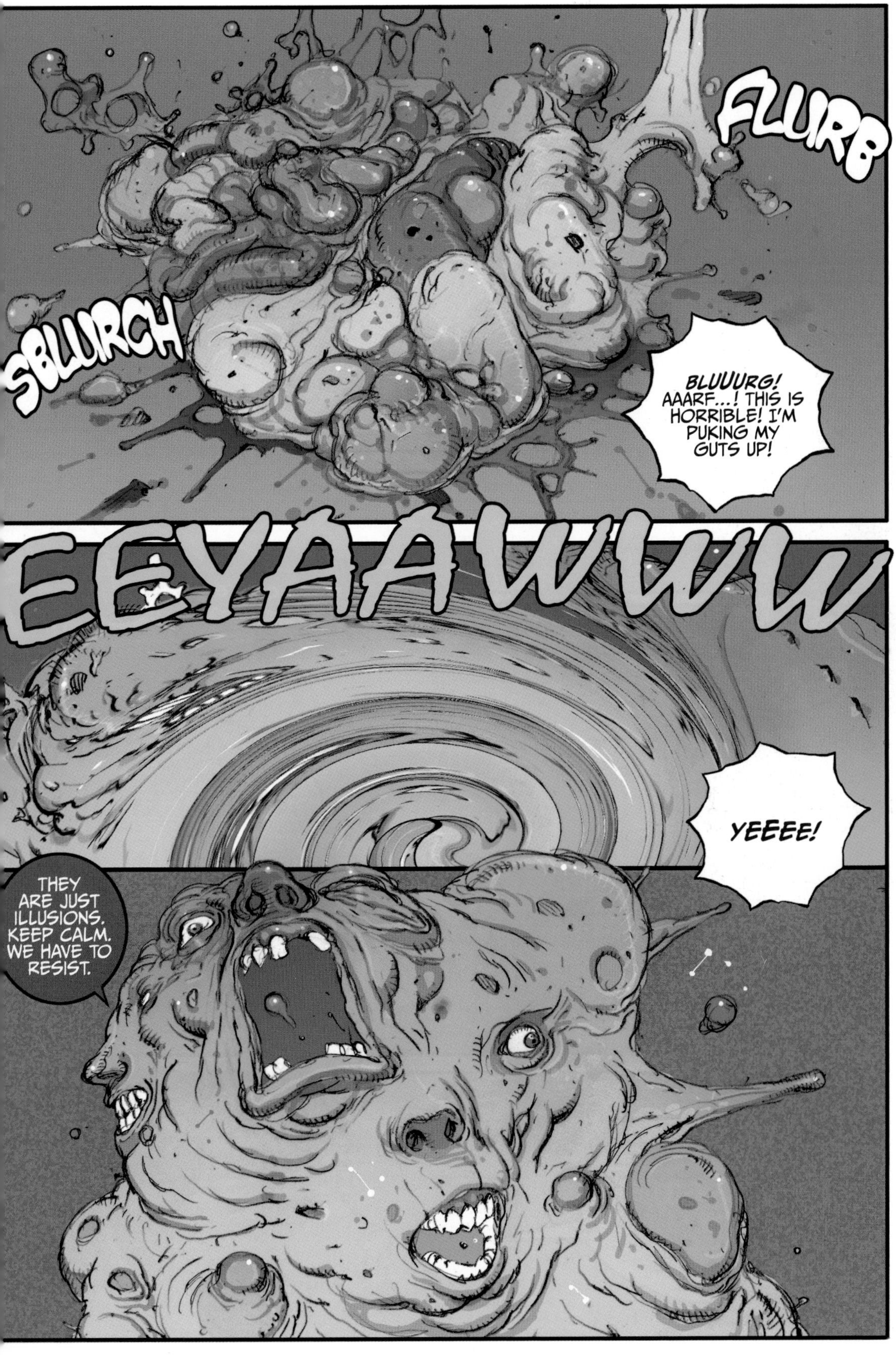
FLURB
SBLURCH
BLUUURG! AAARF...! THIS IS HORRIBLE! I'M PUKING MY GUTS UP!
EEYAAWWW
YEEEE!
THEY ARE JUST ILLUSIONS. KEEP CALM. WE HAVE TO RESIST.

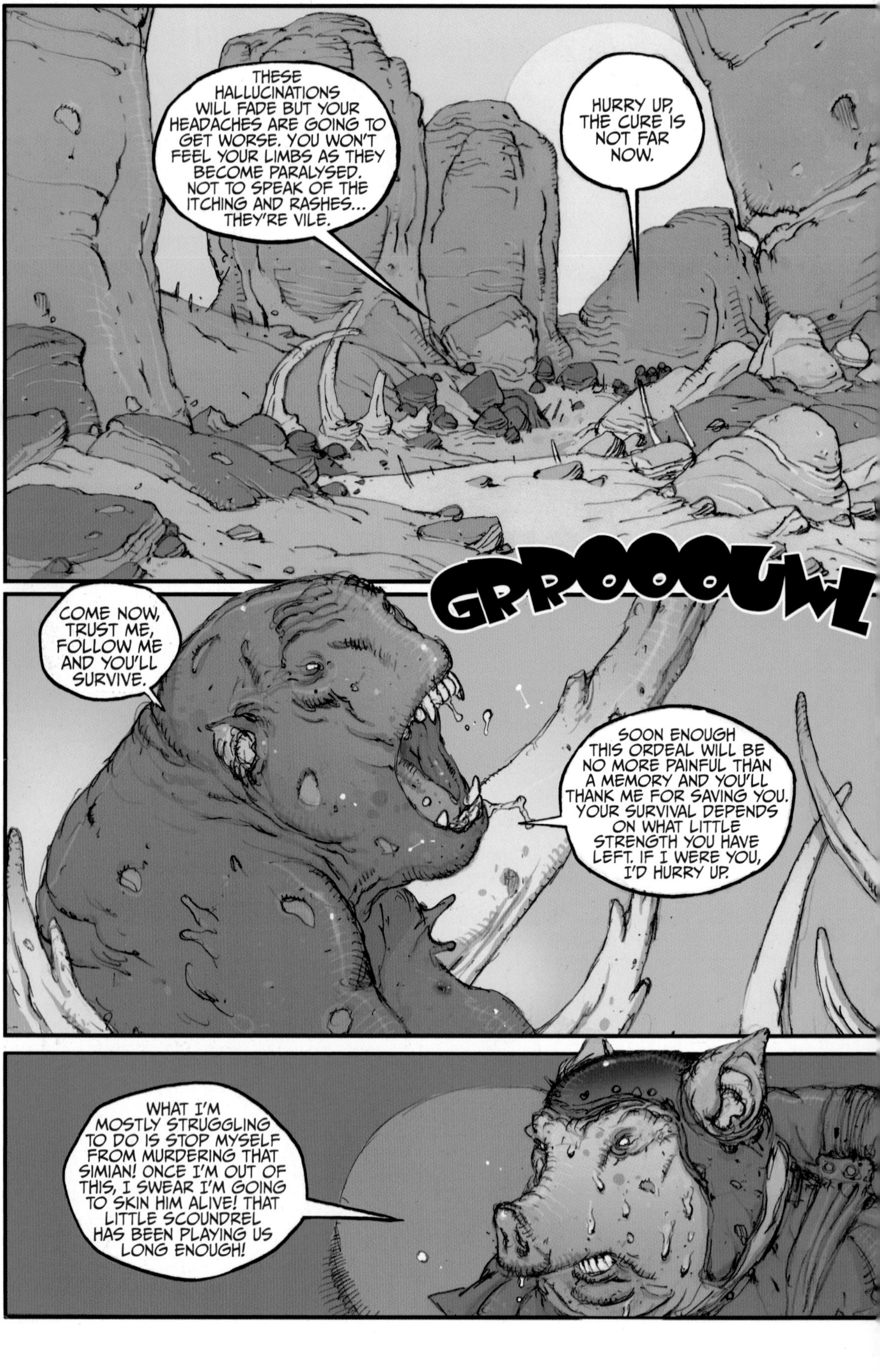
THESE HALLUCINATIONS WILL FADE BUT YOUR HEADACHES ARE GOING TO GET WORSE. YOU WON'T FEEL YOUR LIMBS AS THEY BECOME PARALYSED. NOT TO SPEAK OF THE ITCHING AND RASHES... THEY'RE VILE.
HURRY UP, THE CURE IS NOT FAR NOW.
GRROOOOUWL
COME NOW, TRUST ME, FOLLOW ME AND YOU'LL SURVIVE.
SOON ENOUGH THIS ORDEAL WILL BE NO MORE PAINFUL THAN A MEMORY AND YOU'LL THANK ME FOR SAVING YOU. YOUR SURVIVAL DEPENDS ON WHAT LITTLE STRENGTH YOU HAVE LEFT. IF I WERE YOU, I'D HURRY UP.
WHAT I'M MOSTLY STRUGGLING TO DO IS STOP MYSELF FROM MURDERING THAT SIMIAN! ONCE I'M OUT OF THIS, I SWEAR I'M GOING TO SKIN HIM ALIVE! THAT LITTLE SCOUNDREL HAS BEEN PLAYING US LONG ENOUGH!

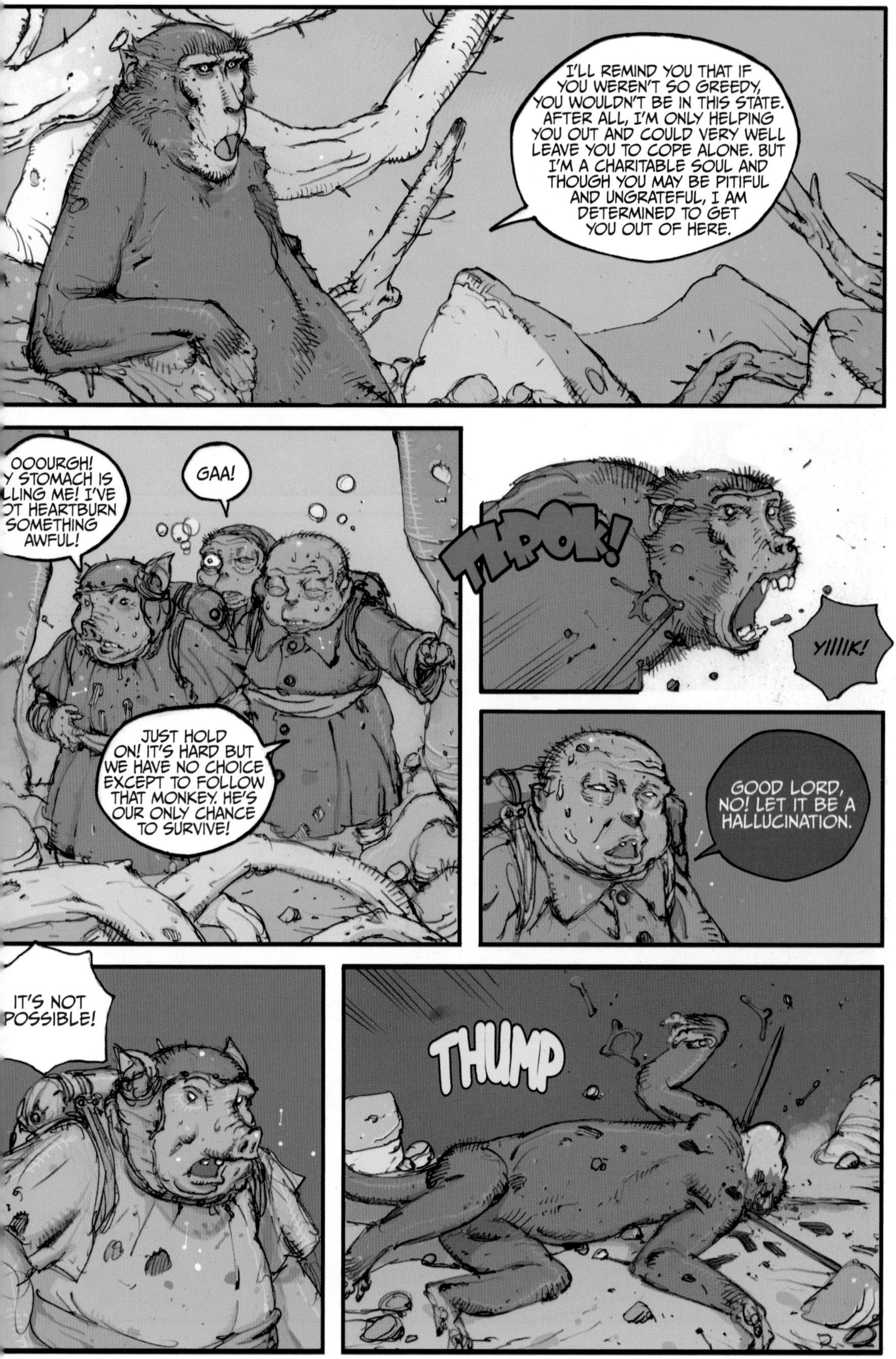
I'LL REMIND YOU THAT IF YOU WEREN'T SO GREEDY, YOU WOULDN'T BE IN THIS STATE. AFTER ALL, I'M ONLY HELPING YOU OUT AND COULD VERY WELL LEAVE YOU TO COPE ALONE. BUT I'M A CHARITABLE SOUL AND THOUGH YOU MAY BE PITIFUL AND UNGRATEFUL, I AM DETERMINED TO GET YOU OUT OF HERE.
OOOURGH! Y STOMACH IS LLING ME! I'VE OT HEARTBURN SOMETHING AWFUL!
GAA!
JUST HOLD ON! IT'S HARD BUT WE HAVE NO CHOICE EXCEPT TO FOLLOW THAT MONKEY. HE'S OUR ONLY CHANCE TO SURVIVE!
THPOK!
YIIIIK!
GOOD LORD, NO! LET IT BE A HALLUCINATION.
IT'S NOT POSSIBLE!
THUMP

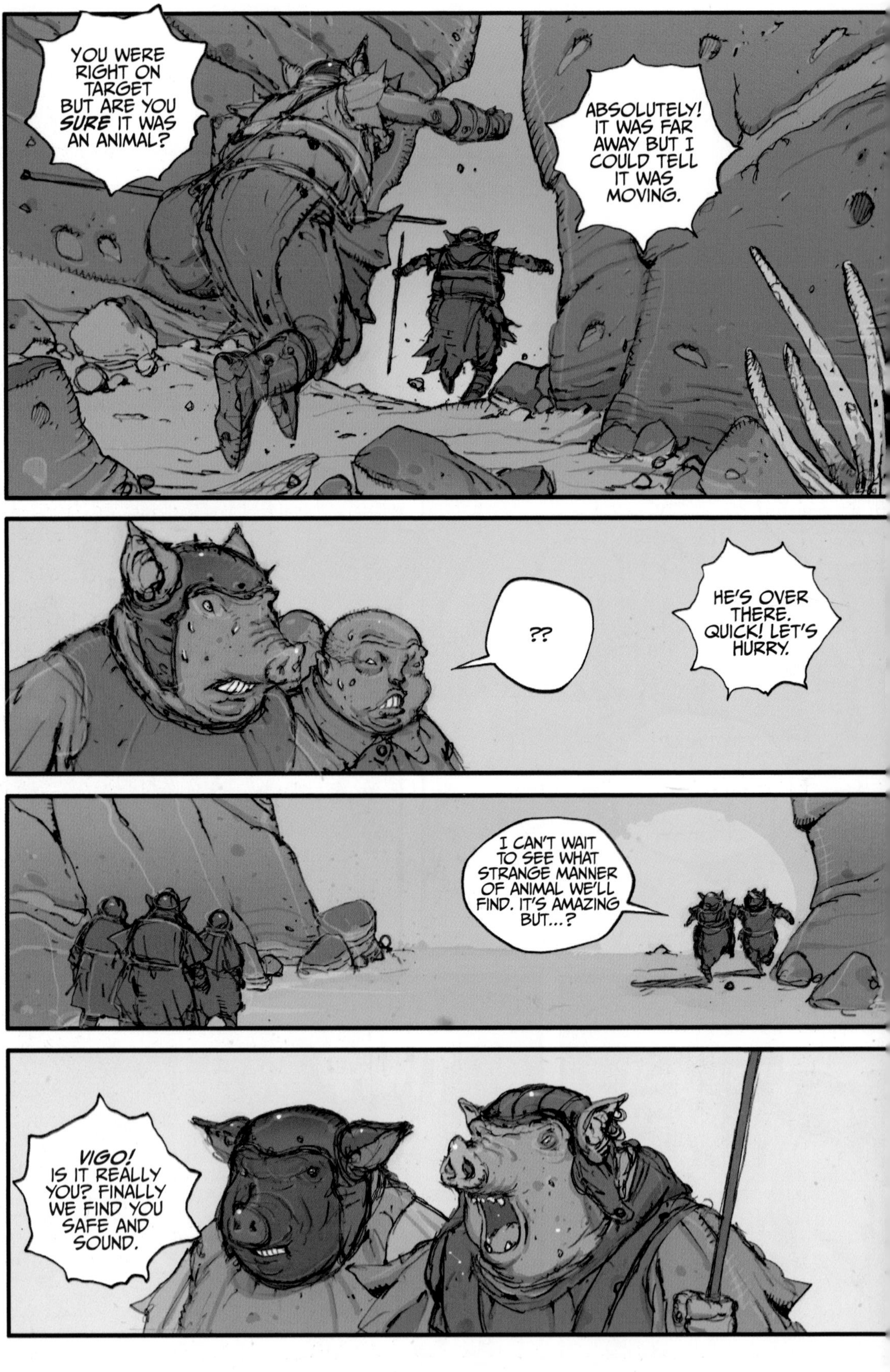
YOU WERE RIGHT ON TARGET BUT ARE YOU *SURE* IT WAS AN ANIMAL?
ABSOLUTELY! IT WAS FAR AWAY BUT I COULD TELL IT WAS MOVING.
??
HE'S OVER THERE. QUICK! LET'S HURRY.
I CAN'T WAIT TO SEE WHAT STRANGE MANNER OF ANIMAL WE'LL FIND. IT'S AMAZING BUT...?
VIGO! IS IT REALLY YOU? FINALLY WE FIND YOU SAFE AND SOUND.

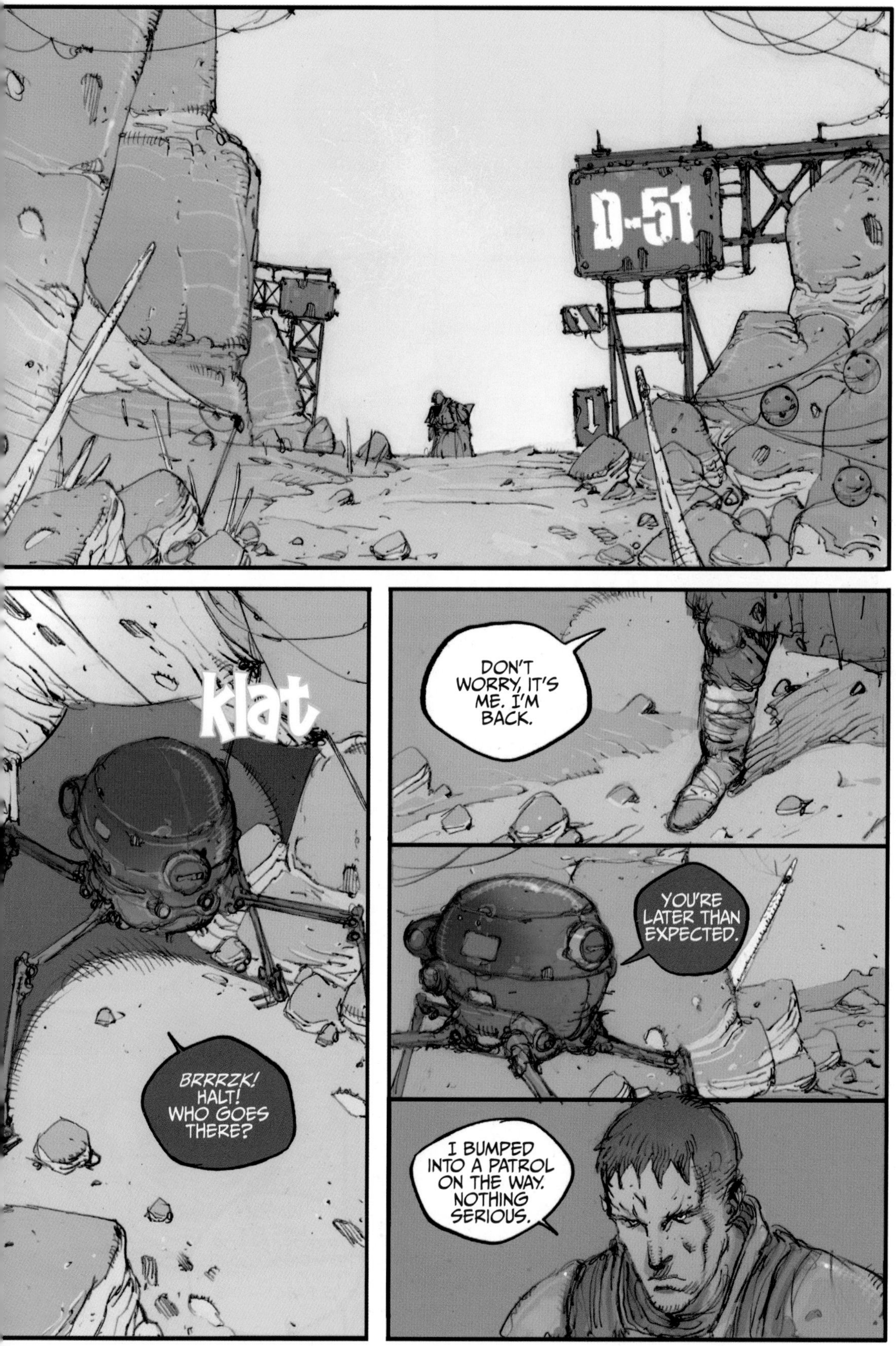
D-51
klat
BRRRZK! HALT! WHO GOES THERE?
DON'T WORRY, IT'S ME. I'M BACK.
YOU'RE LATER THAN EXPECTED.
I BUMPED INTO A PATROL ON THE WAY. NOTHING SERIOUS.

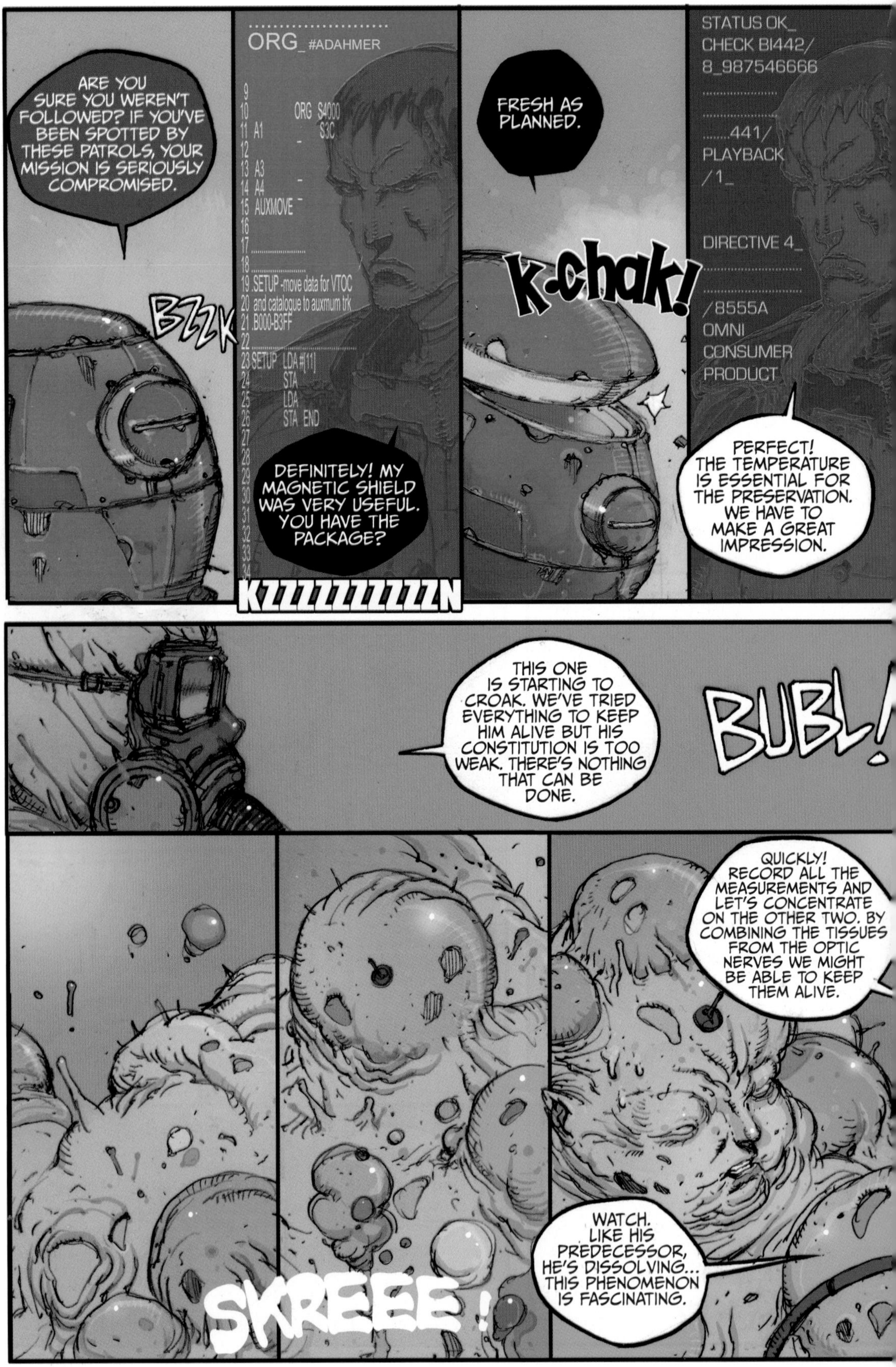
ARE YOU SURE YOU WEREN'T FOLLOWED? IF YOU'VE BEEN SPOTTED BY THESE PATROLS, YOUR MISSION IS SERIOUSLY COMPROMISED.
BZZK
ORG_ #ADAHMER
ORG $4000
A1 S3C
A3
A4
AUXMOVE
.SETUP -move data for VTOC
and catalogue to auxmum trk
.B000-B3FF
SETUP LDA #[11]
STA
LDA
STA END
DEFINITELY! MY MAGNETIC SHIELD WAS VERY USEFUL. YOU HAVE THE PACKAGE?
KZZZZZZZZZZZN
FRESH AS PLANNED.
K-CHAK!
STATUS OK_
CHECK BI442/
8_987546666
.......441/
PLAYBACK
/1_
DIRECTIVE 4_
/8555A
OMNI
CONSUMER
PRODUCT
PERFECT! THE TEMPERATURE IS ESSENTIAL FOR THE PRESERVATION. WE HAVE TO MAKE A GREAT IMPRESSION.
THIS ONE IS STARTING TO CROAK. WE'VE TRIED EVERYTHING TO KEEP HIM ALIVE BUT HIS CONSTITUTION IS TOO WEAK. THERE'S NOTHING THAT CAN BE DONE.
BUBL!
SKREEE!
QUICKLY! RECORD ALL THE MEASUREMENTS AND LET'S CONCENTRATE ON THE OTHER TWO. BY COMBINING THE TISSUES FROM THE OPTIC NERVES WE MIGHT BE ABLE TO KEEP THEM ALIVE.
WATCH. LIKE HIS PREDECESSOR, HE'S DISSOLVING... THIS PHENOMENON IS FASCINATING.

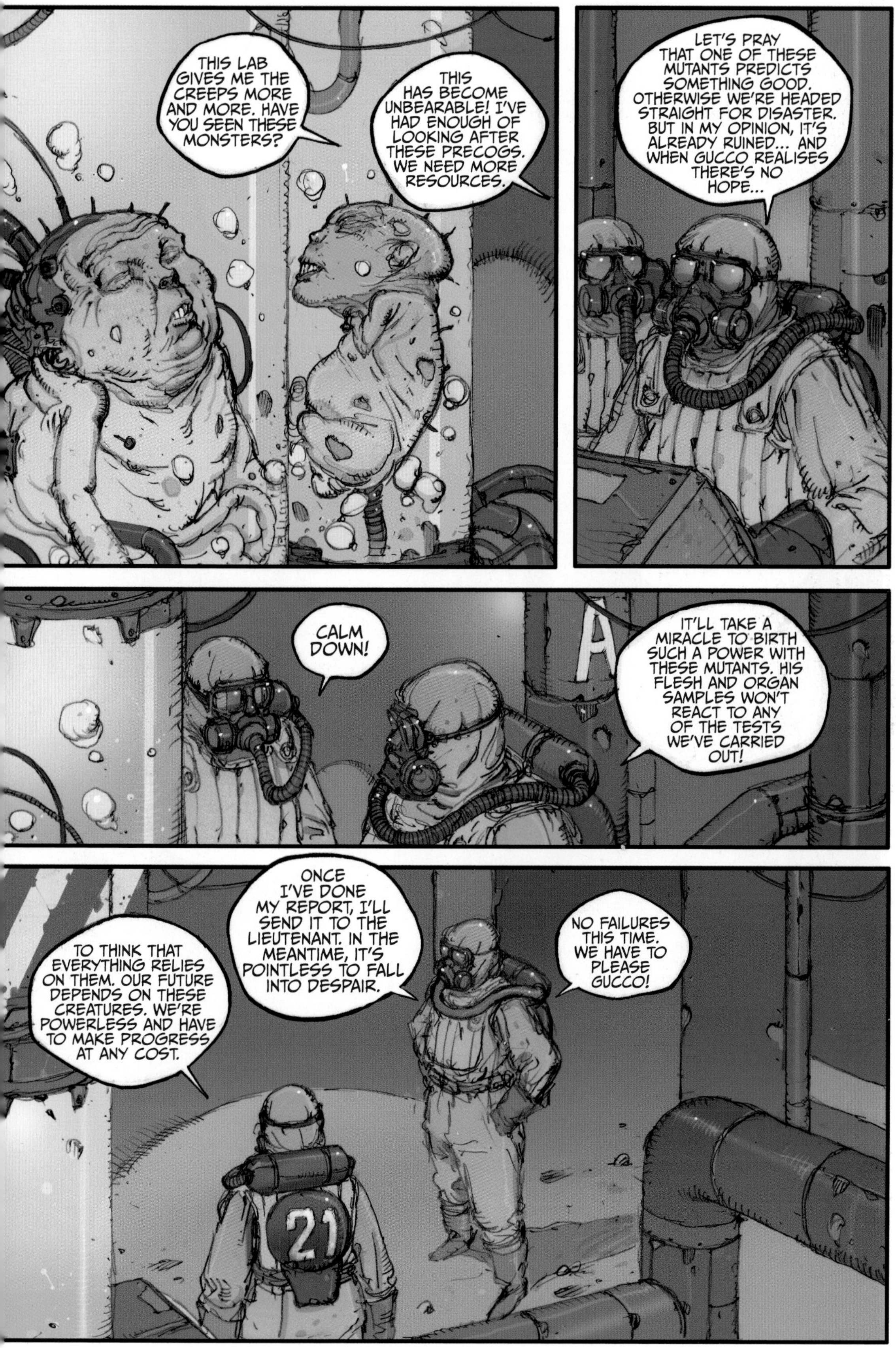
THIS LAB GIVES ME THE CREEPS MORE AND MORE. HAVE YOU SEEN THESE MONSTERS?
THIS HAS BECOME UNBEARABLE! I'VE HAD ENOUGH OF LOOKING AFTER THESE PRECOGS. WE NEED MORE RESOURCES.
LET'S PRAY THAT ONE OF THESE MUTANTS PREDICTS SOMETHING GOOD. OTHERWISE WE'RE HEADED STRAIGHT FOR DISASTER. BUT IN MY OPINION, IT'S ALREADY RUINED... AND WHEN GUCCO REALISES THERE'S NO HOPE...
CALM DOWN!
IT'LL TAKE A MIRACLE TO BIRTH SUCH A POWER WITH THESE MUTANTS. HIS FLESH AND ORGAN SAMPLES WON'T REACT TO ANY OF THE TESTS WE'VE CARRIED OUT!
TO THINK THAT EVERYTHING RELIES ON THEM. OUR FUTURE DEPENDS ON THESE CREATURES. WE'RE POWERLESS AND HAVE TO MAKE PROGRESS AT ANY COST.
ONCE I'VE DONE MY REPORT, I'LL SEND IT TO THE LIEUTENANT. IN THE MEANTIME, IT'S POINTLESS TO FALL INTO DESPAIR.
NO FAILURES THIS TIME. WE HAVE TO PLEASE GUCCO!
21

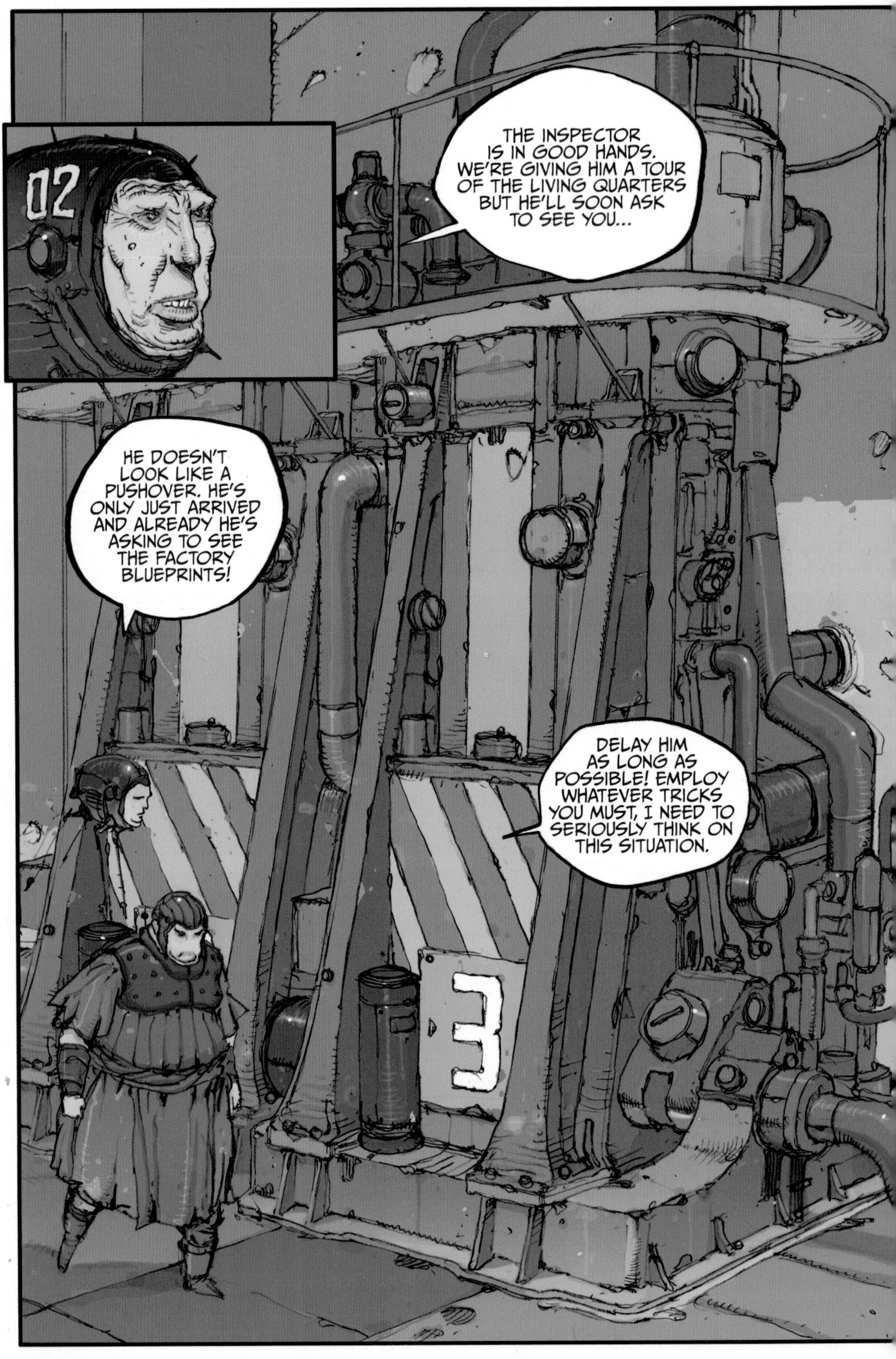
THE INSPECTOR IS IN GOOD HANDS. WE'RE GIVING HIM A TOUR OF THE LIVING QUARTERS BUT HE'LL SOON ASK TO SEE YOU...
HE DOESN'T LOOK LIKE A PUSHOVER. HE'S ONLY JUST ARRIVED AND ALREADY HE'S ASKING TO SEE THE FACTORY BLUEPRINTS!
DELAY HIM AS LONG AS POSSIBLE! EMPLOY WHATEVER TRICKS YOU MUST, I NEED TO SERIOUSLY THINK ON THIS SITUATION.

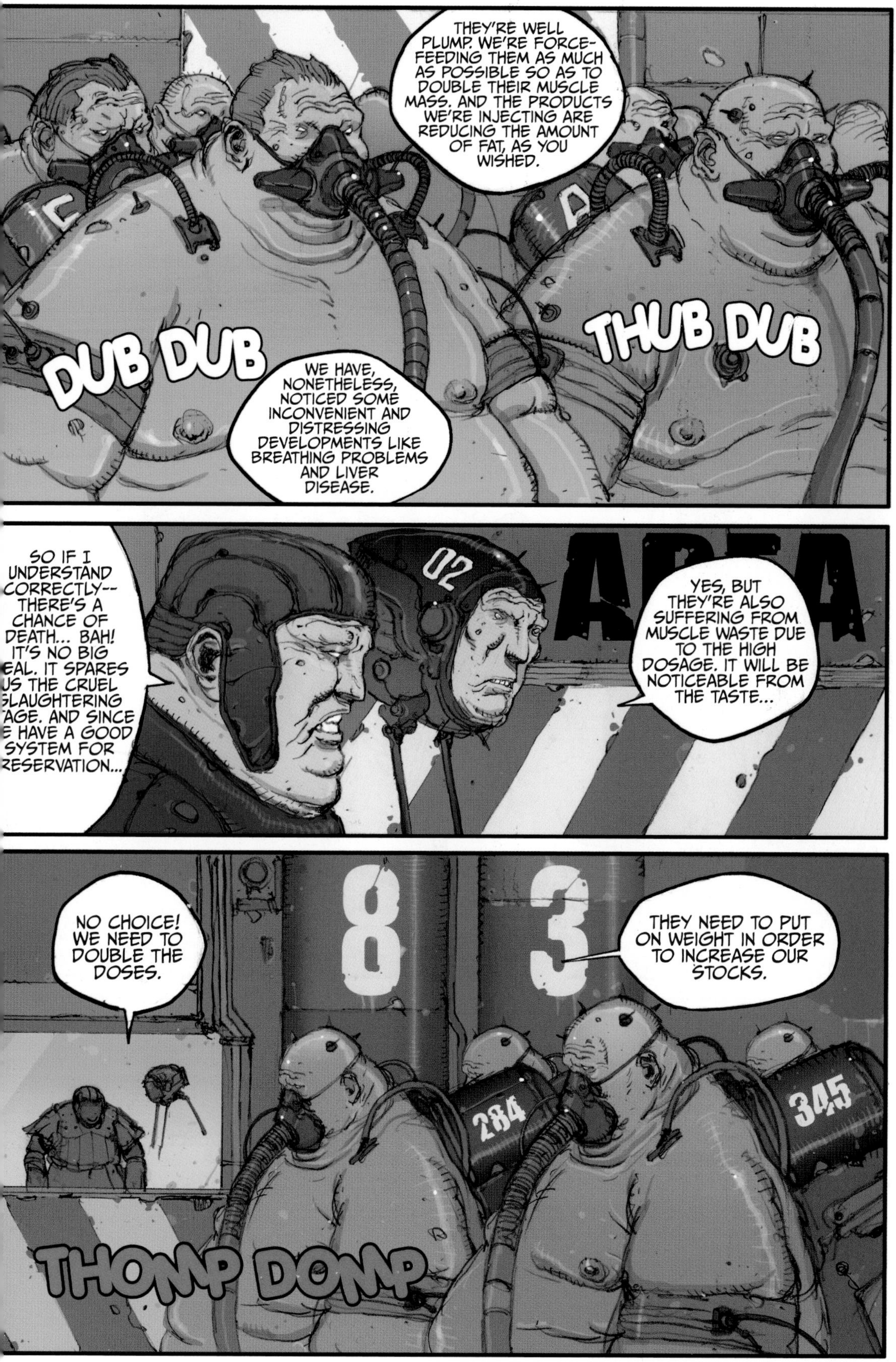
THEY'RE WELL PLUMP. WE'RE FORCE-FEEDING THEM AS MUCH AS POSSIBLE SO AS TO DOUBLE THEIR MUSCLE MASS. AND THE PRODUCTS WE'RE INJECTING ARE REDUCING THE AMOUNT OF FAT, AS YOU WISHED.
DUB DUB
THUB DUB
WE HAVE, NONETHELESS, NOTICED SOME INCONVENIENT AND DISTRESSING DEVELOPMENTS LIKE BREATHING PROBLEMS AND LIVER DISEASE.
SO IF I UNDERSTAND CORRECTLY-- THERE'S A CHANCE OF DEATH... BAH! IT'S NO BIG EAL. IT SPARES US THE CRUEL SLAUGHTERING TAGE. AND SINCE E HAVE A GOOD SYSTEM FOR RESERVATION...
YES, BUT THEY'RE ALSO SUFFERING FROM MUSCLE WASTE DUE TO THE HIGH DOSAGE. IT WILL BE NOTICEABLE FROM THE TASTE...
NO CHOICE! WE NEED TO DOUBLE THE DOSES.
THEY NEED TO PUT ON WEIGHT IN ORDER TO INCREASE OUR STOCKS.
THOMP DOMP

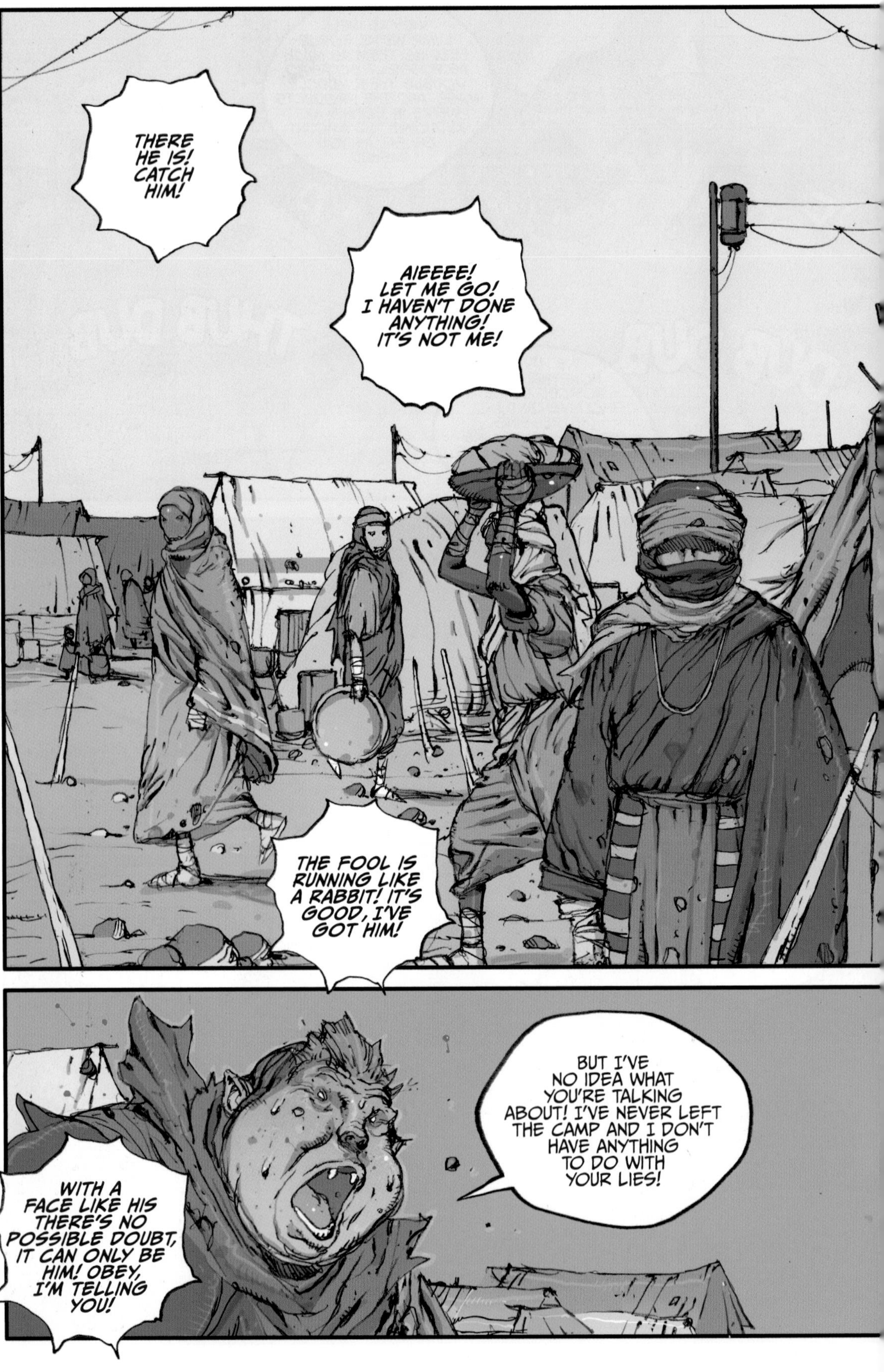
THERE HE IS! CATCH HIM!
AIEEEE! LET ME GO! I HAVEN'T DONE ANYTHING! IT'S NOT ME!
THE FOOL IS RUNNING LIKE A RABBIT! IT'S GOOD, I'VE GOT HIM!
BUT I'VE NO IDEA WHAT YOU'RE TALKING ABOUT! I'VE NEVER LEFT THE CAMP AND I DON'T HAVE ANYTHING TO DO WITH YOUR LIES!
WITH A FACE LIKE HIS THERE'S NO POSSIBLE DOUBT, IT CAN ONLY BE HIM! OBEY, I'M TELLING YOU!

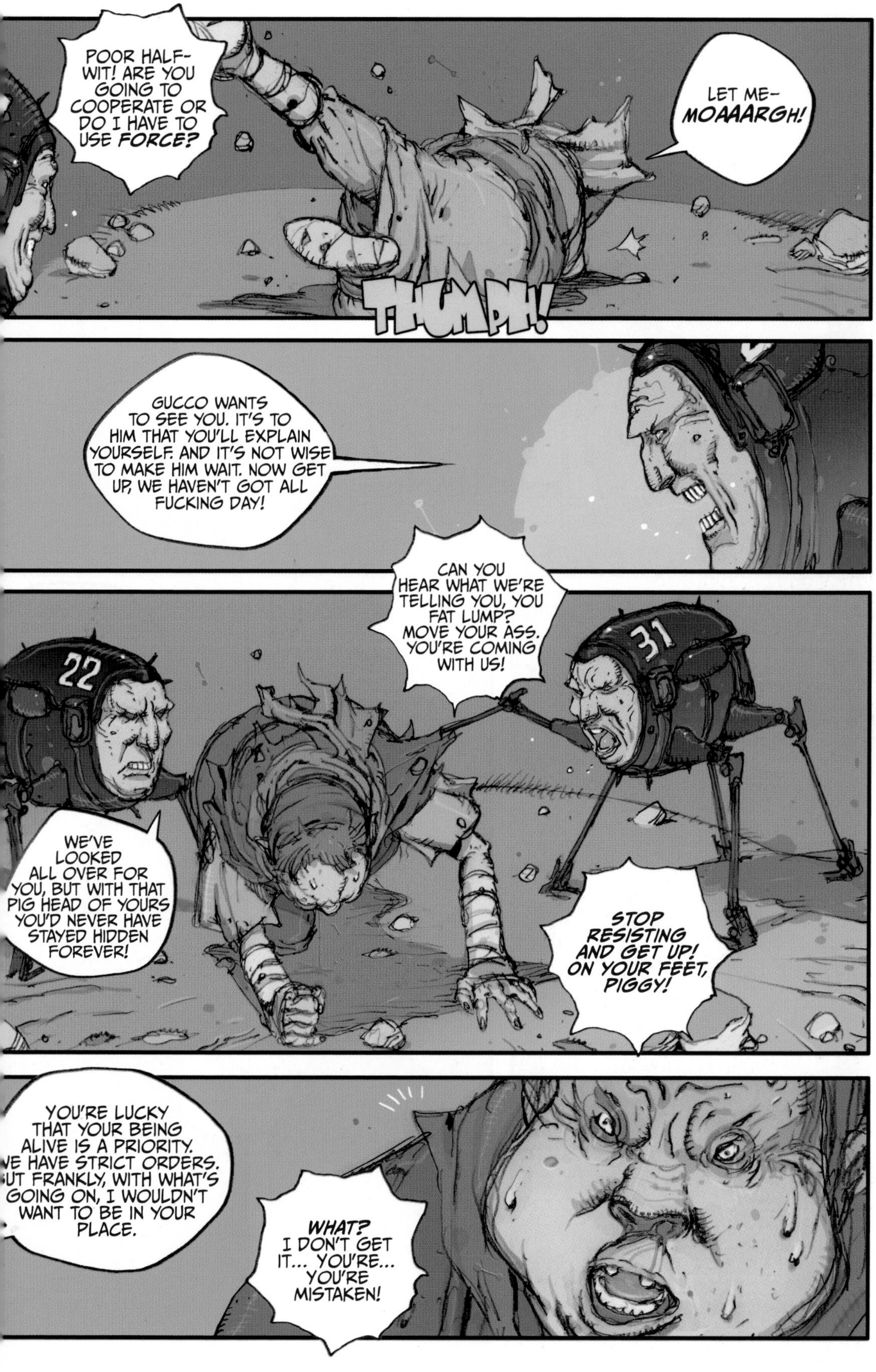
POOR HALF-WIT! ARE YOU GOING TO COOPERATE OR DO I HAVE TO USE *FORCE?*
LET ME- *MOAAARGH!*
THUMPH!
GUCCO WANTS TO SEE YOU. IT'S TO HIM THAT YOU'LL EXPLAIN YOURSELF. AND IT'S NOT WISE TO MAKE HIM WAIT. NOW GET UP, WE HAVEN'T GOT ALL FUCKING DAY!
22
31
CAN YOU HEAR WHAT WE'RE TELLING YOU, YOU FAT LUMP? MOVE YOUR ASS. YOU'RE COMING WITH US!
WE'VE LOOKED ALL OVER FOR YOU, BUT WITH THAT PIG HEAD OF YOURS YOU'D NEVER HAVE STAYED HIDDEN FOREVER!
STOP RESISTING AND GET UP! ON YOUR FEET, PIGGY!
YOU'RE LUCKY THAT YOUR BEING ALIVE IS A PRIORITY. WE HAVE STRICT ORDERS. BUT FRANKLY, WITH WHAT'S GOING ON, I WOULDN'T WANT TO BE IN YOUR PLACE.
WHAT? I DON'T GET IT... YOU'RE... YOU'RE MISTAKEN!

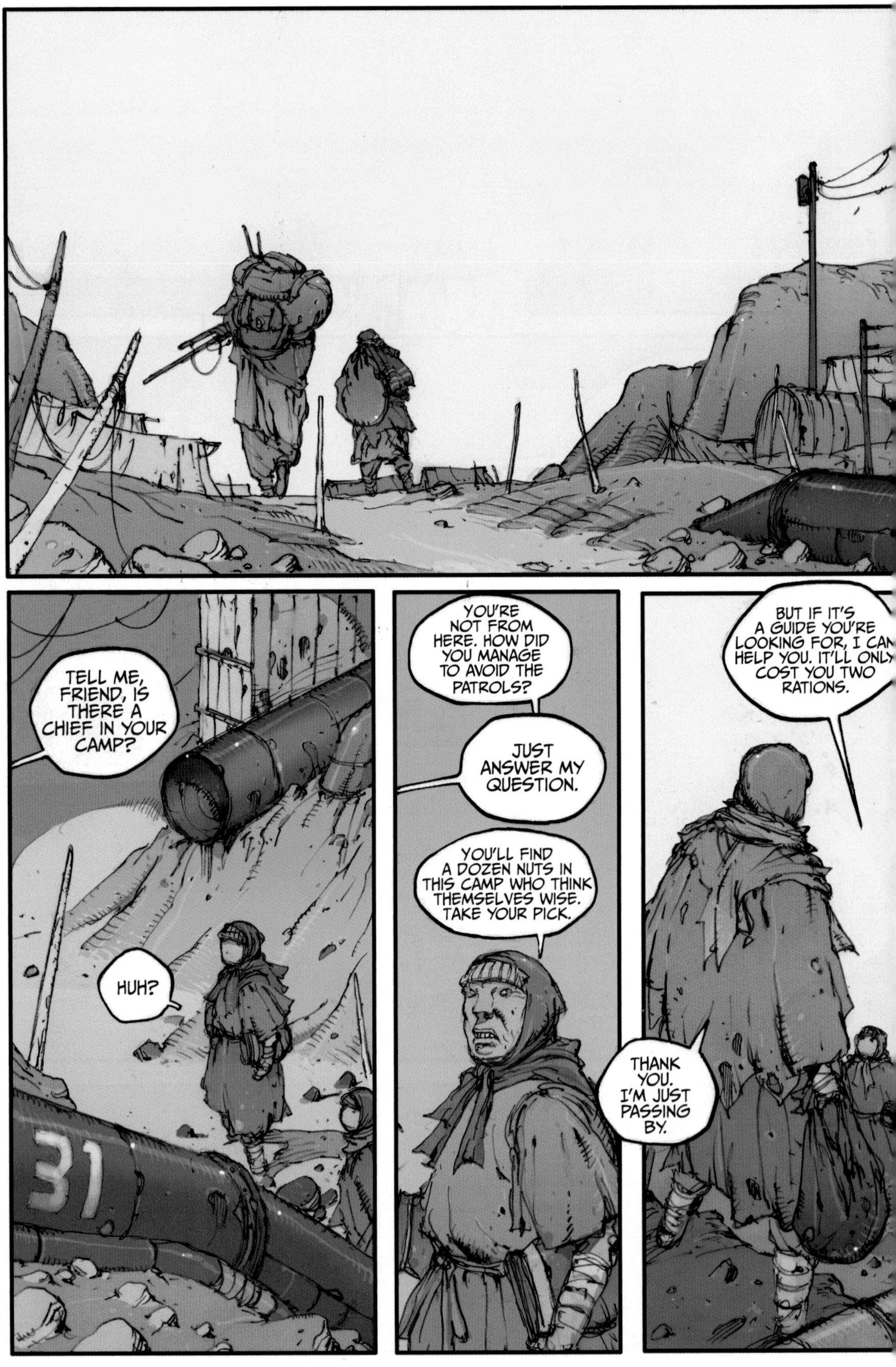
TELL ME, FRIEND, IS THERE A CHIEF IN YOUR CAMP?
HUH?
31
YOU'RE NOT FROM HERE. HOW DID YOU MANAGE TO AVOID THE PATROLS?
JUST ANSWER MY QUESTION.
YOU'LL FIND A DOZEN NUTS IN THIS CAMP WHO THINK THEMSELVES WISE. TAKE YOUR PICK.
BUT IF IT'S A GUIDE YOU'RE LOOKING FOR, I CAN HELP YOU. IT'LL ONLY COST YOU TWO RATIONS.
THANK YOU. I'M JUST PASSING BY.

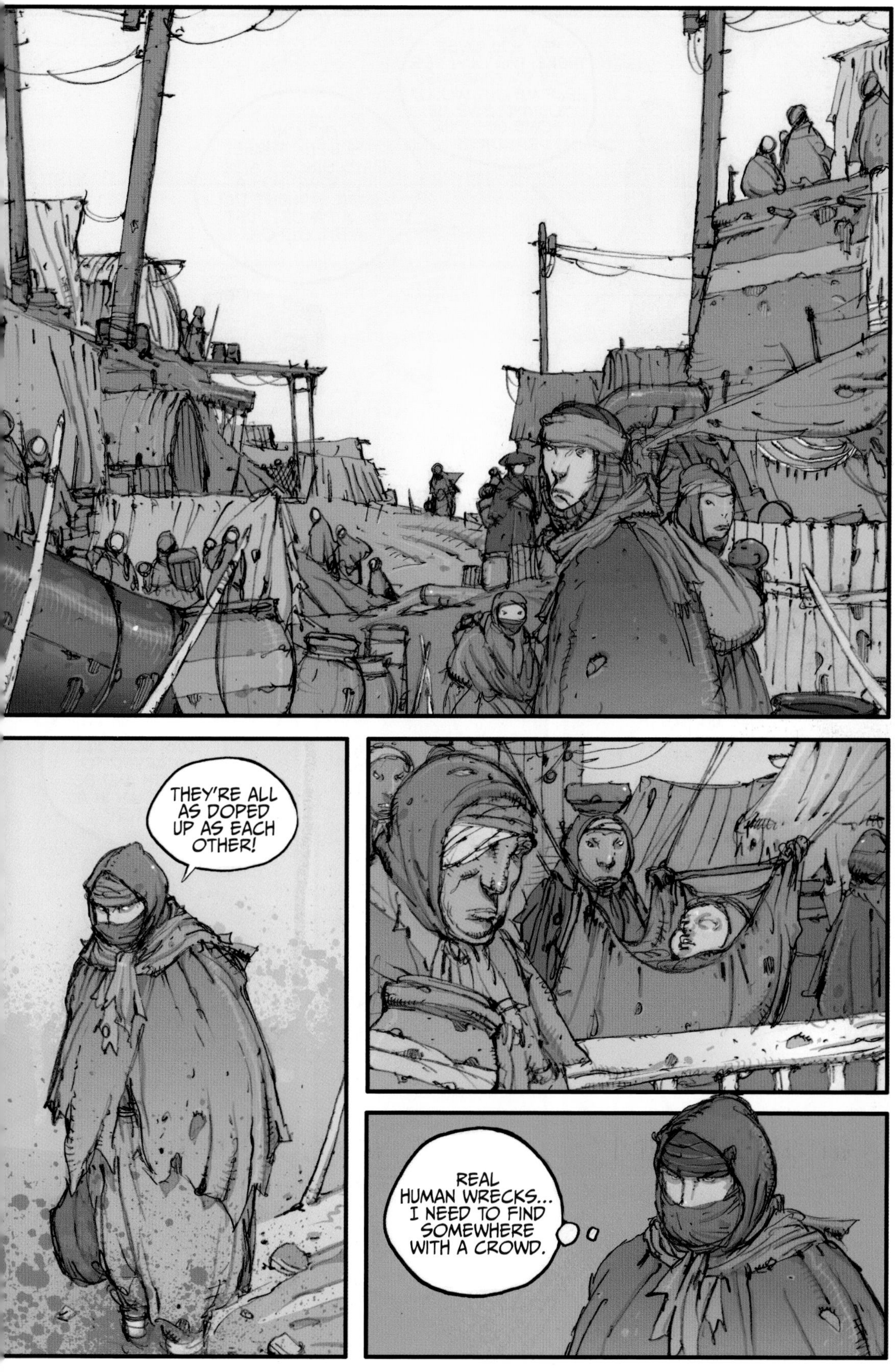
THEY'RE ALL AS DOPED UP AS EACH OTHER!
REAL HUMAN WRECKS... I NEED TO FIND SOMEWHERE WITH A CROWD.

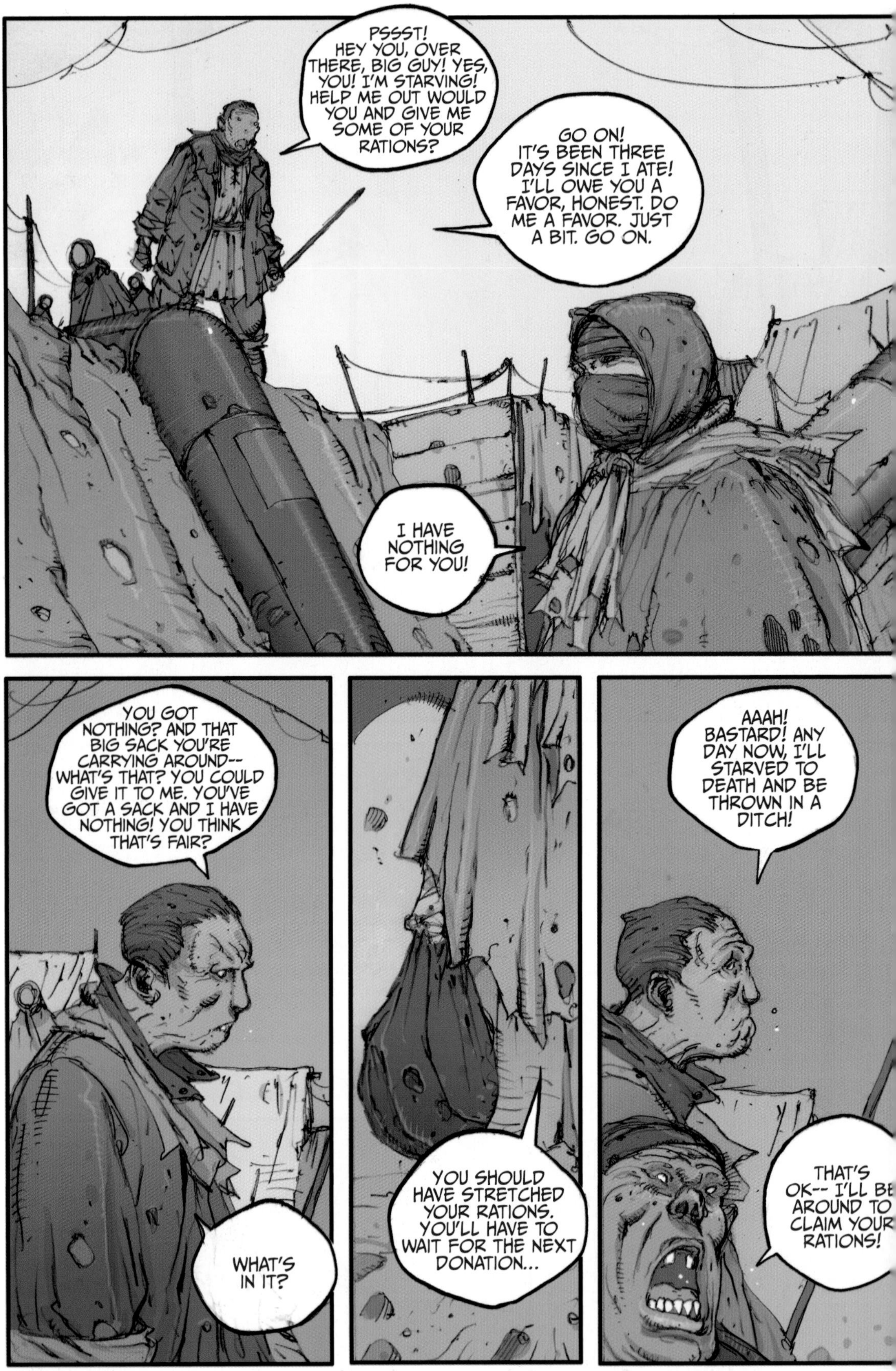
PSSST! HEY YOU, OVER THERE, BIG GUY! YES, YOU! I'M STARVING! HELP ME OUT WOULD YOU AND GIVE ME SOME OF YOUR RATIONS?
GO ON! IT'S BEEN THREE DAYS SINCE I ATE! I'LL OWE YOU A FAVOR, HONEST. DO ME A FAVOR. JUST A BIT. GO ON.
I HAVE NOTHING FOR YOU!
YOU GOT NOTHING? AND THAT BIG SACK YOU'RE CARRYING AROUND-- WHAT'S THAT? YOU COULD GIVE IT TO ME. YOU'VE GOT A SACK AND I HAVE NOTHING! YOU THINK THAT'S FAIR?
WHAT'S IN IT?
YOU SHOULD HAVE STRETCHED YOUR RATIONS. YOU'LL HAVE TO WAIT FOR THE NEXT DONATION...
AAAH! BASTARD! ANY DAY NOW, I'LL STARVED TO DEATH AND BE THROWN IN A DITCH!
THAT'S OK-- I'LL BE AROUND TO CLAIM YOUR RATIONS!

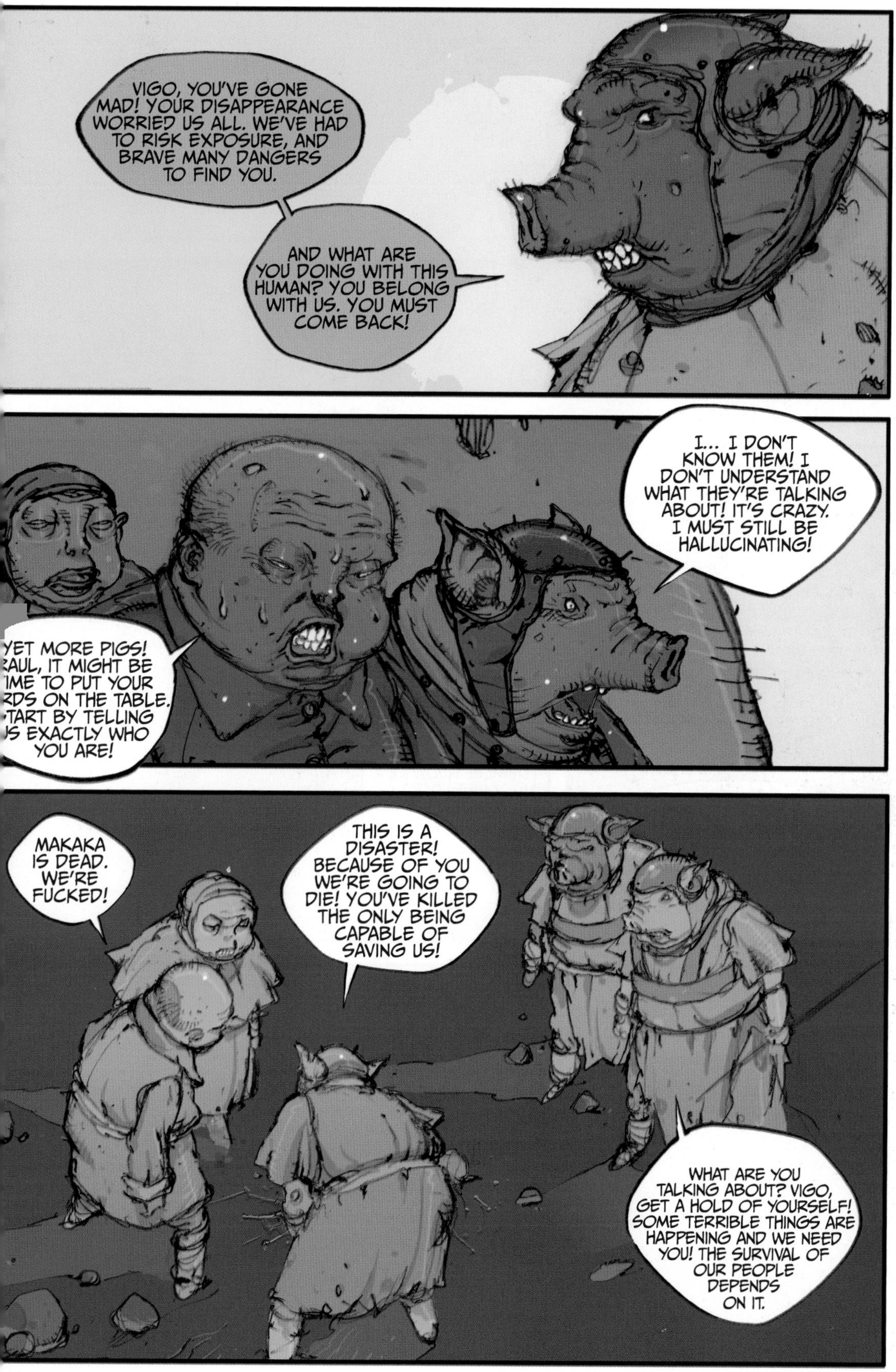
VIGO, YOU'VE GONE MAD! YOUR DISAPPEARANCE WORRIED US ALL. WE'VE HAD TO RISK EXPOSURE, AND BRAVE MANY DANGERS TO FIND YOU.
AND WHAT ARE YOU DOING WITH THIS HUMAN? YOU BELONG WITH US. YOU MUST COME BACK!
I... I DON'T KNOW THEM! I DON'T UNDERSTAND WHAT THEY'RE TALKING ABOUT! IT'S CRAZY. I MUST STILL BE HALLUCINATING!
YET MORE PIGS! AUL, IT MIGHT BE IME TO PUT YOUR RDS ON THE TABLE. TART BY TELLING S EXACTLY WHO YOU ARE!
MAKAKA IS DEAD. WE'RE FUCKED!
THIS IS A DISASTER! BECAUSE OF YOU WE'RE GOING TO DIE! YOU'VE KILLED THE ONLY BEING CAPABLE OF SAVING US!
WHAT ARE YOU TALKING ABOUT? VIGO, GET A HOLD OF YOURSELF! SOME TERRIBLE THINGS ARE HAPPENING AND WE NEED YOU! THE SURVIVAL OF OUR PEOPLE DEPENDS ON IT.

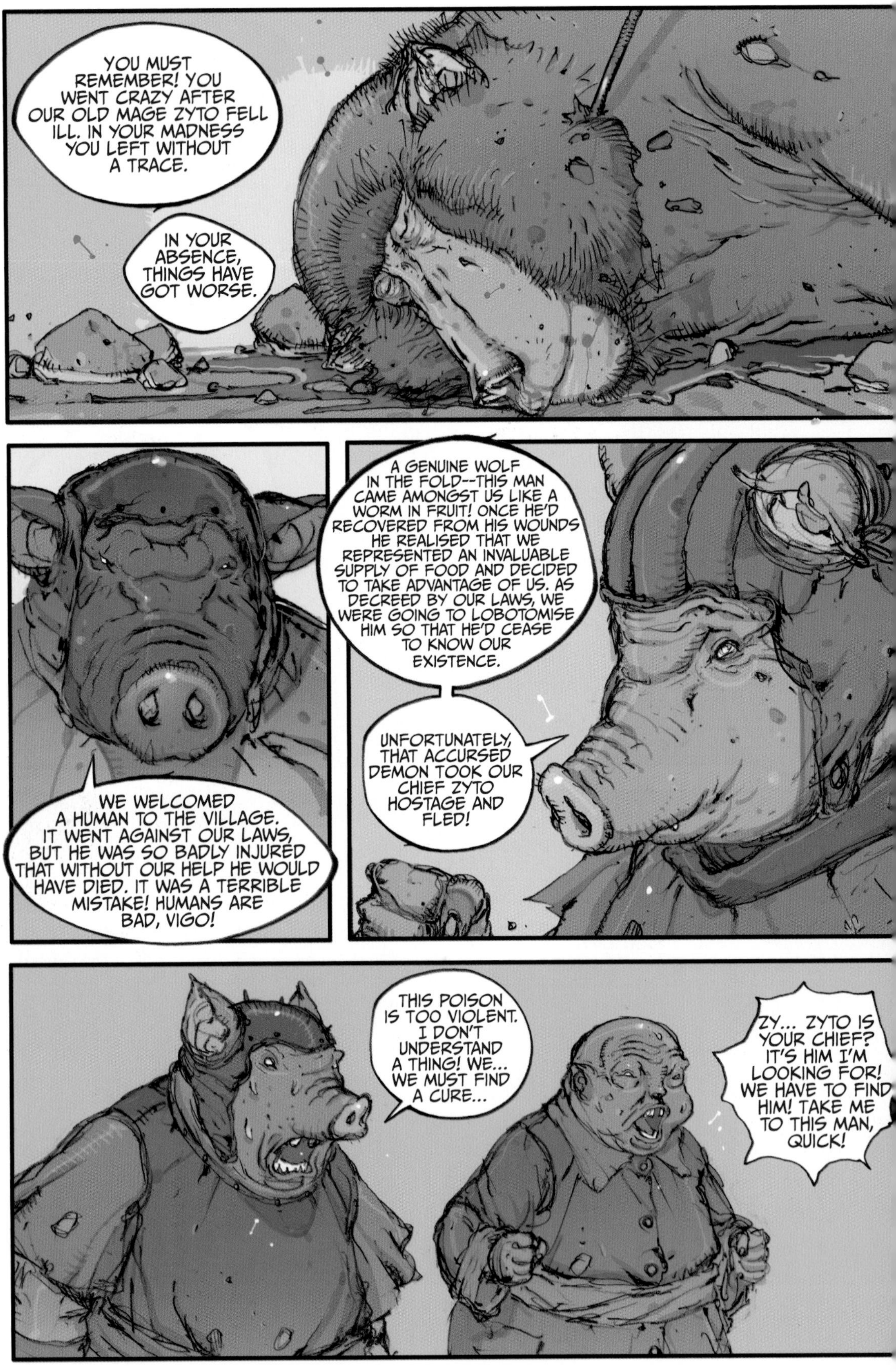
YOU MUST REMEMBER! YOU WENT CRAZY AFTER OUR OLD MAGE ZYTO FELL ILL. IN YOUR MADNESS YOU LEFT WITHOUT A TRACE.
IN YOUR ABSENCE, THINGS HAVE GOT WORSE.
WE WELCOMED A HUMAN TO THE VILLAGE. IT WENT AGAINST OUR LAWS, BUT HE WAS SO BADLY INJURED THAT WITHOUT OUR HELP HE WOULD HAVE DIED. IT WAS A TERRIBLE MISTAKE! HUMANS ARE BAD, VIGO!
A GENUINE WOLF IN THE FOLD--THIS MAN CAME AMONGST US LIKE A WORM IN FRUIT! ONCE HE'D RECOVERED FROM HIS WOUNDS HE REALISED THAT WE REPRESENTED AN INVALUABLE SUPPLY OF FOOD AND DECIDED TO TAKE ADVANTAGE OF US. AS DECREED BY OUR LAWS, WE WERE GOING TO LOBOTOMISE HIM SO THAT HE'D CEASE TO KNOW OUR EXISTENCE.
UNFORTUNATELY, THAT ACCURSED DEMON TOOK OUR CHIEF ZYTO HOSTAGE AND FLED!
THIS POISON IS TOO VIOLENT. I DON'T UNDERSTAND A THING! WE... WE MUST FIND A CURE...
ZY... ZYTO IS YOUR CHIEF? IT'S HIM I'M LOOKING FOR! WE HAVE TO FIND HIM! TAKE ME TO THIS MAN, QUICK!

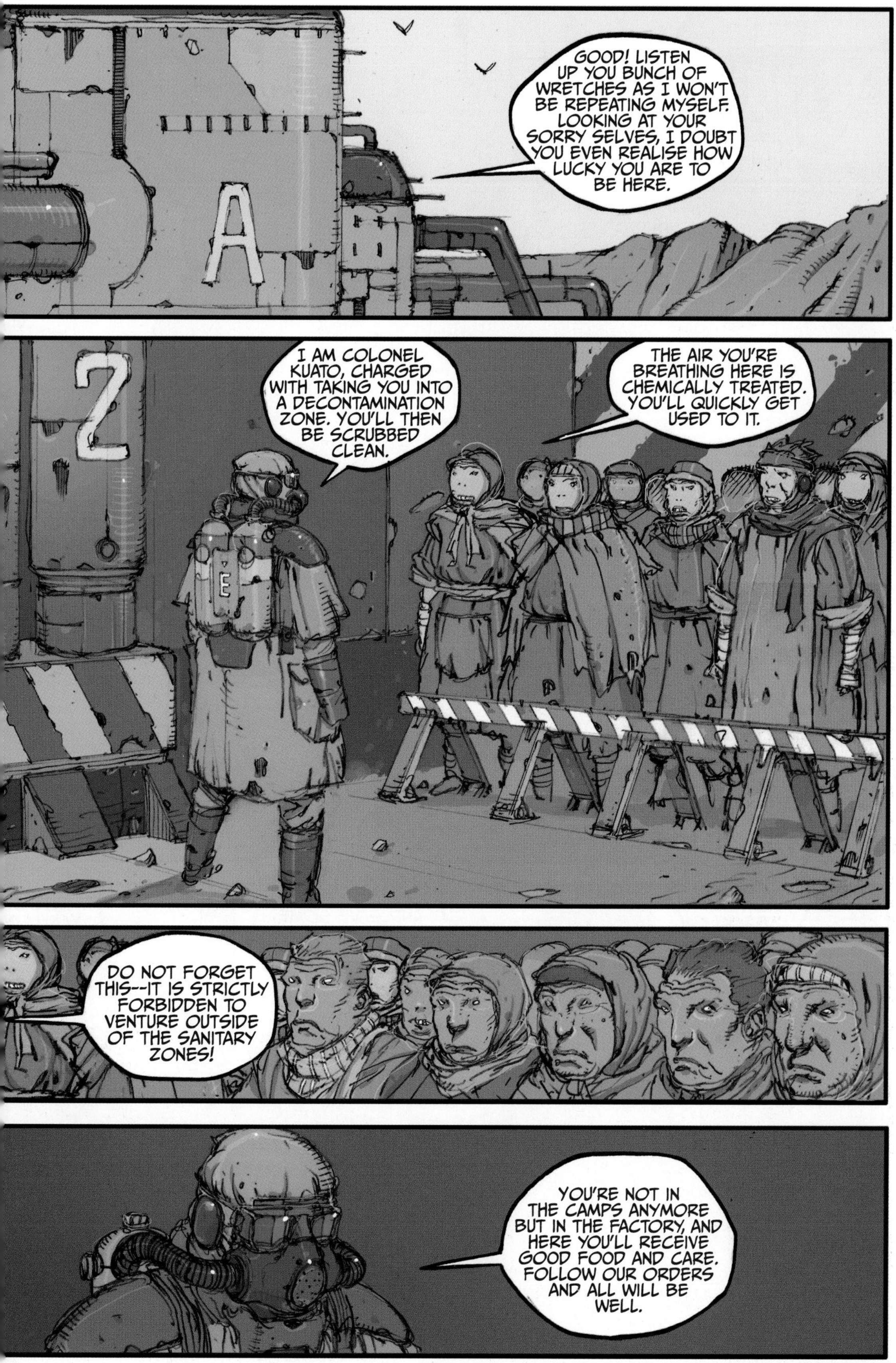
GOOD! LISTEN UP YOU BUNCH OF WRETCHES AS I WON'T BE REPEATING MYSELF. LOOKING AT YOUR SORRY SELVES, I DOUBT YOU EVEN REALISE HOW LUCKY YOU ARE TO BE HERE.
I AM COLONEL KUATO, CHARGED WITH TAKING YOU INTO A DECONTAMINATION ZONE. YOU'LL THEN BE SCRUBBED CLEAN.
THE AIR YOU'RE BREATHING HERE IS CHEMICALLY TREATED. YOU'LL QUICKLY GET USED TO IT.
DO NOT FORGET THIS--IT IS STRICTLY FORBIDDEN TO VENTURE OUTSIDE OF THE SANITARY ZONES!
YOU'RE NOT IN THE CAMPS ANYMORE BUT IN THE FACTORY, AND HERE YOU'LL RECEIVE GOOD FOOD AND CARE. FOLLOW OUR ORDERS AND ALL WILL BE WELL.

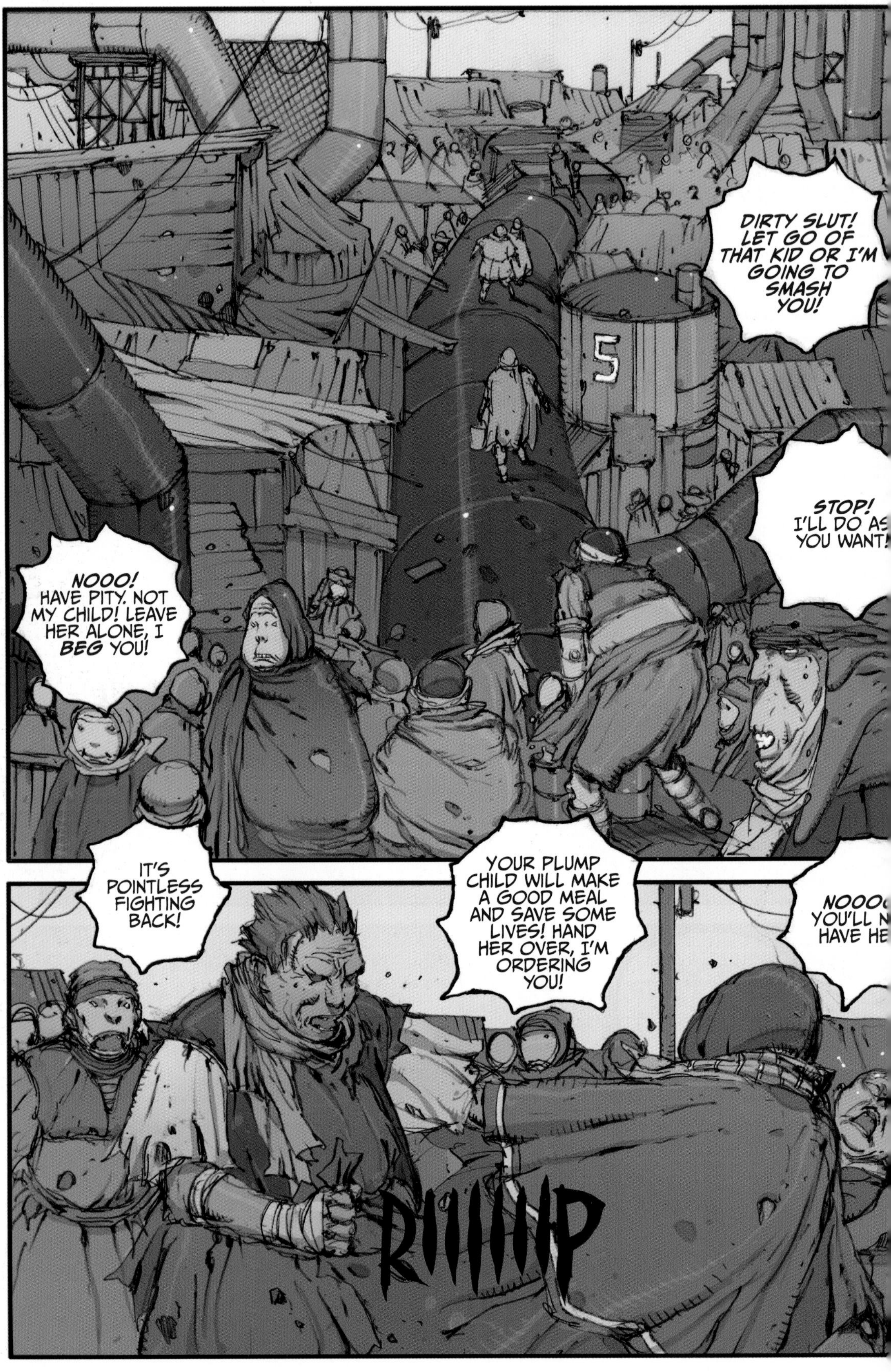
DIRTY SLUT! LET GO OF THAT KID OR I'M GOING TO SMASH YOU!
NOOO! HAVE PITY. NOT MY CHILD! LEAVE HER ALONE, I BEG YOU!
STOP! I'LL DO AS YOU WANT!
IT'S POINTLESS FIGHTING BACK!
YOUR PLUMP CHILD WILL MAKE A GOOD MEAL AND SAVE SOME LIVES! HAND HER OVER, I'M ORDERING YOU!
NOOO YOU'LL N HAVE HE
RIIIIIP

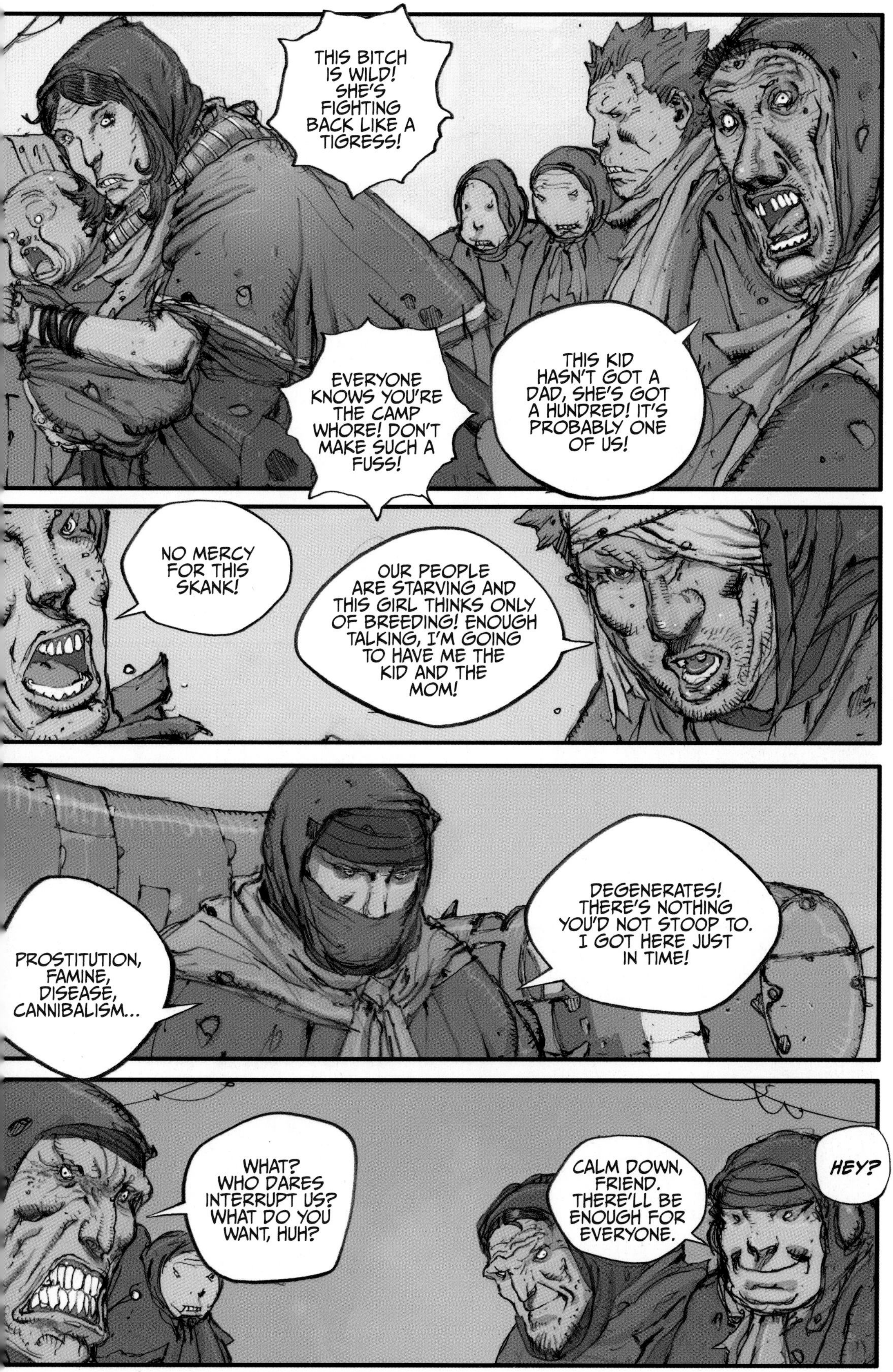
THIS BITCH IS WILD! SHE'S FIGHTING BACK LIKE A TIGRESS!
EVERYONE KNOWS YOU'RE THE CAMP WHORE! DON'T MAKE SUCH A FUSS!
THIS KID HASN'T GOT A DAD, SHE'S GOT A HUNDRED! IT'S PROBABLY ONE OF US!
NO MERCY FOR THIS SKANK!
OUR PEOPLE ARE STARVING AND THIS GIRL THINKS ONLY OF BREEDING! ENOUGH TALKING, I'M GOING TO HAVE ME THE KID AND THE MOM!
PROSTITUTION, FAMINE, DISEASE, CANNIBALISM...
DEGENERATES! THERE'S NOTHING YOU'D NOT STOOP TO. I GOT HERE JUST IN TIME!
WHAT? WHO DARES INTERRUPT US? WHAT DO YOU WANT, HUH?
CALM DOWN, FRIEND. THERE'LL BE ENOUGH FOR EVERYONE.
HEY?

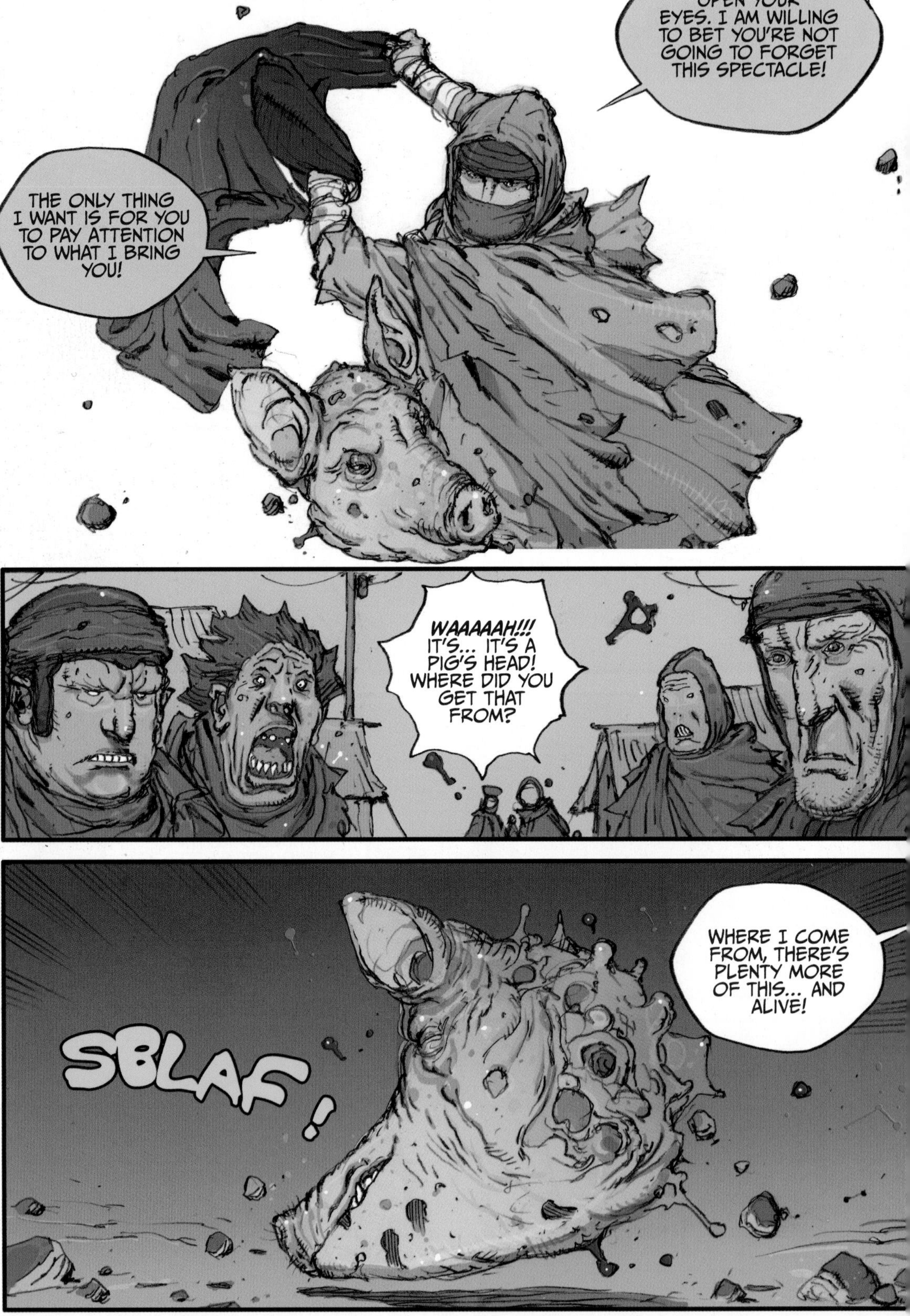
THE ONLY THING I WANT IS FOR YOU TO PAY ATTENTION TO WHAT I BRING YOU!
OPEN YOUR EYES. I AM WILLING TO BET YOU'RE NOT GOING TO FORGET THIS SPECTACLE!
WAAAAAH!!! IT'S... IT'S A PIG'S HEAD! WHERE DID YOU GET THAT FROM?
SBLAF!
WHERE I COME FROM, THERE'S PLENTY MORE OF THIS... AND ALIVE!

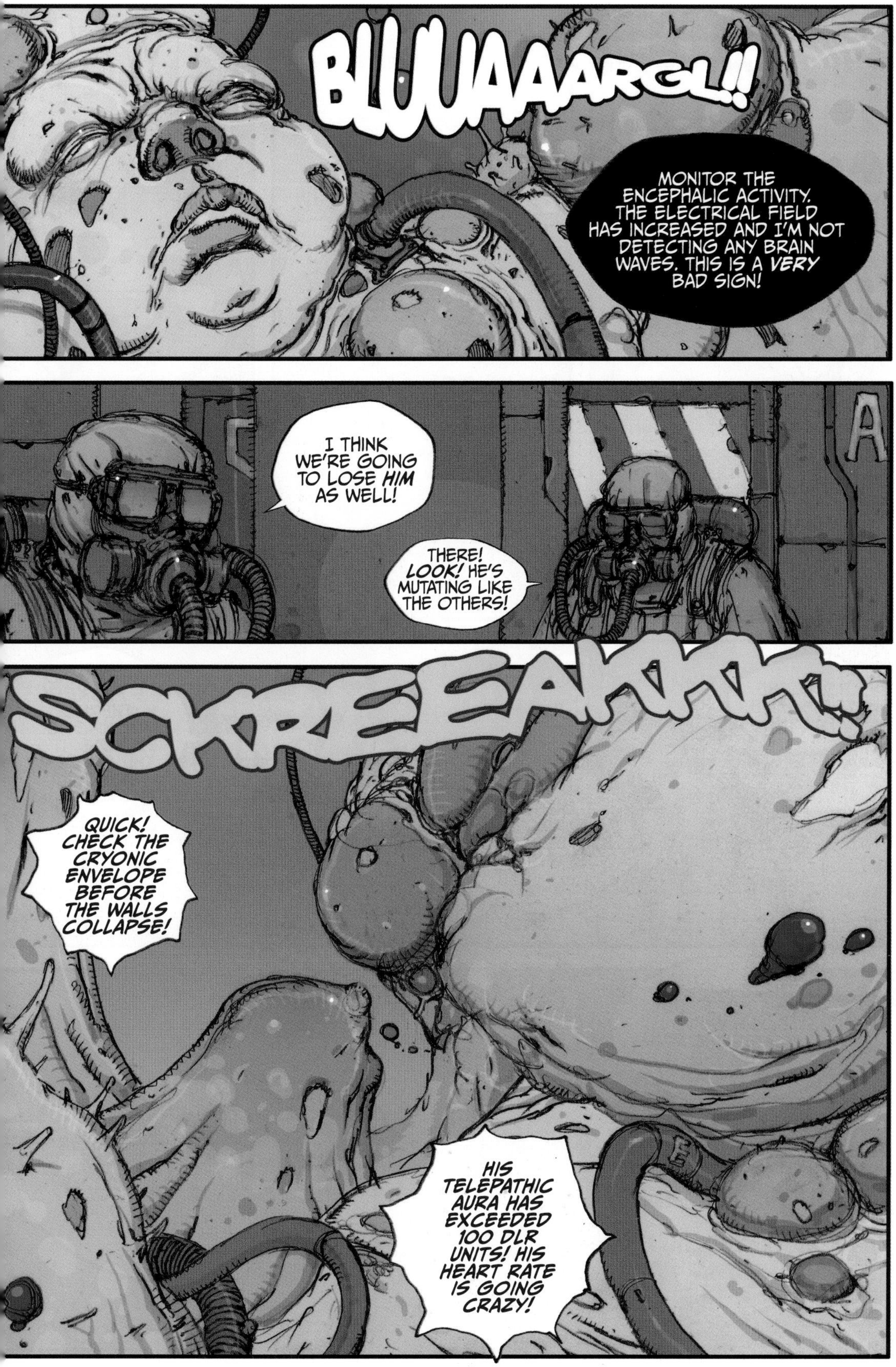
BLUUAAARGL!!
MONITOR THE ENCEPHALIC ACTIVITY. THE ELECTRICAL FIELD HAS INCREASED AND I'M NOT DETECTING ANY BRAIN WAVES. THIS IS A VERY BAD SIGN!
I THINK WE'RE GOING TO LOSE HIM AS WELL!
THERE! LOOK! HE'S MUTATING LIKE THE OTHERS!
SCKREEAKKK!!
QUICK! CHECK THE CRYONIC ENVELOPE BEFORE THE WALLS COLLAPSE!
HIS TELEPATHIC AURA HAS EXCEEDED 100 DLR UNITS! HIS HEART RATE IS GOING CRAZY!

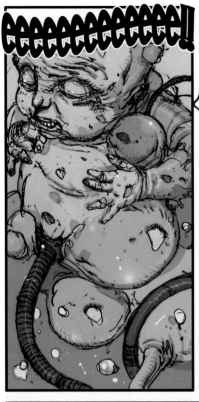

eeeeeeeeeeeeel!

TOO LATE! THE PSI FIELD IS ABOUT TO EXPLODE! WE'VE TRIED EVERYTHING!

WE... WE NEED TO WARN GUCCO!

flurb!

TWeeep

BOSS, THE TESTS HAVE FAILED!

I KNEW IT! I'M SURROUNDED BY A BUNCH OF INCOMPETENTS!

EVERYTHING IS FUCKED! THERE'S NOTHING TO BE DONE. IT'S THE END! I'M GOING TO CROAK!

THERE MAY BE SOME HOPE LEFT, BOSS. WE'VE LOCATED THE MAN WITH THE PIG FACE...

WH... WHAT? YOU'VE LAID YOUR HANDS ON THIS MONSTER AND I WASN'T INFORMED? SO WHAT ARE YOU WAITING FOR, USELESS FOOL?! HURRY UP, IT'S OUR LAST CHANCE!

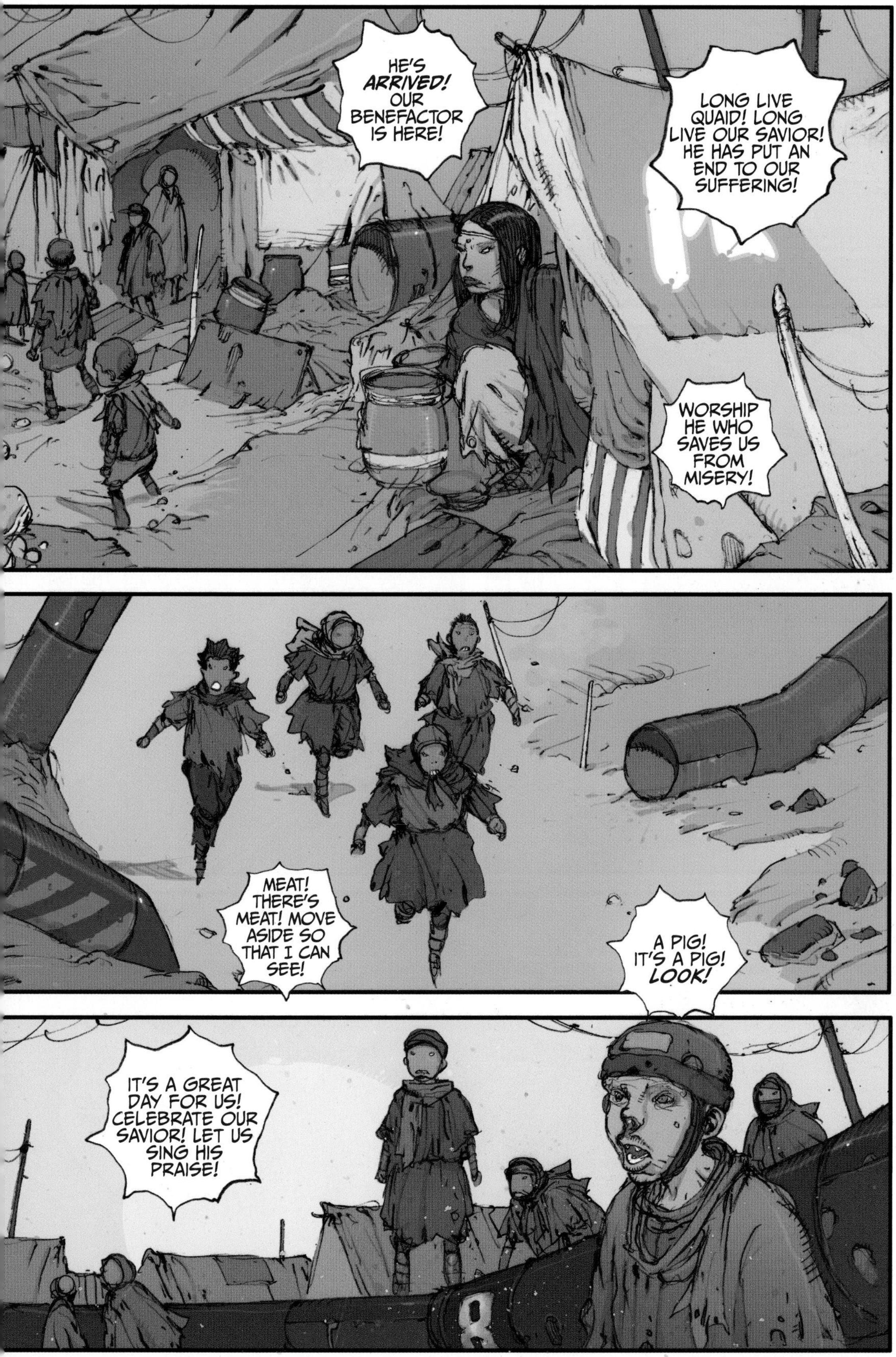
HE'S ARRIVED! OUR BENEFACTOR IS HERE!
LONG LIVE QUAID! LONG LIVE OUR SAVIOR! HE HAS PUT AN END TO OUR SUFFERING!
WORSHIP HE WHO SAVES US FROM MISERY!
MEAT! THERE'S MEAT! MOVE ASIDE SO THAT I CAN SEE!
A PIG! IT'S A PIG! LOOK!
IT'S A GREAT DAY FOR US! CELEBRATE OUR SAVIOR! LET US SING HIS PRAISE!

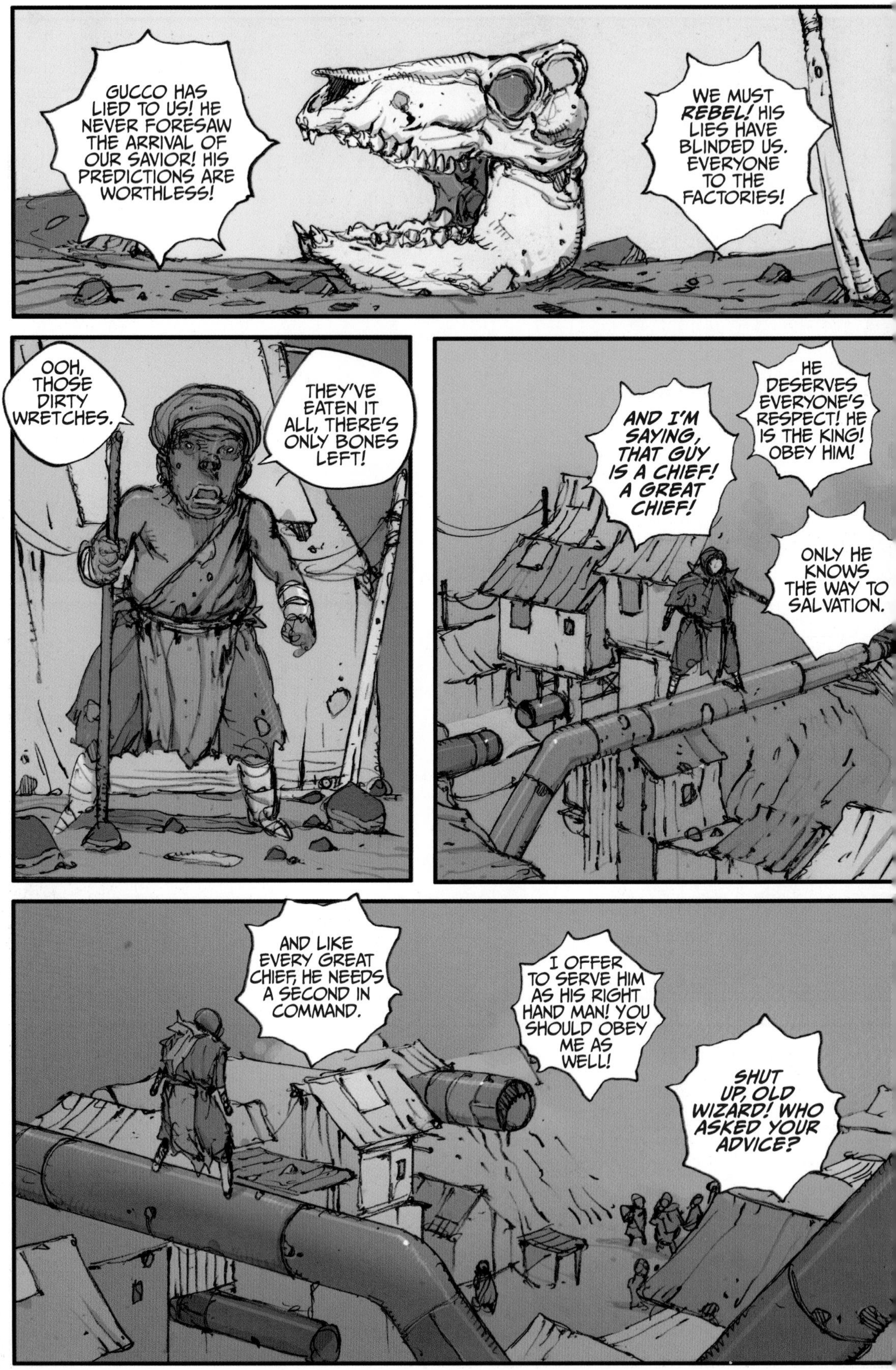
GUCCO HAS LIED TO US! HE NEVER FORESAW THE ARRIVAL OF OUR SAVIOR! HIS PREDICTIONS ARE WORTHLESS!
WE MUST REBEL! HIS LIES HAVE BLINDED US. EVERYONE TO THE FACTORIES!
OOH, THOSE DIRTY WRETCHES.
THEY'VE EATEN IT ALL, THERE'S ONLY BONES LEFT!
AND I'M SAYING, THAT GUY IS A CHIEF! A GREAT CHIEF!
HE DESERVES EVERYONE'S RESPECT! HE IS THE KING! OBEY HIM!
ONLY HE KNOWS THE WAY TO SALVATION.
AND LIKE EVERY GREAT CHIEF, HE NEEDS A SECOND IN COMMAND.
I OFFER TO SERVE HIM AS HIS RIGHT HAND MAN! YOU SHOULD OBEY ME AS WELL!
SHUT UP, OLD WIZARD! WHO ASKED YOUR ADVICE?

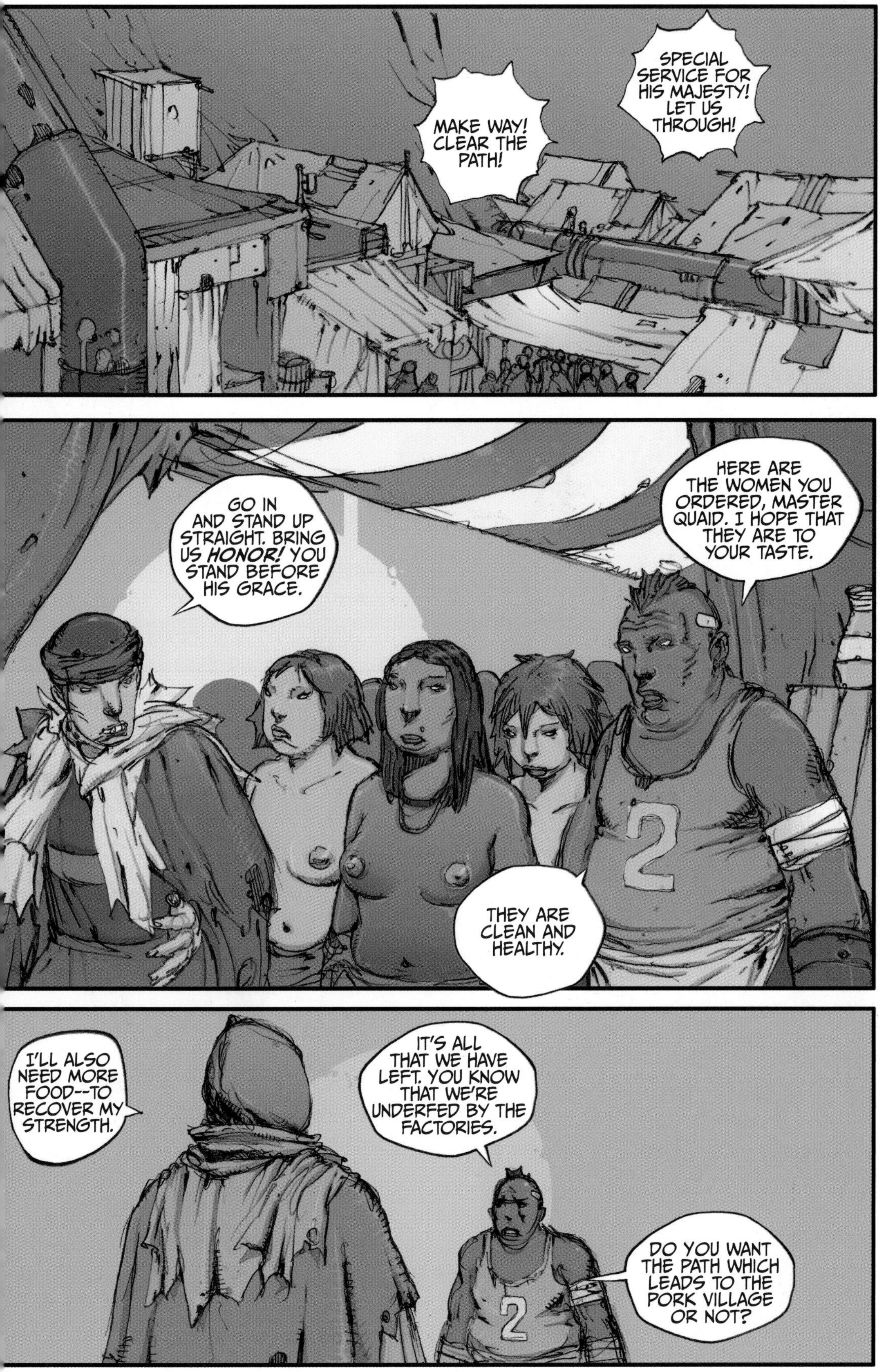
MAKE WAY! CLEAR THE PATH!
SPECIAL SERVICE FOR HIS MAJESTY! LET US THROUGH!
GO IN AND STAND UP STRAIGHT. BRING US HONOR! YOU STAND BEFORE HIS GRACE.
HERE ARE THE WOMEN YOU ORDERED, MASTER QUAID. I HOPE THAT THEY ARE TO YOUR TASTE.
THEY ARE CLEAN AND HEALTHY.
I'LL ALSO NEED MORE FOOD--TO RECOVER MY STRENGTH.
IT'S ALL THAT WE HAVE LEFT. YOU KNOW THAT WE'RE UNDERFED BY THE FACTORIES.
DO YOU WANT THE PATH WHICH LEADS TO THE PORK VILLAGE OR NOT?

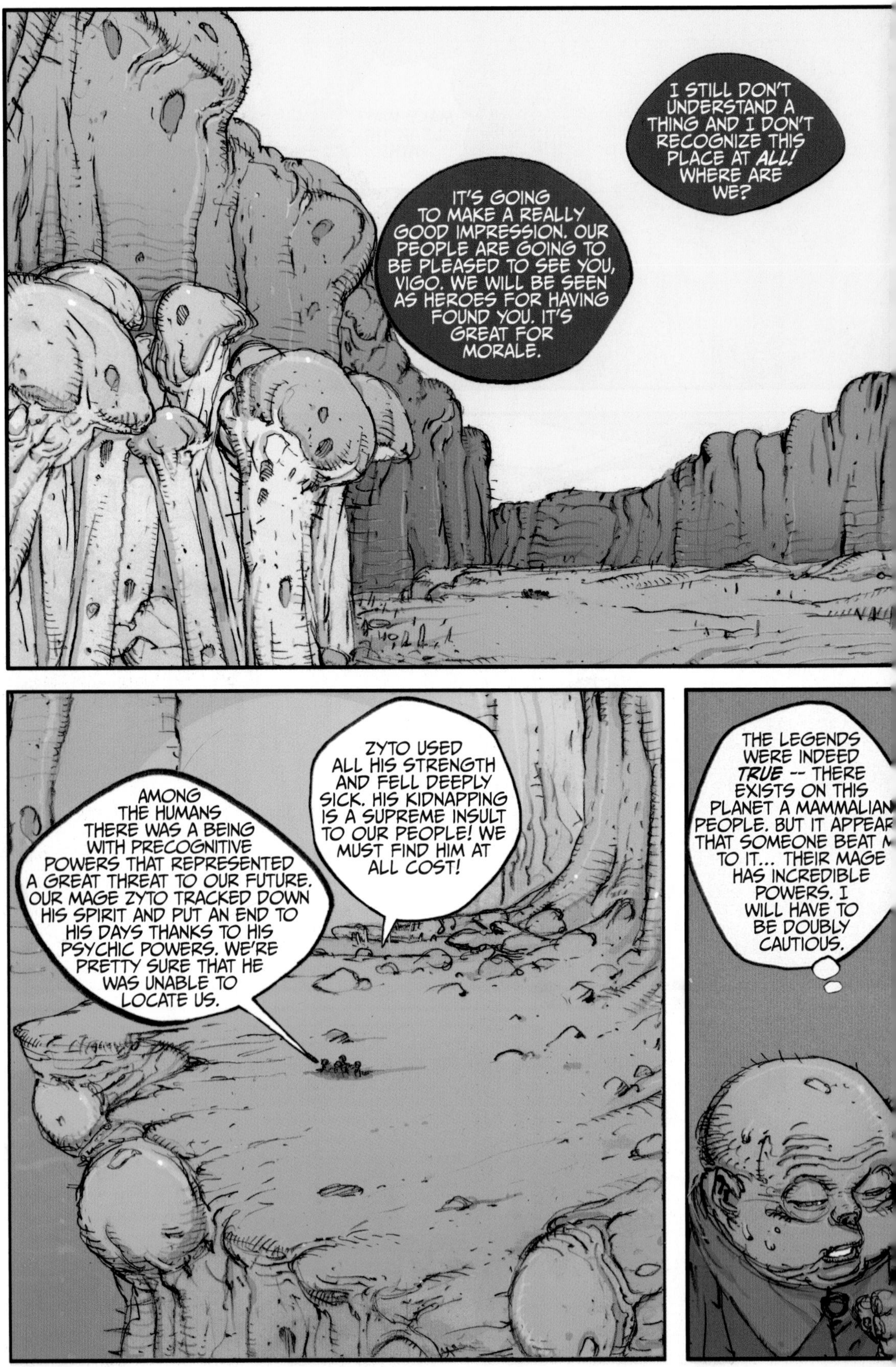

I STILL DON'T UNDERSTAND A THING AND I DON'T RECOGNIZE THIS PLACE AT ALL! WHERE ARE WE?
IT'S GOING TO MAKE A REALLY GOOD IMPRESSION. OUR PEOPLE ARE GOING TO BE PLEASED TO SEE YOU, VIGO. WE WILL BE SEEN AS HEROES FOR HAVING FOUND YOU. IT'S GREAT FOR MORALE.
AMONG THE HUMANS THERE WAS A BEING WITH PRECOGNITIVE POWERS THAT REPRESENTED A GREAT THREAT TO OUR FUTURE. OUR MAGE ZYTO TRACKED DOWN HIS SPIRIT AND PUT AN END TO HIS DAYS THANKS TO HIS PSYCHIC POWERS. WE'RE PRETTY SURE THAT HE WAS UNABLE TO LOCATE US.
ZYTO USED ALL HIS STRENGTH AND FELL DEEPLY SICK. HIS KIDNAPPING IS A SUPREME INSULT TO OUR PEOPLE! WE MUST FIND HIM AT ALL COST!
THE LEGENDS WERE INDEED TRUE -- THERE EXISTS ON THIS PLANET A MAMMALIAN PEOPLE. BUT IT APPEAR THAT SOMEONE BEAT M TO IT... THEIR MAGE HAS INCREDIBLE POWERS. I WILL HAVE TO BE DOUBLY CAUTIOUS.

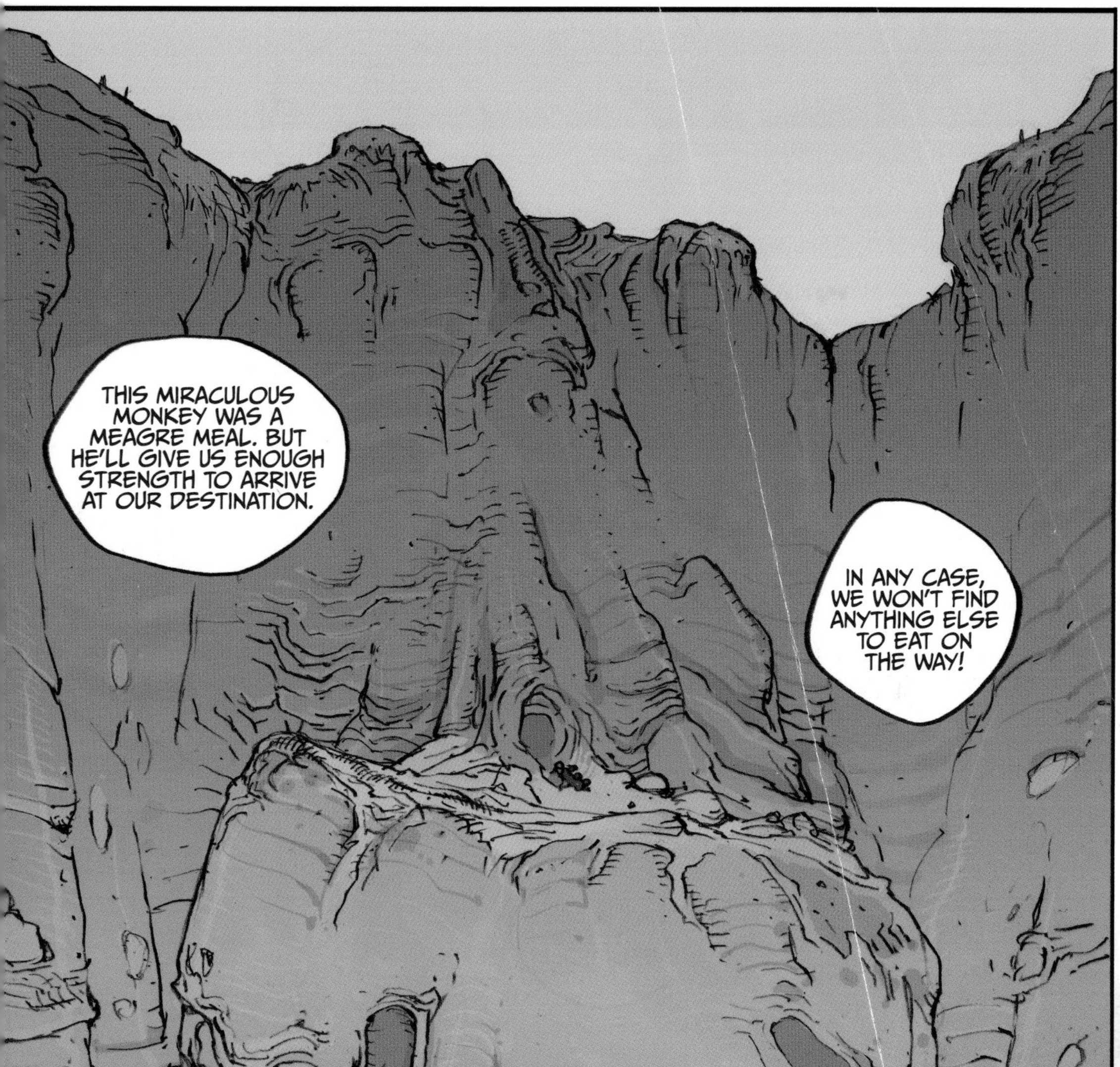
THIS MIRACULOUS MONKEY WAS A MEAGRE MEAL. BUT HE'LL GIVE US ENOUGH STRENGTH TO ARRIVE AT OUR DESTINATION.
IN ANY CASE, WE WON'T FIND ANYTHING ELSE TO EAT ON THE WAY!

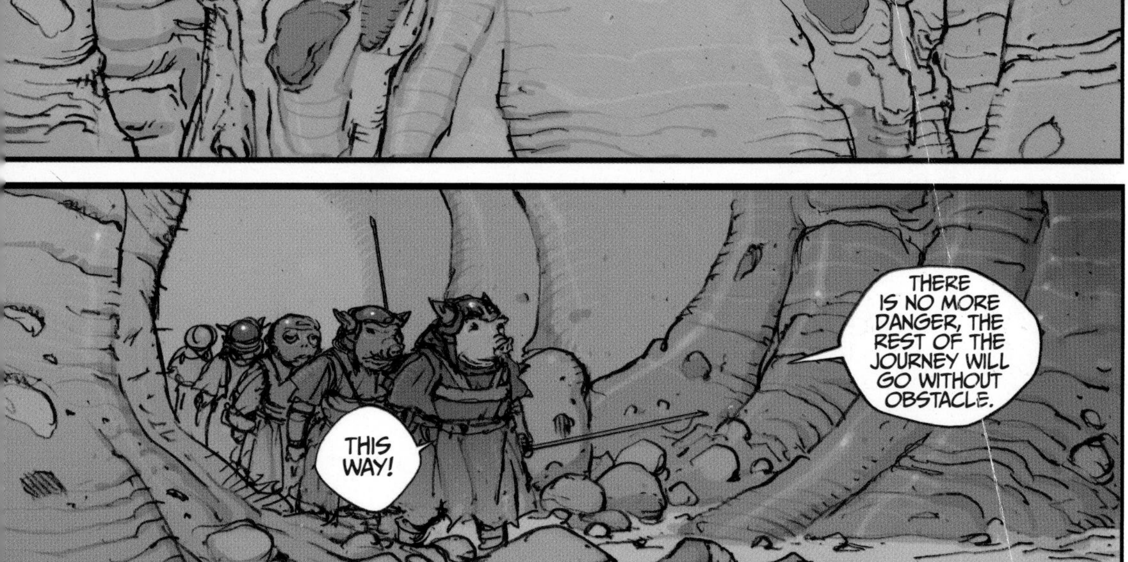
THERE IS NO MORE DANGER, THE REST OF THE JOURNEY WILL GO WITHOUT OBSTACLE.
THIS WAY!

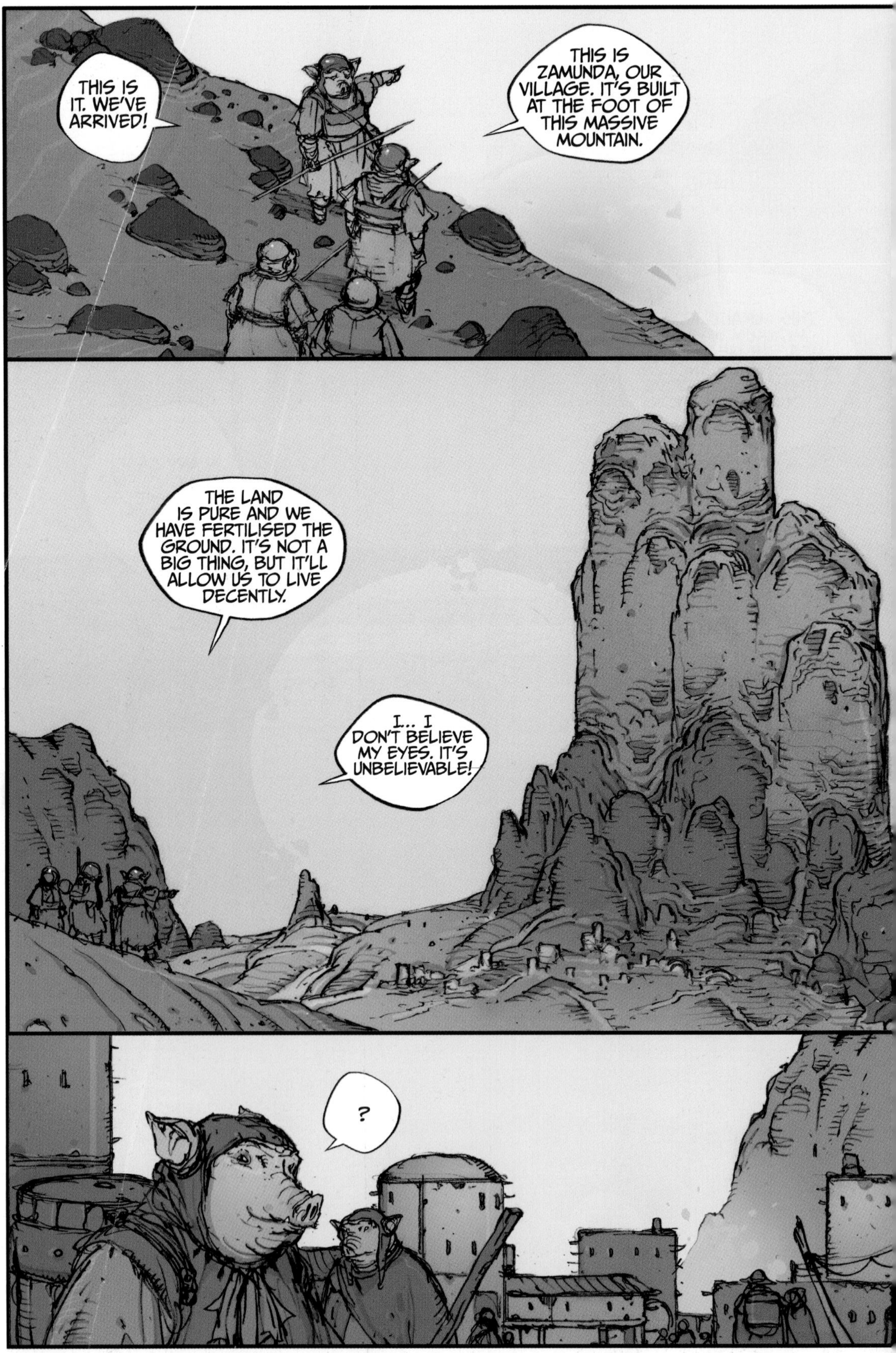
THIS IS IT. WE'VE ARRIVED!
THIS IS ZAMUNDA, OUR VILLAGE. IT'S BUILT AT THE FOOT OF THIS MASSIVE MOUNTAIN.
THE LAND IS PURE AND WE HAVE FERTILISED THE GROUND. IT'S NOT A BIG THING, BUT IT'LL ALLOW US TO LIVE DECENTLY.
I... I DON'T BELIEVE MY EYES. IT'S UNBELIEVABLE!
?

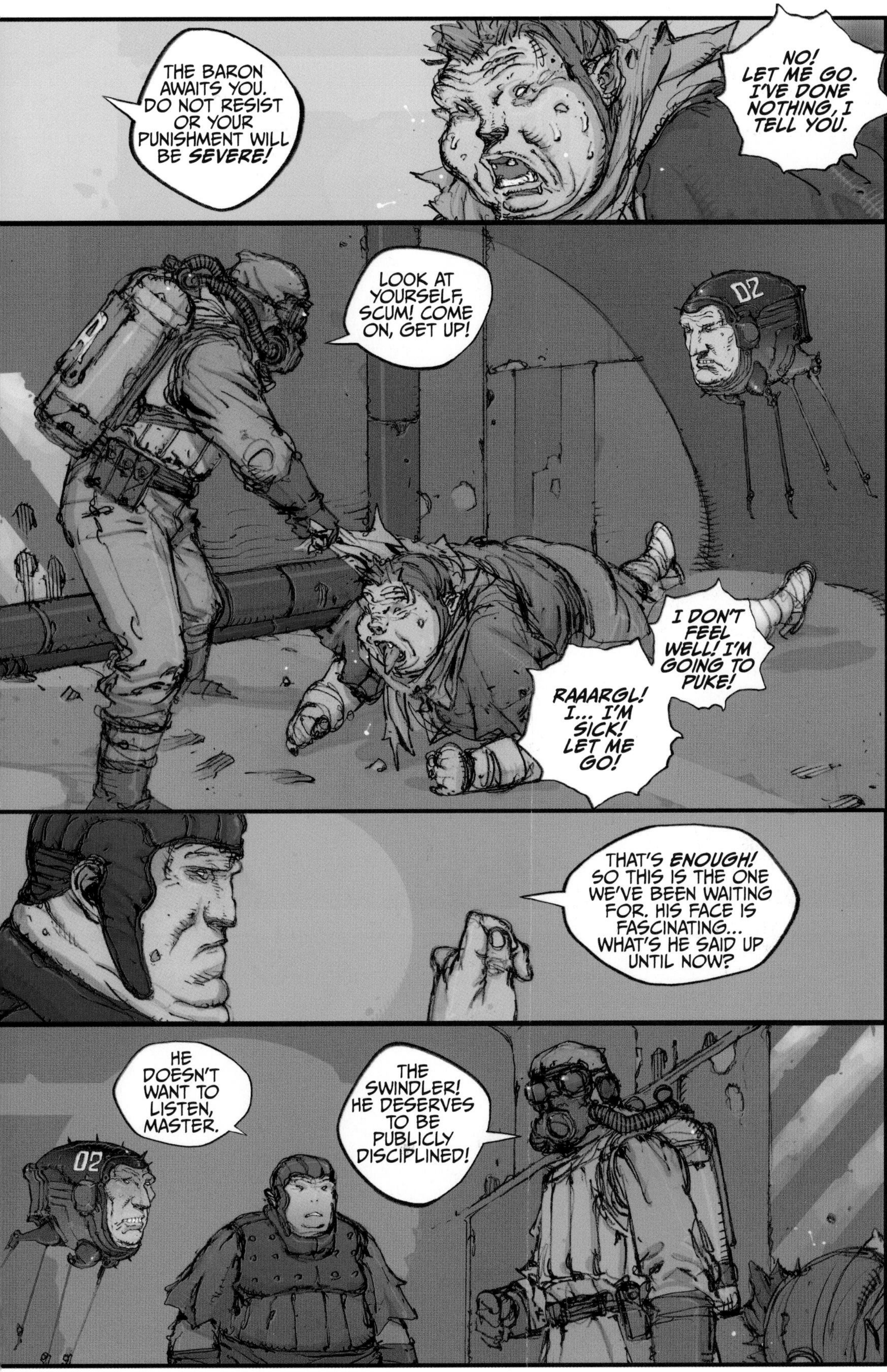
THE BARON AWAITS YOU. DO NOT RESIST OR YOUR PUNISHMENT WILL BE *SEVERE!*
NO! LET ME GO. I'VE DONE NOTHING, I TELL YOU.
LOOK AT YOURSELF, SCUM! COME ON, GET UP!
I DON'T FEEL WELL! I'M GOING TO PUKE!
RAAARGL! I... I'M SICK! LET ME GO!
THAT'S *ENOUGH!* SO THIS IS THE ONE WE'VE BEEN WAITING FOR. HIS FACE IS FASCINATING... WHAT'S HE SAID UP UNTIL NOW?
HE DOESN'T WANT TO LISTEN, MASTER.
THE SWINDLER! HE DESERVES TO BE PUBLICLY DISCIPLINED!
02

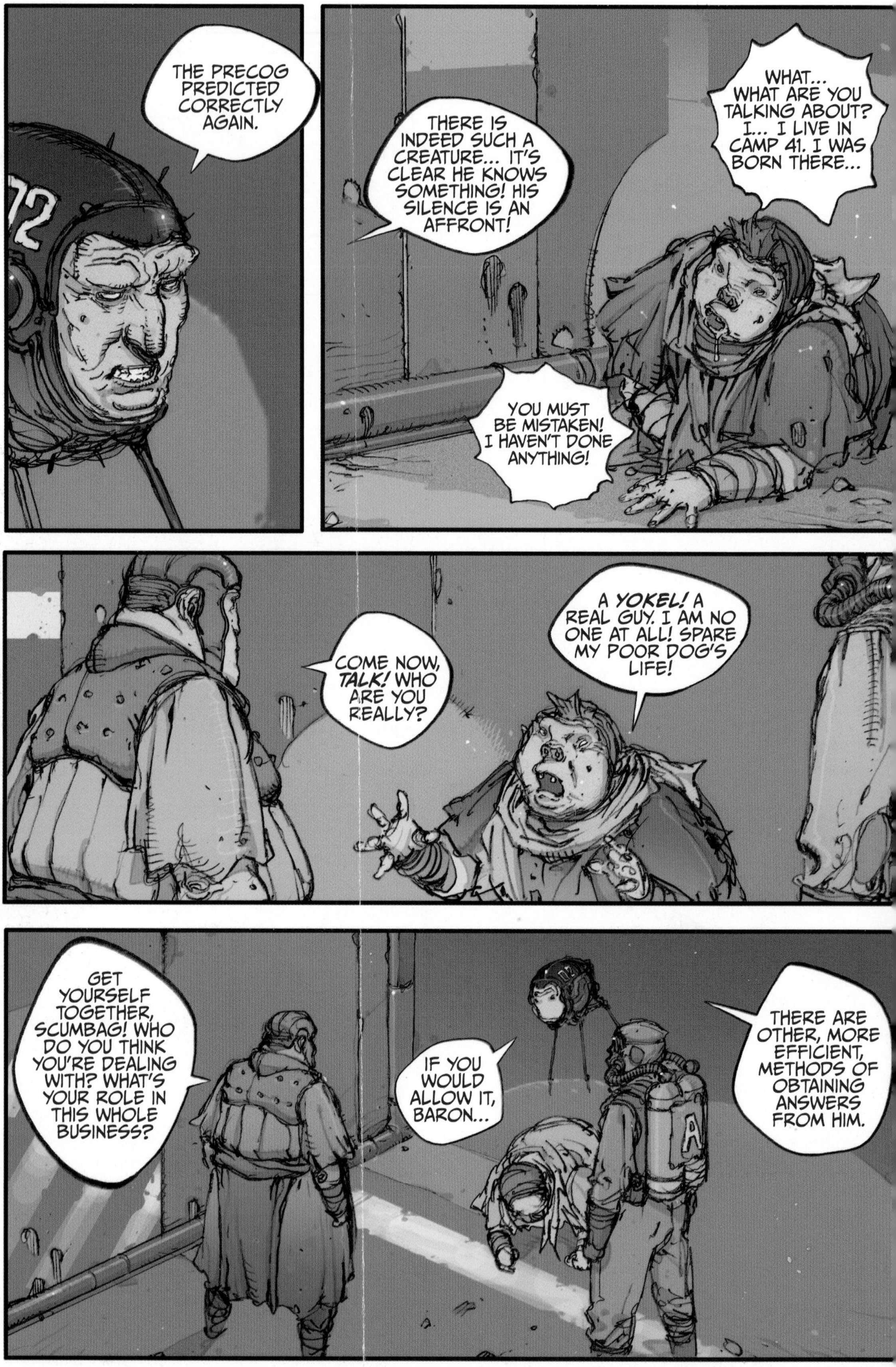
THE PRECOG PREDICTED CORRECTLY AGAIN.
THERE IS INDEED SUCH A CREATURE... IT'S CLEAR HE KNOWS SOMETHING! HIS SILENCE IS AN AFFRONT!
WHAT... WHAT ARE YOU TALKING ABOUT? I... I LIVE IN CAMP 41. I WAS BORN THERE...
YOU MUST BE MISTAKEN! I HAVEN'T DONE ANYTHING!
COME NOW, *TALK!* WHO ARE YOU REALLY?
A *YOKEL!* A REAL GUY. I AM NO ONE AT ALL! SPARE MY POOR DOG'S LIFE!
GET YOURSELF TOGETHER, SCUMBAG! WHO DO YOU THINK YOU'RE DEALING WITH? WHAT'S YOUR ROLE IN THIS WHOLE BUSINESS?
IF YOU WOULD ALLOW IT, BARON...
THERE ARE OTHER, MORE EFFICIENT, METHODS OF OBTAINING ANSWERS FROM HIM.

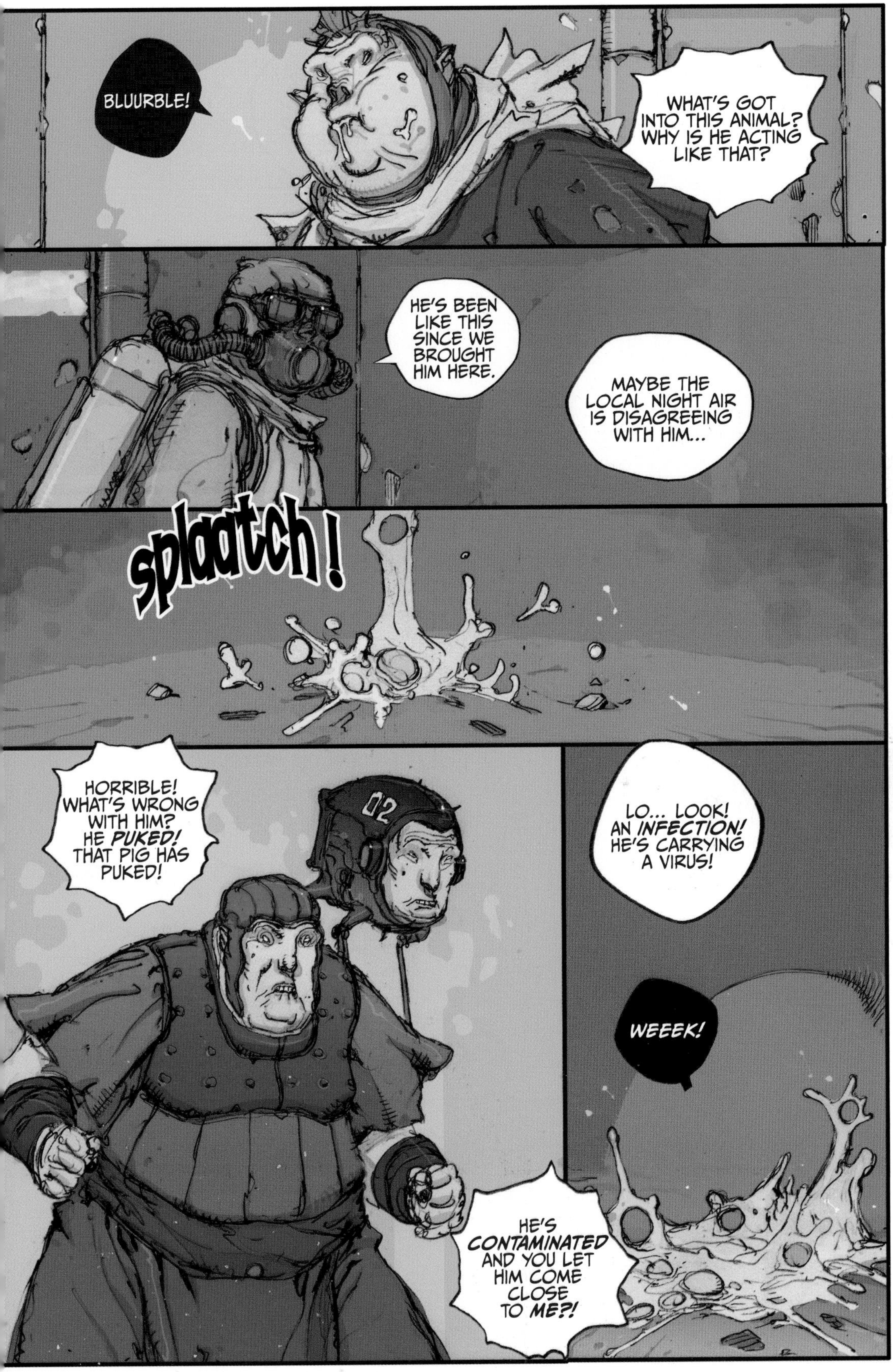
BLUURBLE!
WHAT'S GOT INTO THIS ANIMAL? WHY IS HE ACTING LIKE THAT?
HE'S BEEN LIKE THIS SINCE WE BROUGHT HIM HERE.
MAYBE THE LOCAL NIGHT AIR IS DISAGREEING WITH HIM...
splaatch!
HORRIBLE! WHAT'S WRONG WITH HIM? HE PUKED! THAT PIG HAS PUKED!
02
LO... LOOK! AN INFECTION! HE'S CARRYING A VIRUS!
WEEEK!
HE'S CONTAMINATED AND YOU LET HIM COME CLOSE TO ME?!

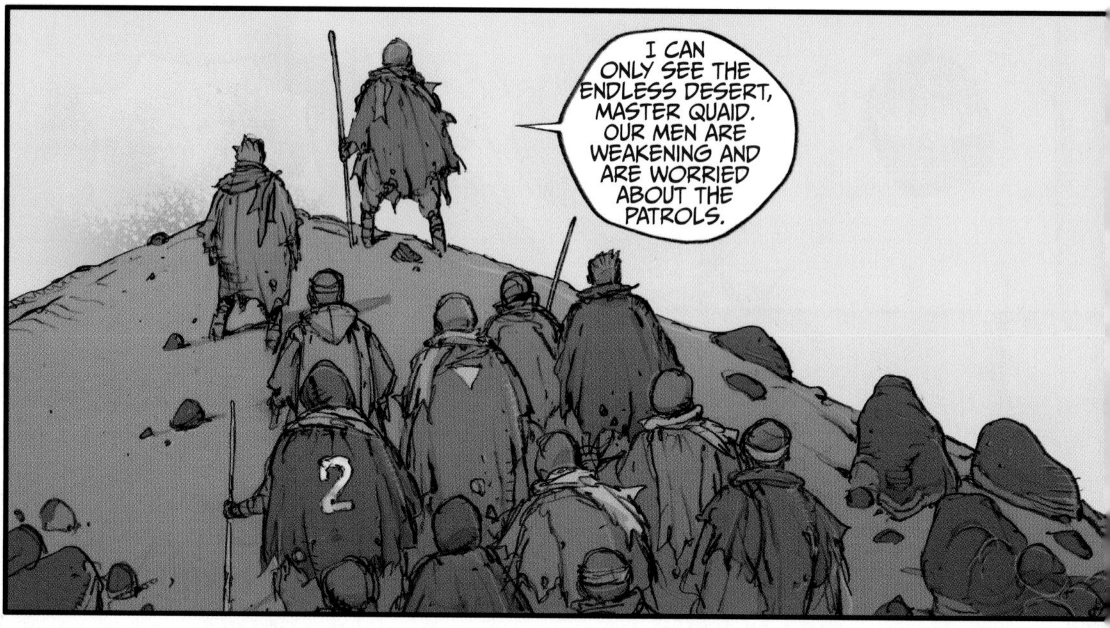
I CAN ONLY SEE THE ENDLESS DESERT, MASTER QUAID. OUR MEN ARE WEAKENING AND ARE WORRIED ABOUT THE PATROLS.
2
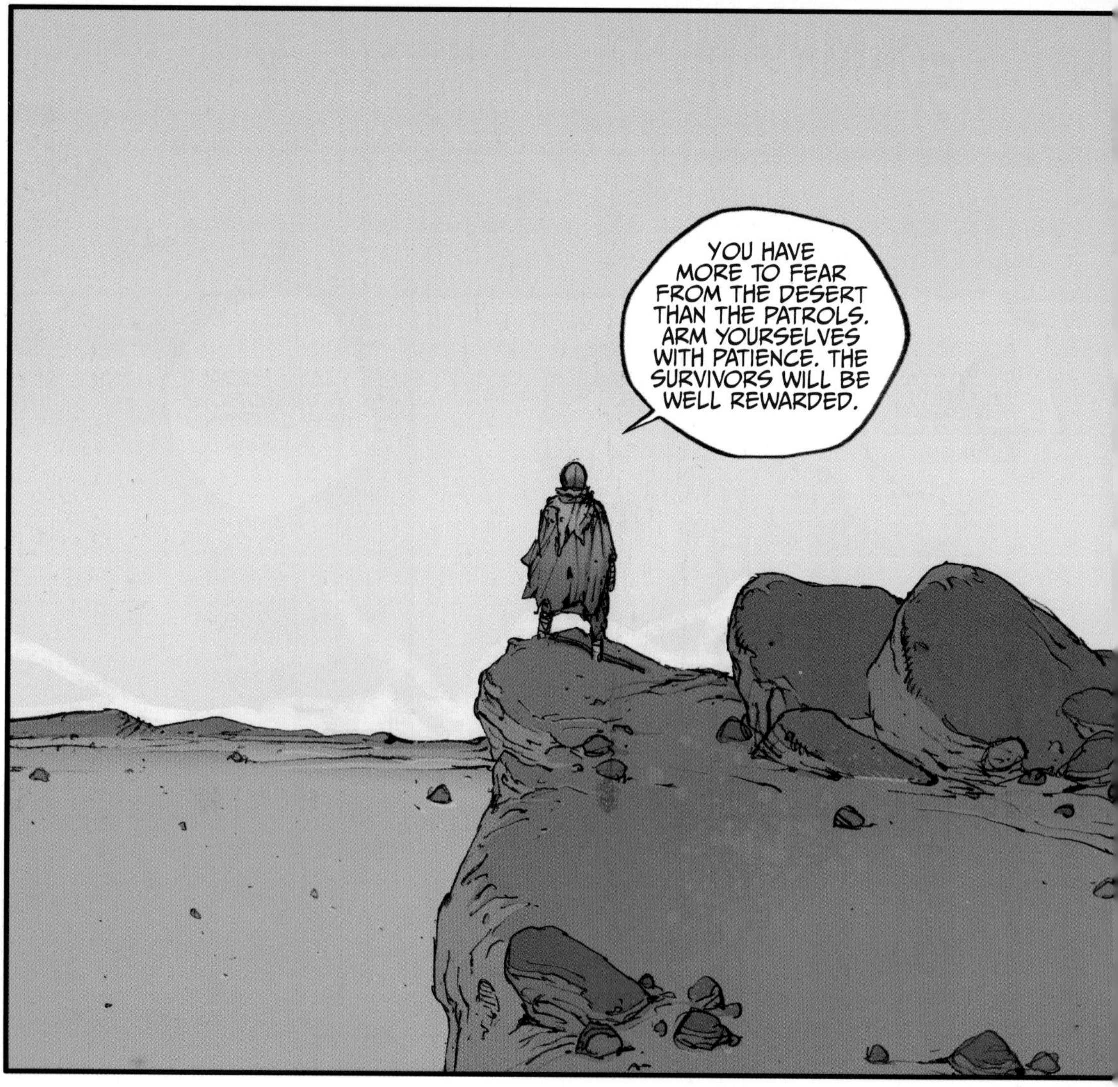
YOU HAVE MORE TO FEAR FROM THE DESERT THAN THE PATROLS. ARM YOURSELVES WITH PATIENCE. THE SURVIVORS WILL BE WELL REWARDED.

IMAGE ENHANCE
MODE 008 0065

IMAGE LEVEL // S

SPEED PARAMETE
54826 256.02
54879 256.00
84721 258.65
54800 000.02
54800 000.00
15899 999.65
54888 555.52
71541 112.11_//

154879 256.00
184721 258.65
154800 000.02
154800 000.00

BZZZK! ALERT! STRONG MASS ACTIVITY DETECTED. INDIVIDUALS ARE MOVING OUTSIDE THE CAMPS.

POSITION NORTH NORTH EAST. GEOTECH SYSTEMS AND ANALYSIS ENGAGED.

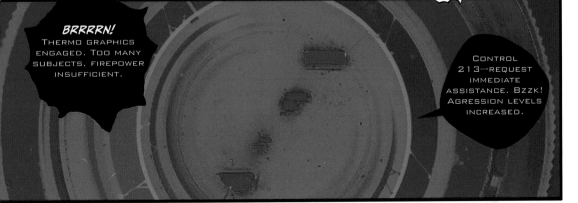

BRRRRN! THERMO GRAPHICS ENGAGED. TOO MANY SUBJECTS. FIREPOWER INSUFFICIENT.

CONTROL 213--REQUEST IMMEDIATE ASSISTANCE. BZZK! AGRESSION LEVELS INCREASED.

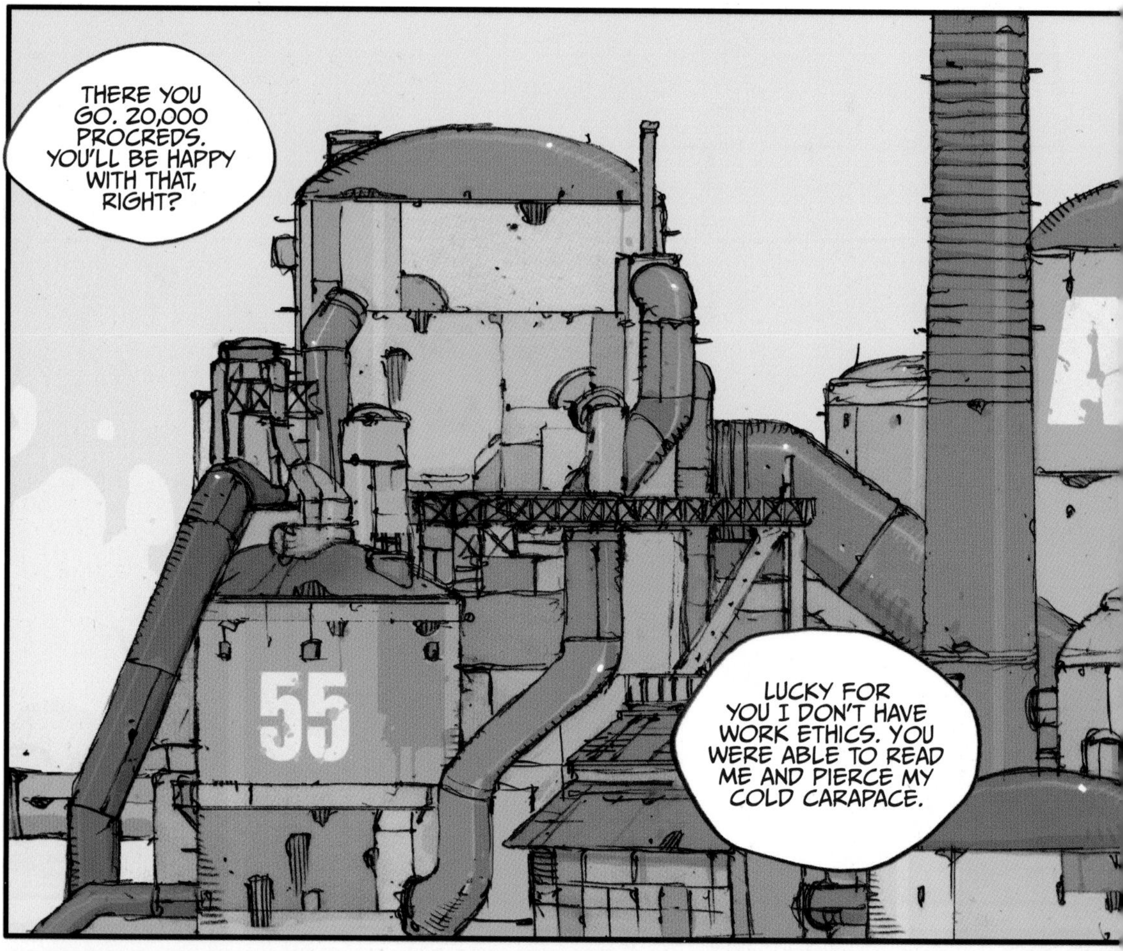
THERE YOU GO. 20,000 PROCREDS. YOU'LL BE HAPPY WITH THAT, RIGHT?
LUCKY FOR YOU I DON'T HAVE WORK ETHICS. YOU WERE ABLE TO READ ME AND PIERCE MY COLD CARAPACE.
55

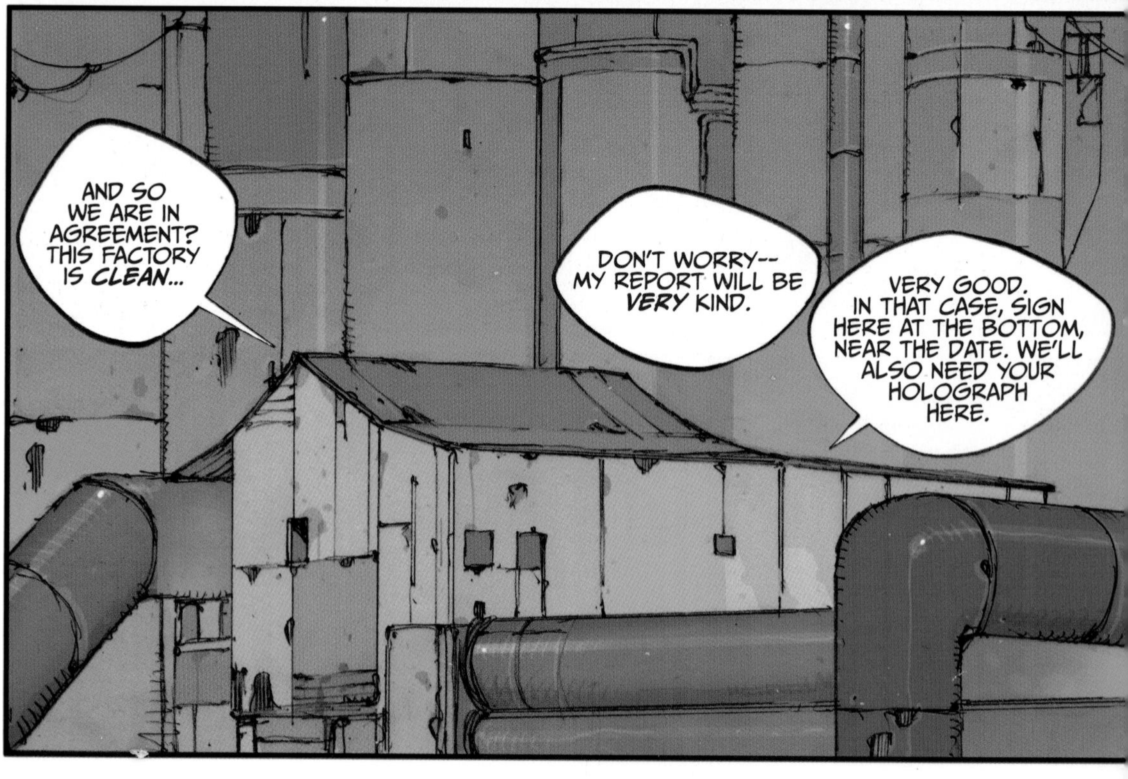
AND SO WE ARE IN AGREEMENT? THIS FACTORY IS *CLEAN*...
DON'T WORRY-- MY REPORT WILL BE *VERY* KIND.
VERY GOOD. IN THAT CASE, SIGN HERE AT THE BOTTOM, NEAR THE DATE. WE'LL ALSO NEED YOUR HOLOGRAPH HERE.

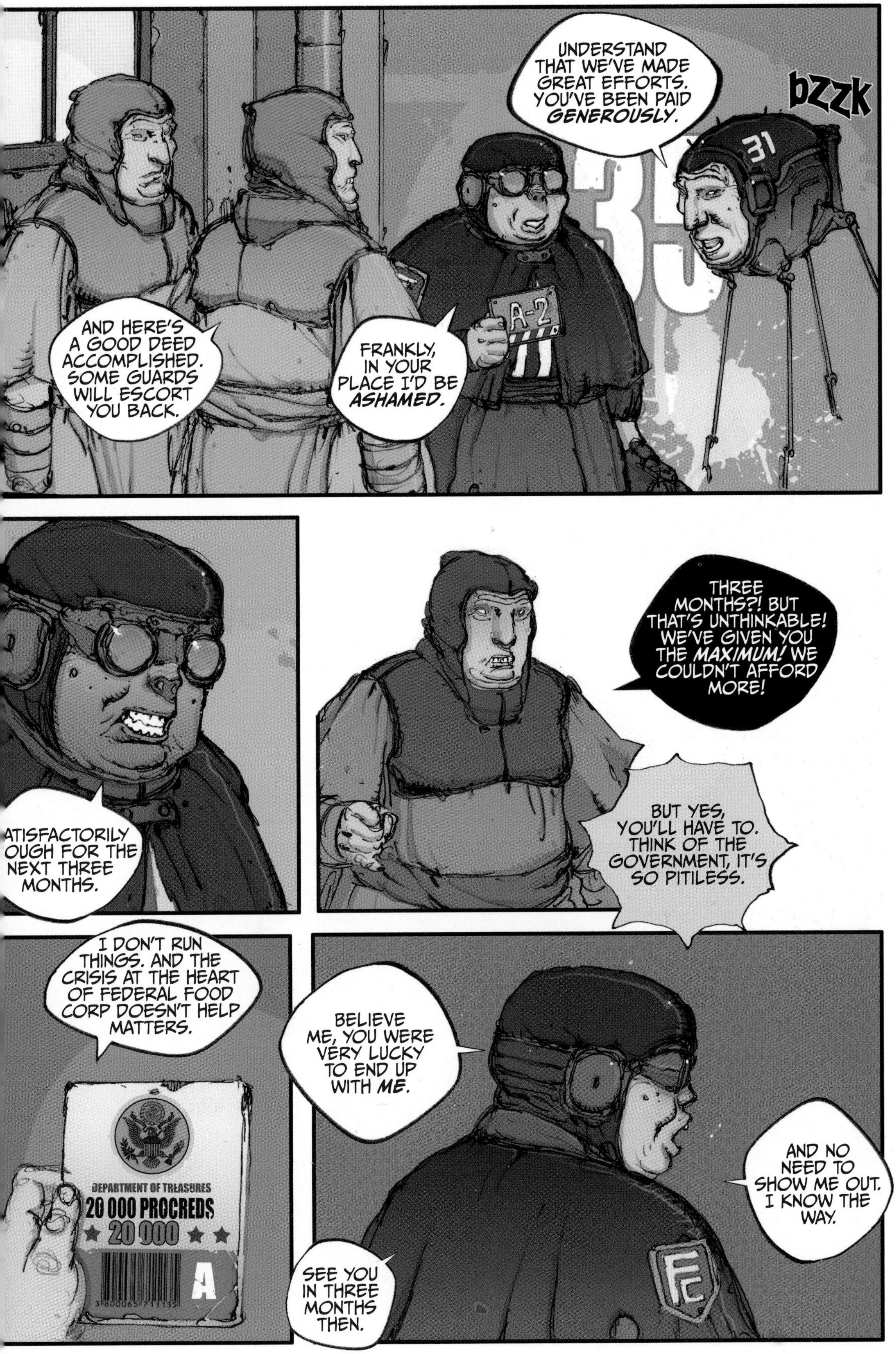
bzzk
UNDERSTAND THAT WE'VE MADE GREAT EFFORTS. YOU'VE BEEN PAID GENEROUSLY.
FRANKLY, IN YOUR PLACE I'D BE ASHAMED.
AND HERE'S A GOOD DEED ACCOMPLISHED. SOME GUARDS WILL ESCORT YOU BACK.
31
A-2
ATISFACTORILY
OUGH FOR THE NEXT THREE MONTHS.
THREE MONTHS?! BUT THAT'S UNTHINKABLE! WE'VE GIVEN YOU THE MAXIMUM! WE COULDN'T AFFORD MORE!
BUT YES, YOU'LL HAVE TO. THINK OF THE GOVERNMENT, IT'S SO PITILESS.
I DON'T RUN THINGS. AND THE CRISIS AT THE HEART OF FEDERAL FOOD CORP DOESN'T HELP MATTERS.
DEPARTMENT OF TREASURES
20 000 PROCREDS
20 000
A
BELIEVE ME, YOU WERE VERY LUCKY TO END UP WITH ME.
AND NO NEED TO SHOW ME OUT. I KNOW THE WAY.
SEE YOU IN THREE MONTHS THEN.
FC

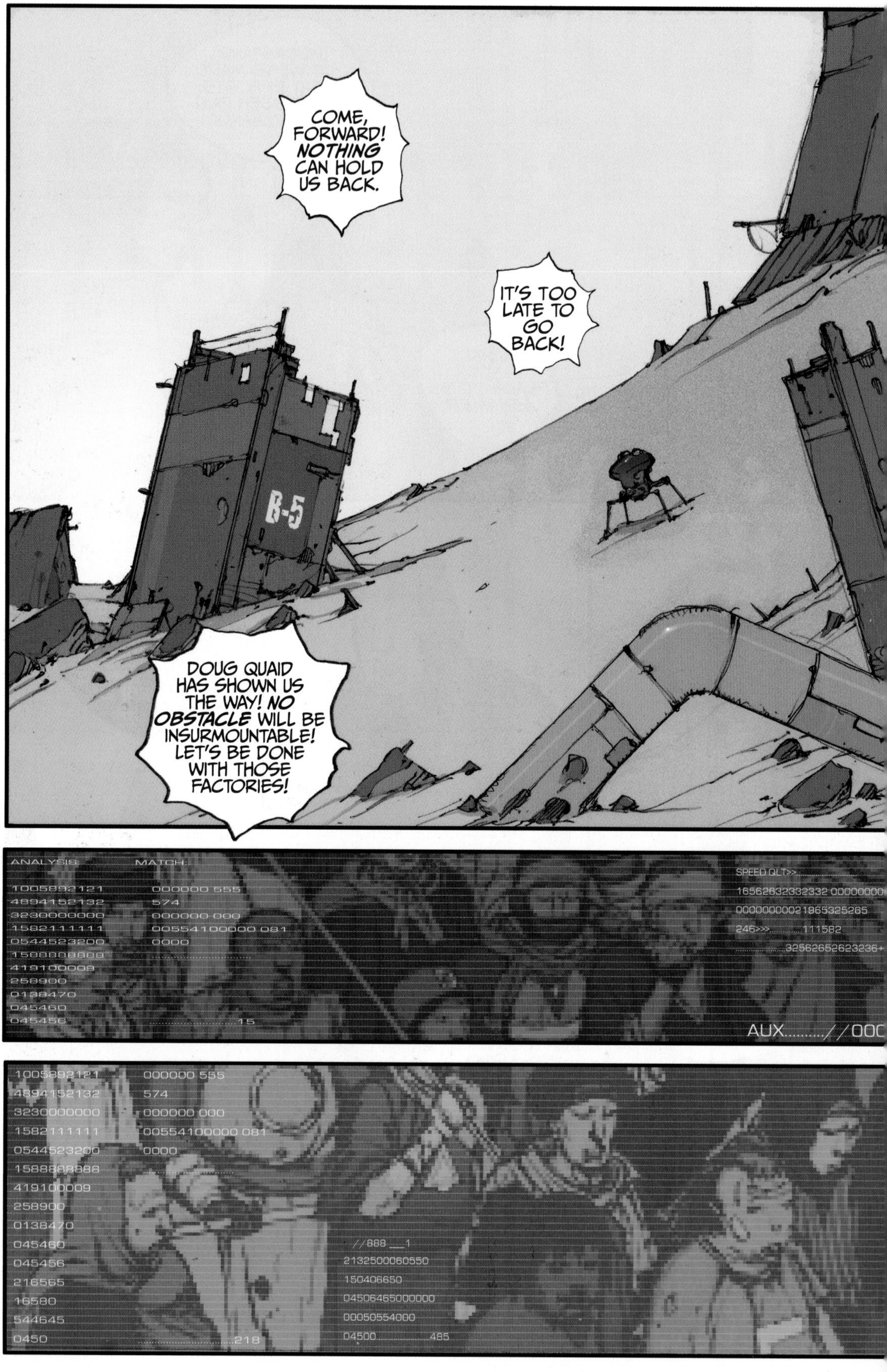
COME, FORWARD! NOTHING CAN HOLD US BACK.
IT'S TOO LATE TO GO BACK!
DOUG QUAID HAS SHOWN US THE WAY! NO OBSTACLE WILL BE INSURMOUNTABLE! LET'S BE DONE WITH THOSE FACTORIES!
B-5
ANALYSIS
MATCH
SPEED QLT>>
AUX........//000
//888 __1
2132500060550
150406650
04506465000000
00050554000
04500..................485

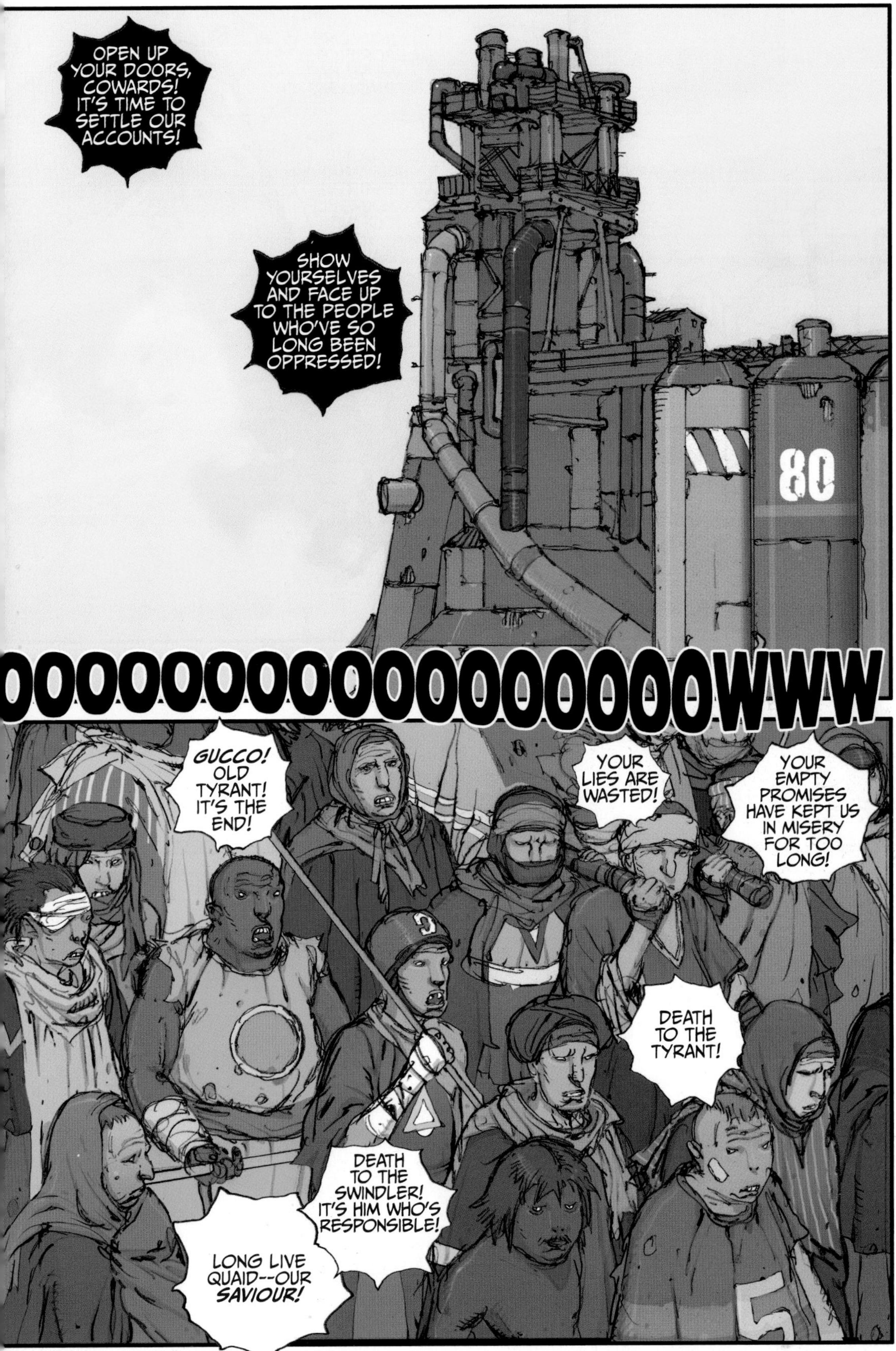
OPEN UP YOUR DOORS, COWARDS! IT'S TIME TO SETTLE OUR ACCOUNTS!
SHOW YOURSELVES AND FACE UP TO THE PEOPLE WHO'VE SO LONG BEEN OPPRESSED!
80
OOOOOOOOOOOOOOOOOOOWWW
GUCCO! OLD TYRANT! IT'S THE END!
YOUR LIES ARE WASTED!
YOUR EMPTY PROMISES HAVE KEPT US IN MISERY FOR TOO LONG!
DEATH TO THE TYRANT!
DEATH TO THE SWINDLER! IT'S HIM WHO'S RESPONSIBLE!
LONG LIVE QUAID--OUR SAVIOUR!

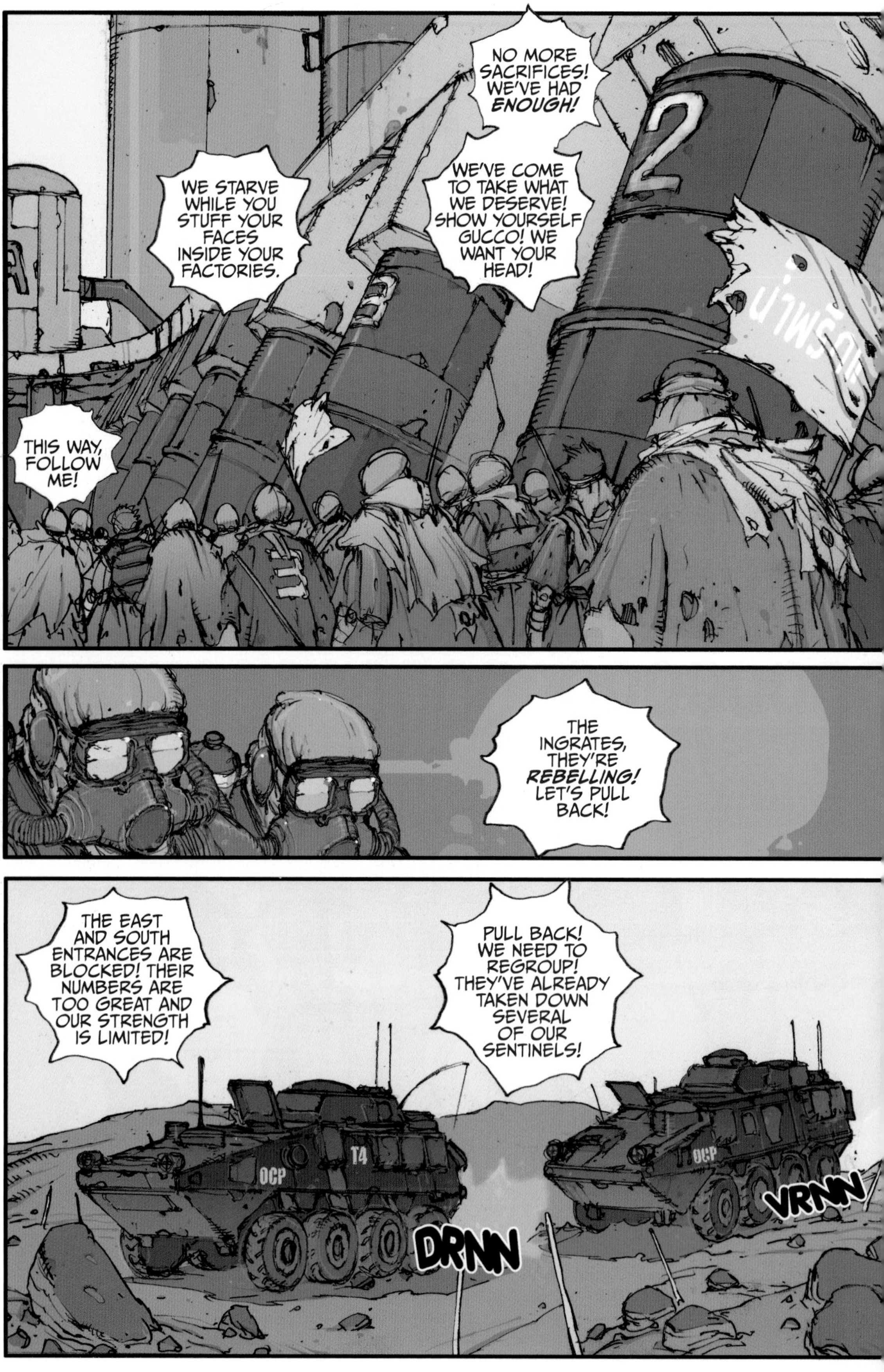
NO MORE SACRIFICES! WE'VE HAD ENOUGH!
WE STARVE WHILE YOU STUFF YOUR FACES INSIDE YOUR FACTORIES.
WE'VE COME TO TAKE WHAT WE DESERVE! SHOW YOURSELF GUCCO! WE WANT YOUR HEAD!
THIS WAY, FOLLOW ME!
THE INGRATES, THEY'RE REBELLING! LET'S PULL BACK!
THE EAST AND SOUTH ENTRANCES ARE BLOCKED! THEIR NUMBERS ARE TOO GREAT AND OUR STRENGTH IS LIMITED!
PULL BACK! WE NEED TO REGROUP! THEY'VE ALREADY TAKEN DOWN SEVERAL OF OUR SENTINELS!
T4
OCP
OCP
DRNN
VRNN

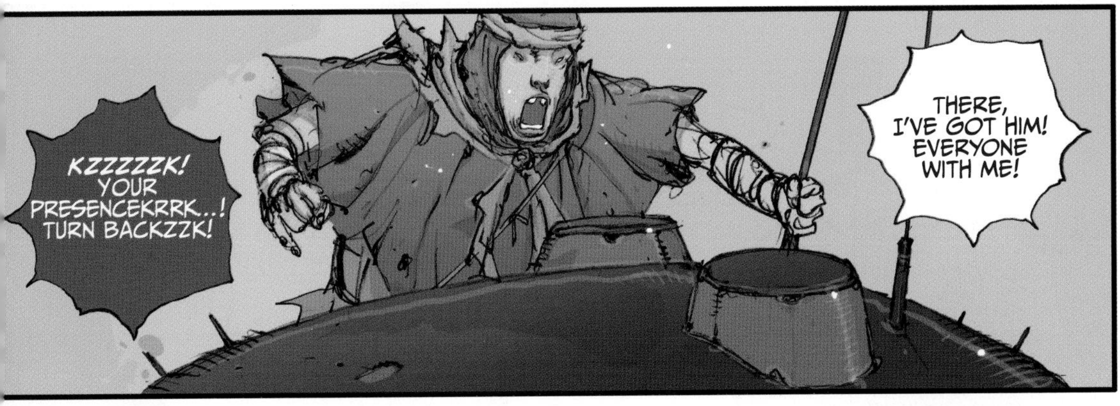
KZZZZZK! YOUR PRESENCEKRRK...! TURN BACKZZK!
THERE, I'VE GOT HIM! EVERYONE WITH ME!

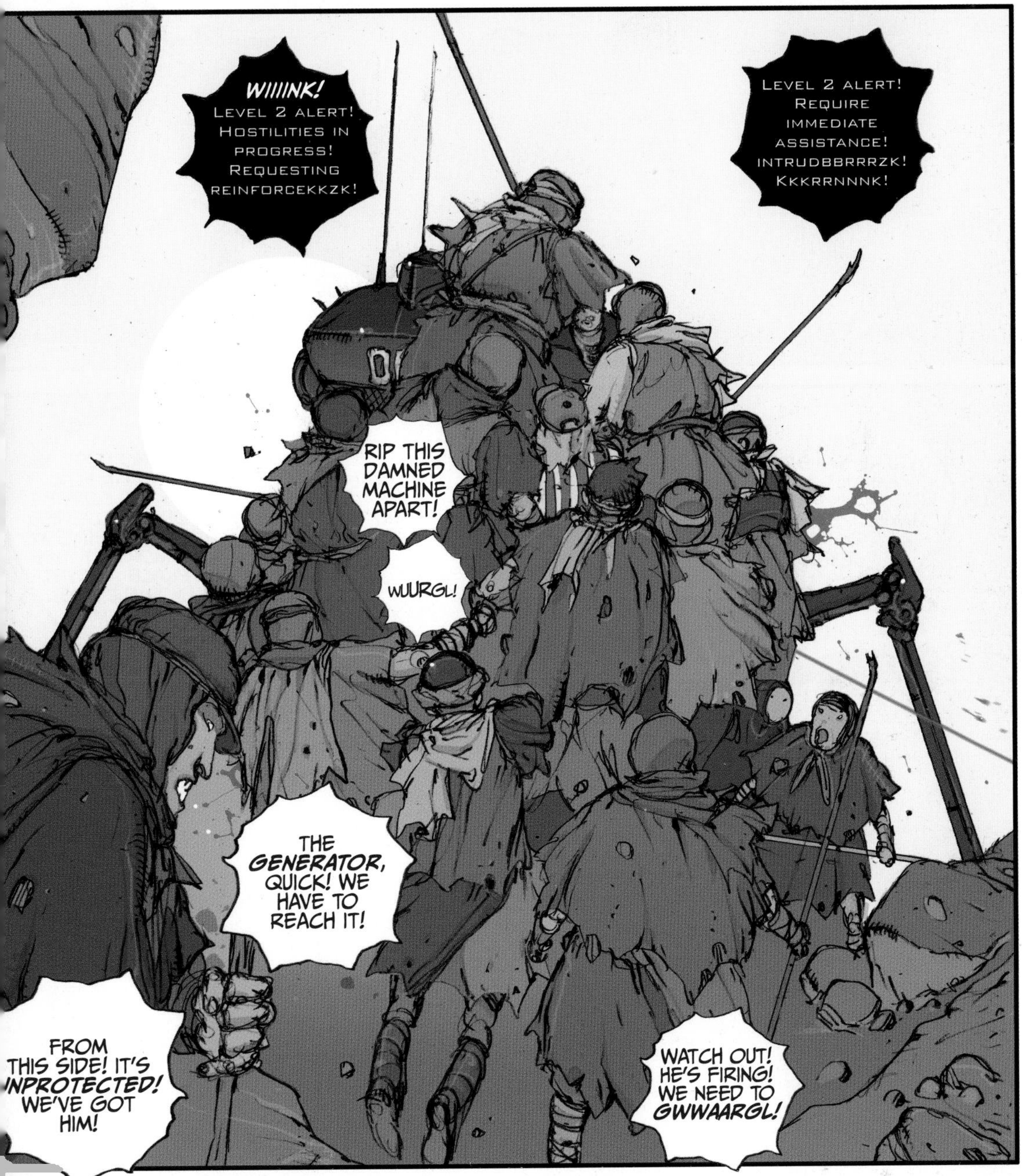
WIIIINK! Level 2 alert! Hostilities in progress! Requesting reinforcekkzk!
Level 2 alert! Require immediate assistance! intrudbbrrrzk! Kkkrrnnnk!
RIP THIS DAMNED MACHINE APART!
WUURGL!
THE GENERATOR, QUICK! WE HAVE TO REACH IT!
FROM THIS SIDE! IT'S UNPROTECTED! WE'VE GOT HIM!
WATCH OUT! HE'S FIRING! WE NEED TO GWWAARGL!

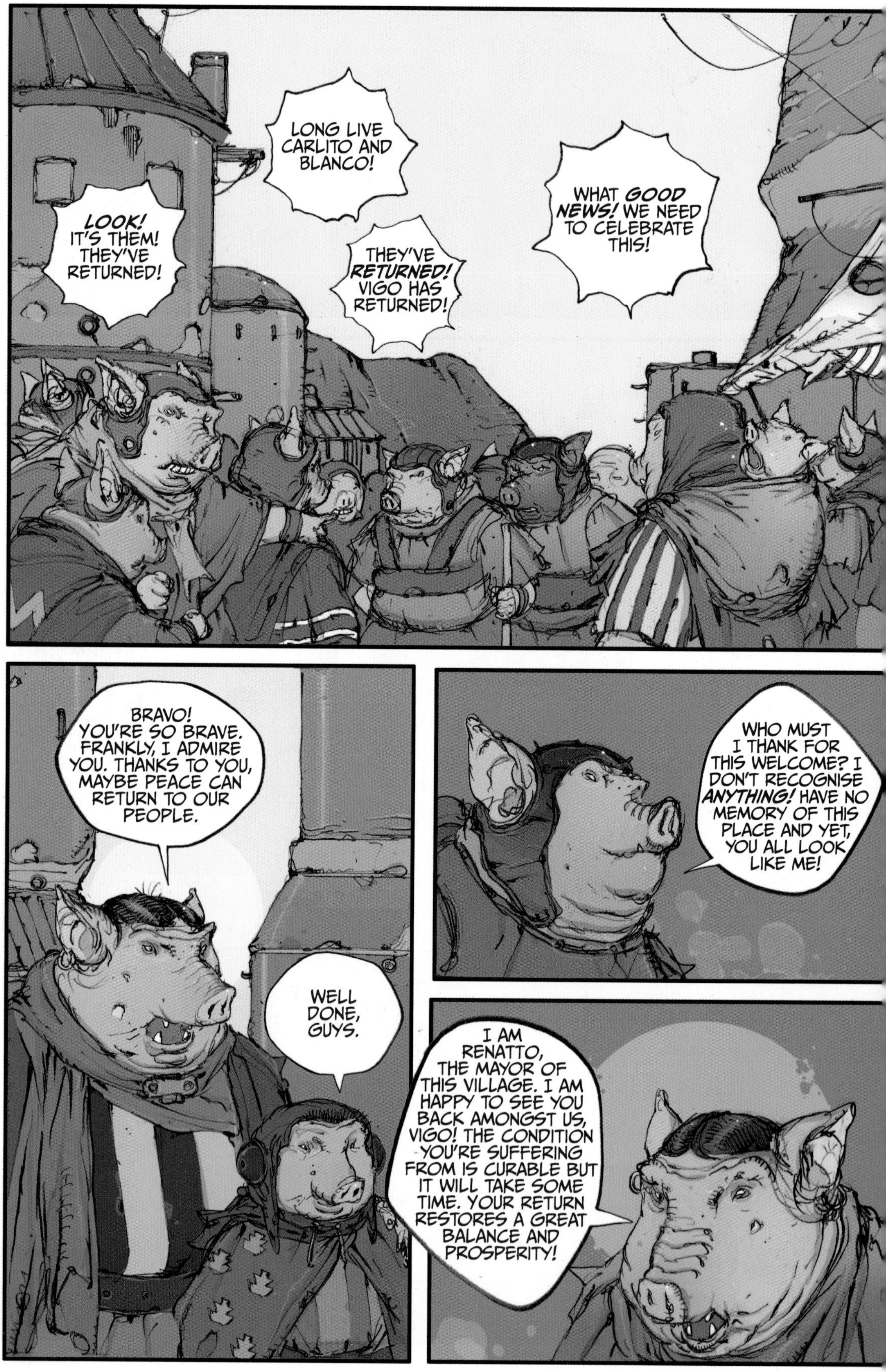
LOOK! IT'S THEM! THEY'VE RETURNED!
LONG LIVE CARLITO AND BLANCO!
THEY'VE RETURNED! VIGO HAS RETURNED!
WHAT GOOD NEWS! WE NEED TO CELEBRATE THIS!
BRAVO! YOU'RE SO BRAVE. FRANKLY, I ADMIRE YOU. THANKS TO YOU, MAYBE PEACE CAN RETURN TO OUR PEOPLE.
WELL DONE, GUYS.
WHO MUST I THANK FOR THIS WELCOME? I DON'T RECOGNISE ANYTHING! HAVE NO MEMORY OF THIS PLACE AND YET, YOU ALL LOOK LIKE ME!
I AM RENATTO, THE MAYOR OF THIS VILLAGE. I AM HAPPY TO SEE YOU BACK AMONGST US, VIGO! THE CONDITION YOU'RE SUFFERING FROM IS CURABLE BUT IT WILL TAKE SOME TIME. YOUR RETURN RESTORES A GREAT BALANCE AND PROSPERITY!

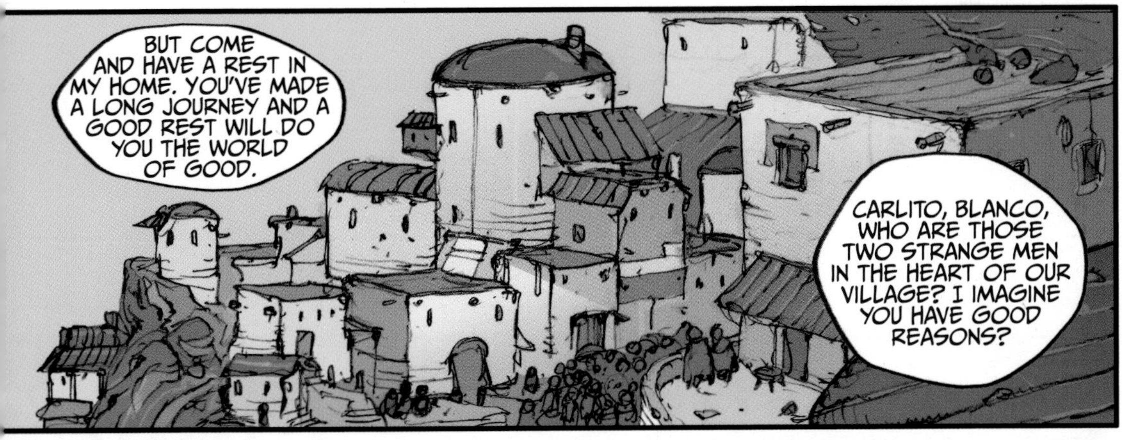
BUT COME AND HAVE A REST IN MY HOME. YOU'VE MADE A LONG JOURNEY AND A GOOD REST WILL DO YOU THE WORLD OF GOOD.
CARLITO, BLANCO, WHO ARE THOSE TWO STRANGE MEN IN THE HEART OF OUR VILLAGE? I IMAGINE YOU HAVE GOOD REASONS?

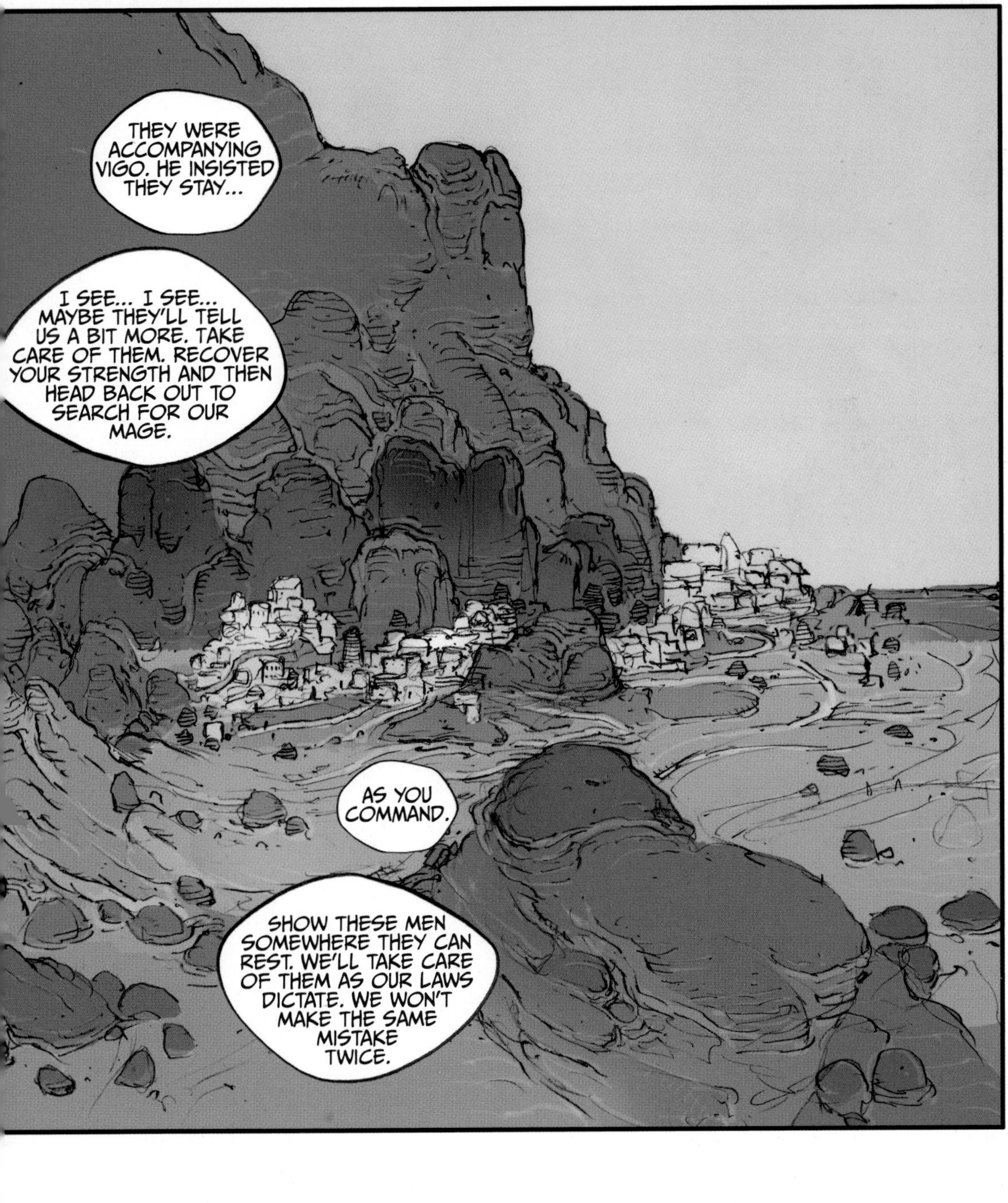
THEY WERE ACCOMPANYING VIGO. HE INSISTED THEY STAY...
I SEE... I SEE... MAYBE THEY'LL TELL US A BIT MORE. TAKE CARE OF THEM. RECOVER YOUR STRENGTH AND THEN HEAD BACK OUT TO SEARCH FOR OUR MAGE.
AS YOU COMMAND.
SHOW THESE MEN SOMEWHERE THEY CAN REST. WE'LL TAKE CARE OF THEM AS OUR LAWS DICTATE. WE WON'T MAKE THE SAME MISTAKE TWICE.

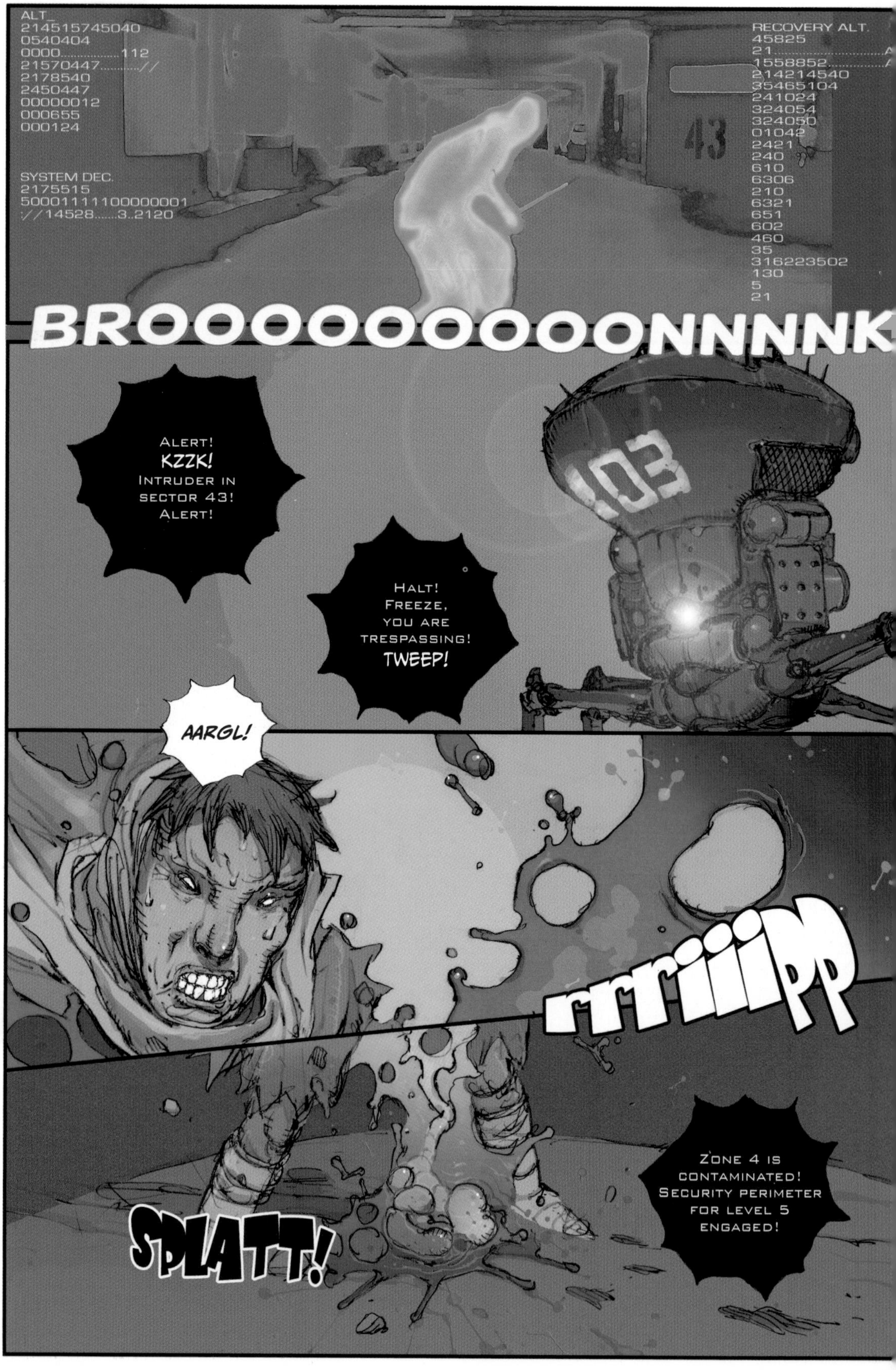
ALT_
214515745040
0540404
0000..................112
21570447............//
2178540
2450447
00000012
000655
000124
SYSTEM DEC.
2175515
50001111100000001
://14528.......3..2120
RECOVERY ALT.
45825
214214540
35465104
241024
324054
324050
01042
2421
240
610
6306
210
6321
651
602
460
35
316223502
130
5
21
BROOOOOOOOONNNNK
Alert! KZZK! Intruder in sector 43! Alert!
Halt! Freeze, you are trespassing! TWEEP!
AARGL!
rrriiiipp
SPLATT!
Zone 4 is contaminated! Security perimeter for level 5 engaged!

ORDER IS RESTORED, BARON.

THE INSPECTOR HAS BEEN SKILFULLY TURNED AWAY AND HANDSOMELY BRIBED. THE VERMIN NONETHELESS RISKS GIVING US SOME PROBLEMS IN THE FUTURE.

IN OTHER NEWS, WE HAVE DETECTED A DEGREE OF UNREST IN THE CAMPS. WE WERE THINKING THAT-- HUH?

SLUURB

GOOD GOD! WHAT'S GOING ON??

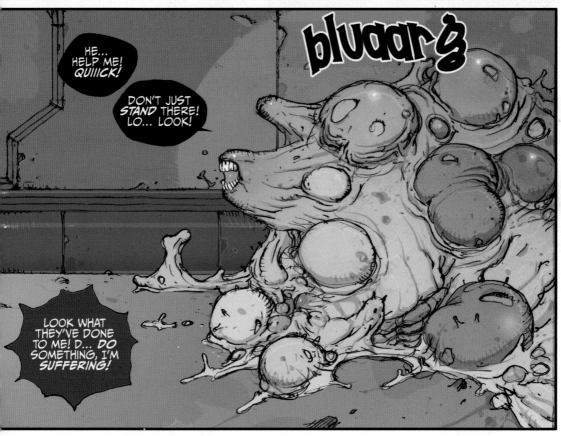

HE... HELP ME! QUIIICK!

DON'T JUST STAND THERE! LO... LOOK!

bluaarg

LOOK WHAT THEY'VE DONE TO ME! D... DO SOMETHING, I'M SUFFERING!

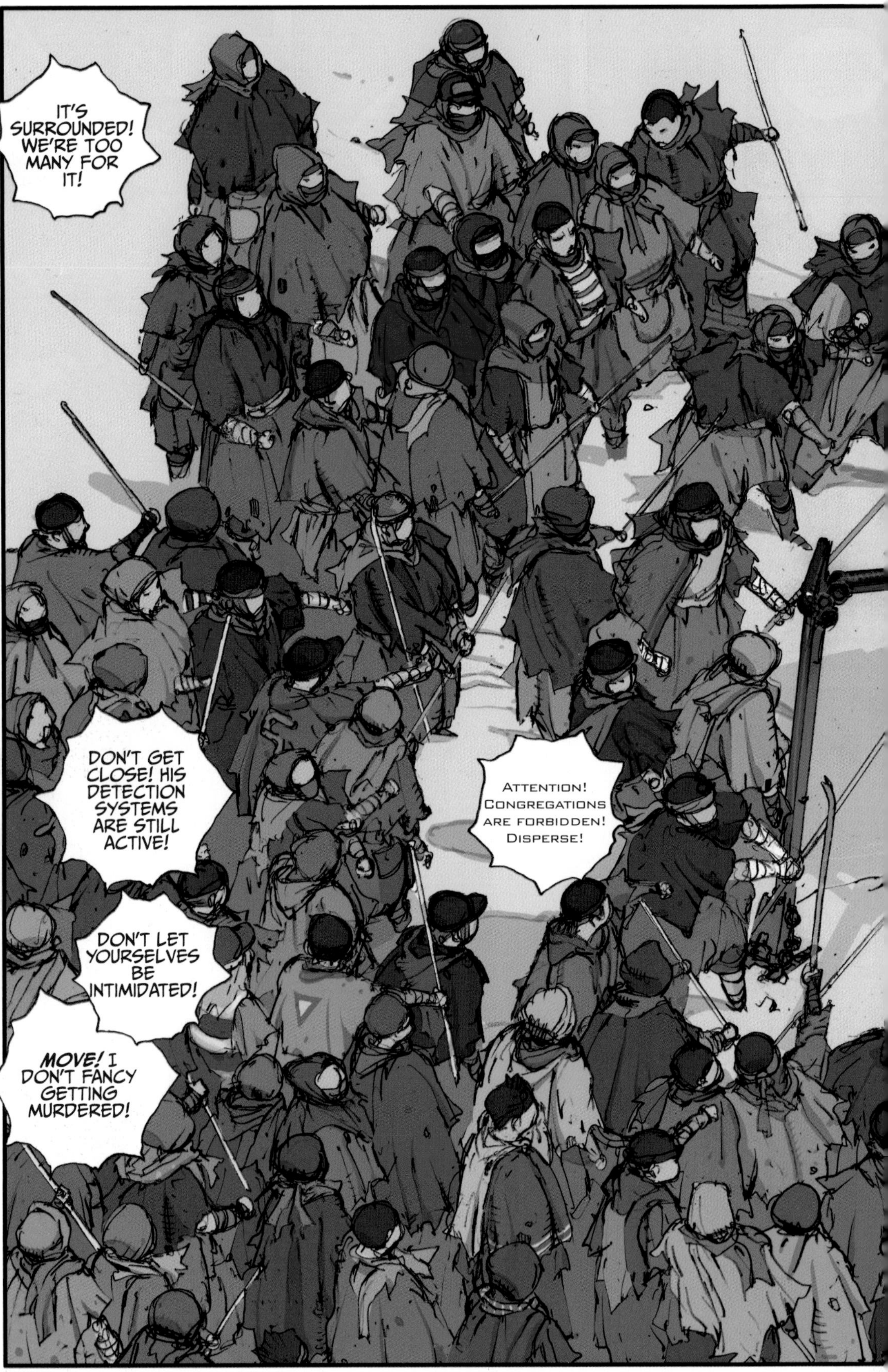
IT'S SURROUNDED! WE'RE TOO MANY FOR IT!
DON'T GET CLOSE! HIS DETECTION SYSTEMS ARE STILL ACTIVE!
ATTENTION! CONGREGATIONS ARE FORBIDDEN! DISPERSE!
DON'T LET YOURSELVES BE INTIMIDATED!
MOVE! I DON'T FANCY GETTING MURDERED!

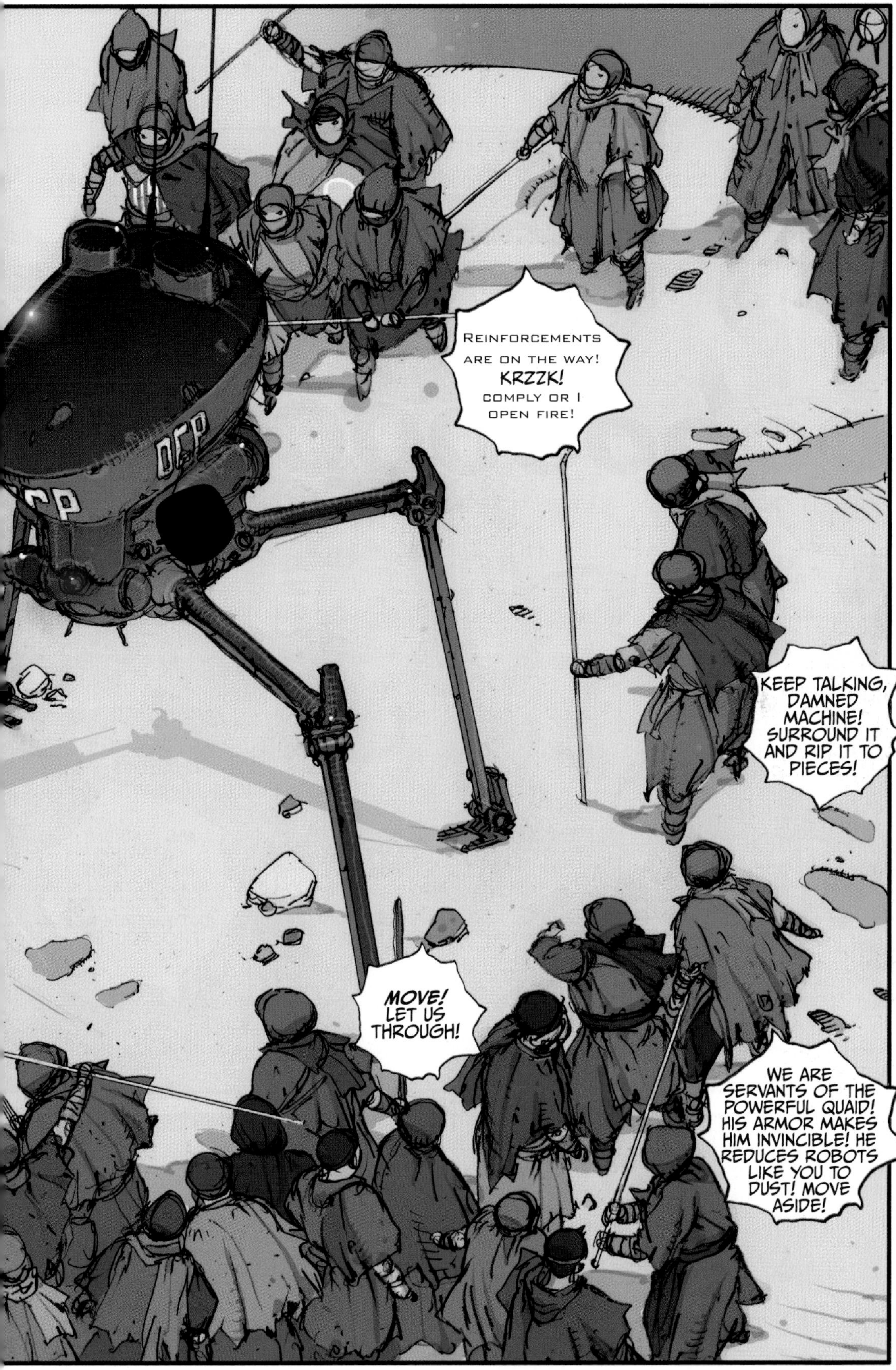
OCP
Reinforcements are on the way! KRZZK! comply or I open fire!
KEEP TALKING, DAMNED MACHINE! SURROUND IT AND RIP IT TO PIECES!
MOVE! LET US THROUGH!
WE ARE SERVANTS OF THE POWERFUL QUAID! HIS ARMOR MAKES HIM INVINCIBLE! HE REDUCES ROBOTS LIKE YOU TO DUST! MOVE ASIDE!

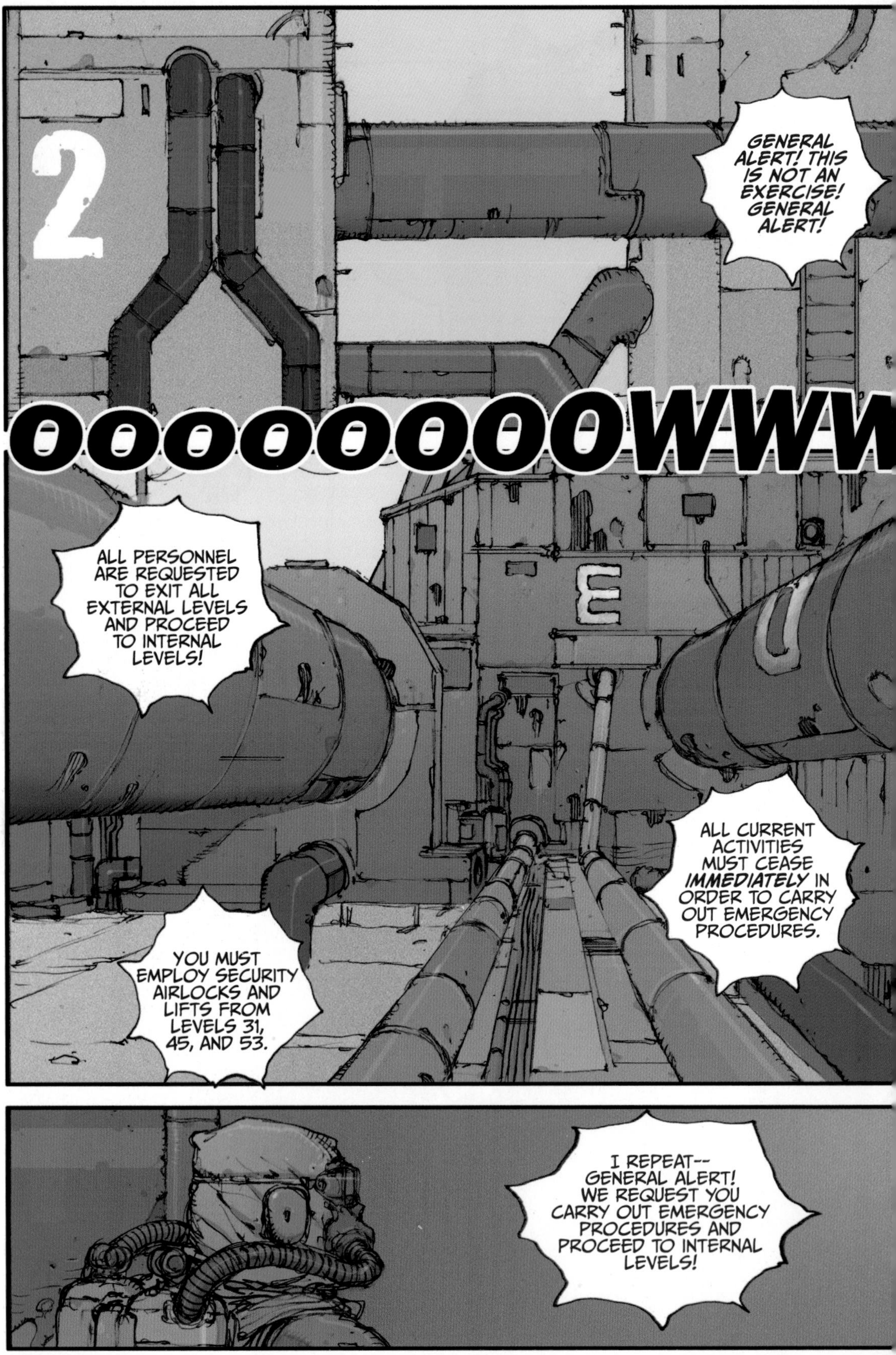
2
GENERAL ALERT! THIS IS NOT AN EXERCISE! GENERAL ALERT!
OOOOOOOOWWW
ALL PERSONNEL ARE REQUESTED TO EXIT ALL EXTERNAL LEVELS AND PROCEED TO INTERNAL LEVELS!
ALL CURRENT ACTIVITIES MUST CEASE *IMMEDIATELY* IN ORDER TO CARRY OUT EMERGENCY PROCEDURES.
YOU MUST EMPLOY SECURITY AIRLOCKS AND LIFTS FROM LEVELS 31, 45, AND 53.
I REPEAT-- GENERAL ALERT! WE REQUEST YOU CARRY OUT EMERGENCY PROCEDURES AND PROCEED TO INTERNAL LEVELS!

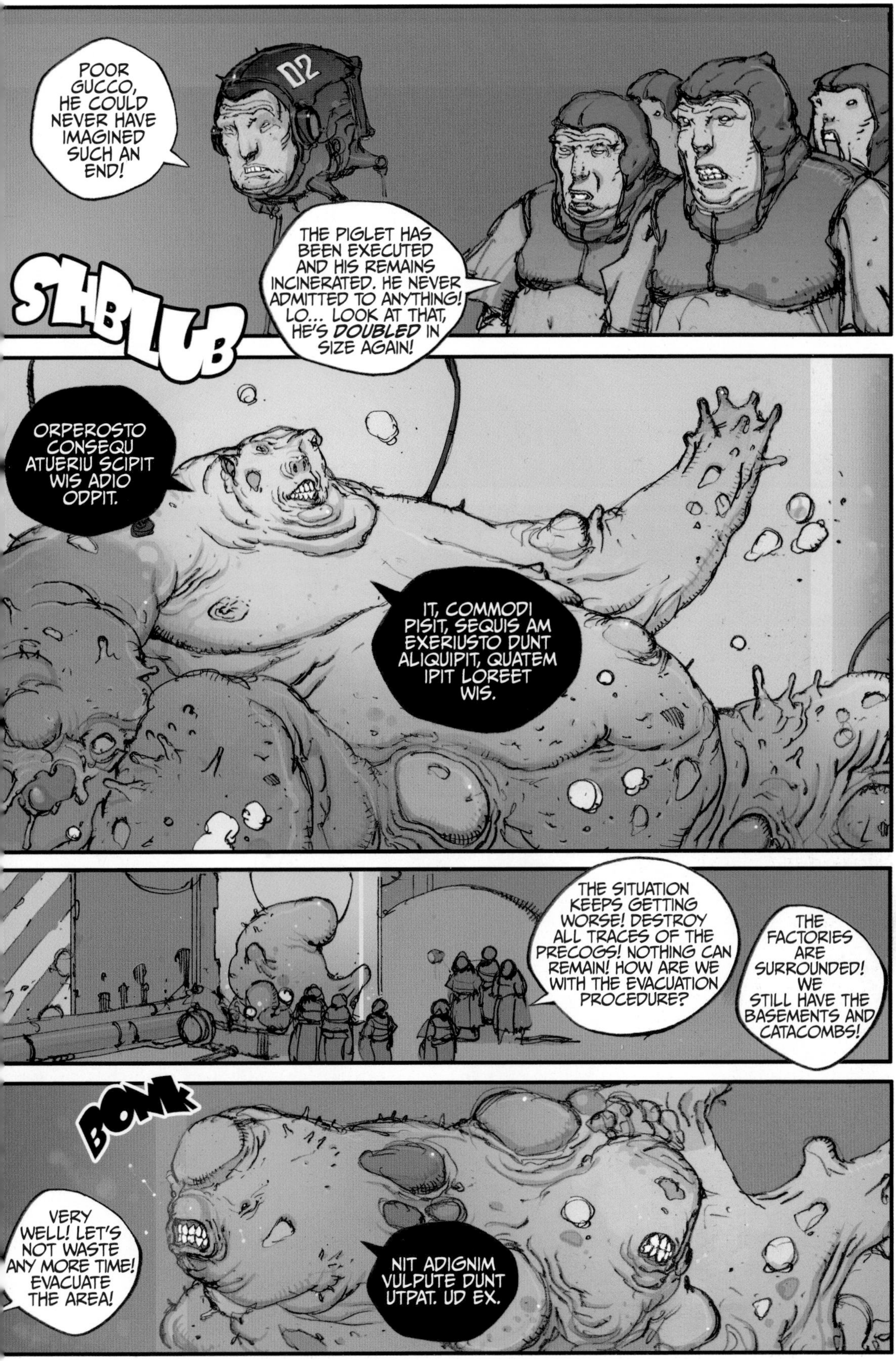
POOR GUCCO, HE COULD NEVER HAVE IMAGINED SUCH AN END!
D2
THE PIGLET HAS BEEN EXECUTED AND HIS REMAINS INCINERATED. HE NEVER ADMITTED TO ANYTHING! LO... LOOK AT THAT, HE'S DOUBLED IN SIZE AGAIN!
SHBLUB
ORPEROSTO CONSEQU ATUERIU SCIPIT WIS ADIO ODPIT.
IT, COMMODI PISIT, SEQUIS AM EXERIUSTO DUNT ALIQUIPIT, QUATEM IPIT LOREET WIS.
THE SITUATION KEEPS GETTING WORSE! DESTROY ALL TRACES OF THE PRECOGS! NOTHING CAN REMAIN! HOW ARE WE WITH THE EVACUATION PROCEDURE?
THE FACTORIES ARE SURROUNDED! WE STILL HAVE THE BASEMENTS AND CATACOMBS!
BOMK
VERY WELL! LET'S NOT WASTE ANY MORE TIME! EVACUATE THE AREA!
NIT ADIGNIM VULPUTE DUNT UTPAT. UD EX.

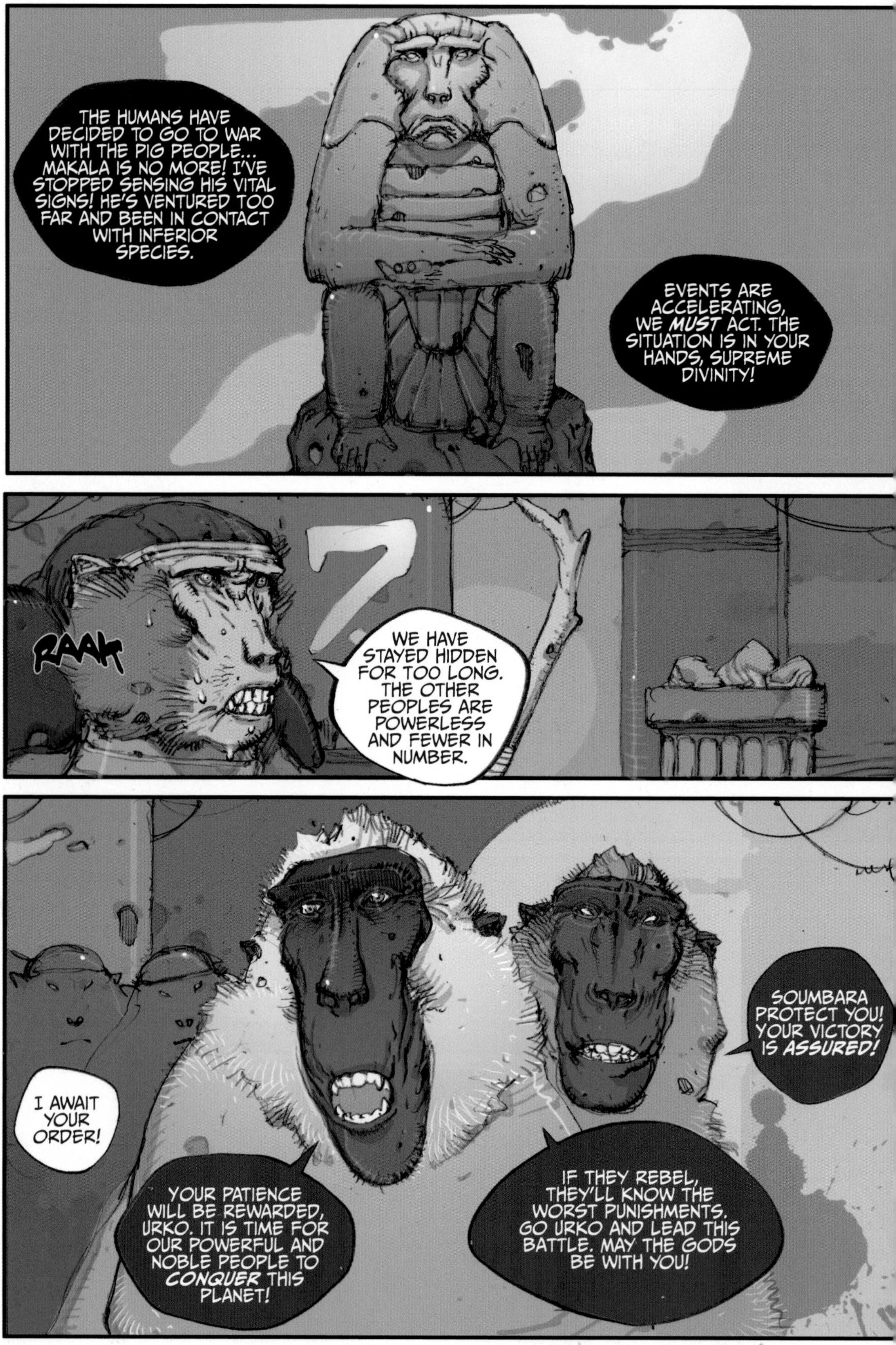
THE HUMANS HAVE DECIDED TO GO TO WAR WITH THE PIG PEOPLE... MAKALA IS NO MORE! I'VE STOPPED SENSING HIS VITAL SIGNS! HE'S VENTURED TOO FAR AND BEEN IN CONTACT WITH INFERIOR SPECIES.
EVENTS ARE ACCELERATING, WE *MUST* ACT. THE SITUATION IS IN YOUR HANDS, SUPREME DIVINITY!
RAAK
WE HAVE STAYED HIDDEN FOR TOO LONG. THE OTHER PEOPLES ARE POWERLESS AND FEWER IN NUMBER.
SOUMBARA PROTECT YOU! YOUR VICTORY IS *ASSURED!*
I AWAIT YOUR ORDER!
YOUR PATIENCE WILL BE REWARDED, URKO. IT IS TIME FOR OUR POWERFUL AND NOBLE PEOPLE TO *CONQUER* THIS PLANET!
IF THEY REBEL, THEY'LL KNOW THE WORST PUNISHMENTS. GO URKO AND LEAD THIS BATTLE. MAY THE GODS BE WITH YOU!

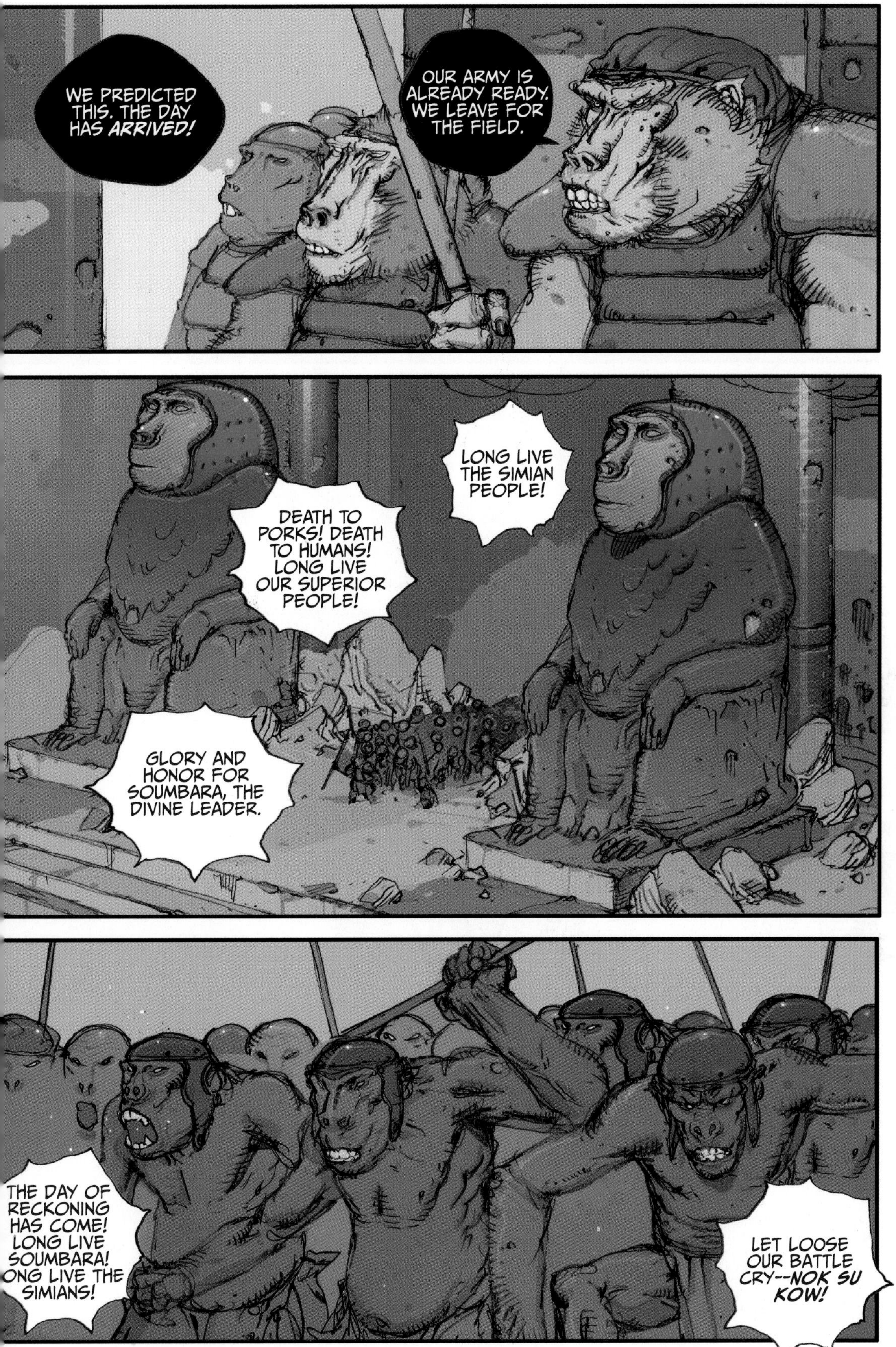

WE PREDICTED THIS. THE DAY HAS *ARRIVED!*
OUR ARMY IS ALREADY READY. WE LEAVE FOR THE FIELD.
LONG LIVE THE SIMIAN PEOPLE!
DEATH TO PORKS! DEATH TO HUMANS! LONG LIVE OUR SUPERIOR PEOPLE!
GLORY AND HONOR FOR SOUMBARA, THE DIVINE LEADER.
THE DAY OF RECKONING HAS COME! LONG LIVE SOUMBARA! ONG LIVE THE SIMIANS!
LET LOOSE OUR BATTLE CRY--*NOK SU KOW!*

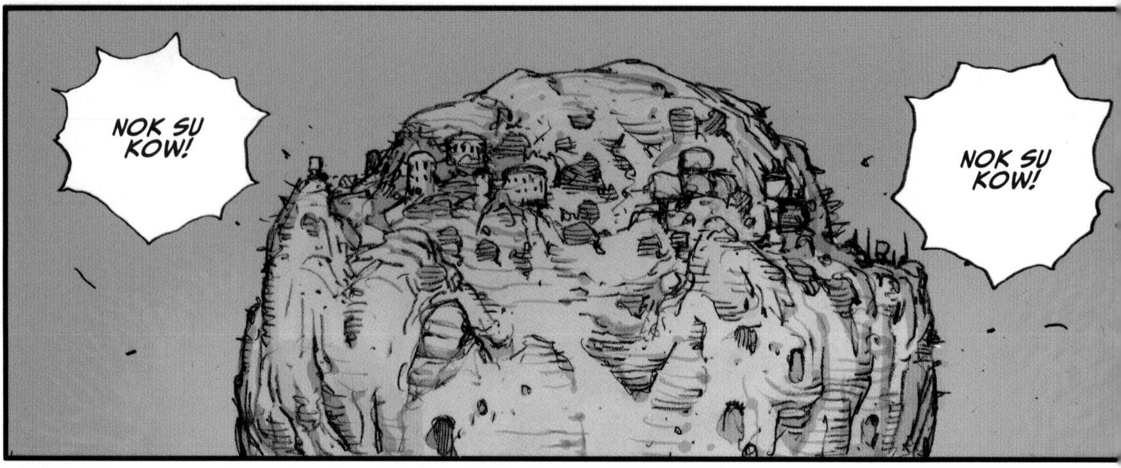
NOK SU KOW!
NOK SU KOW!
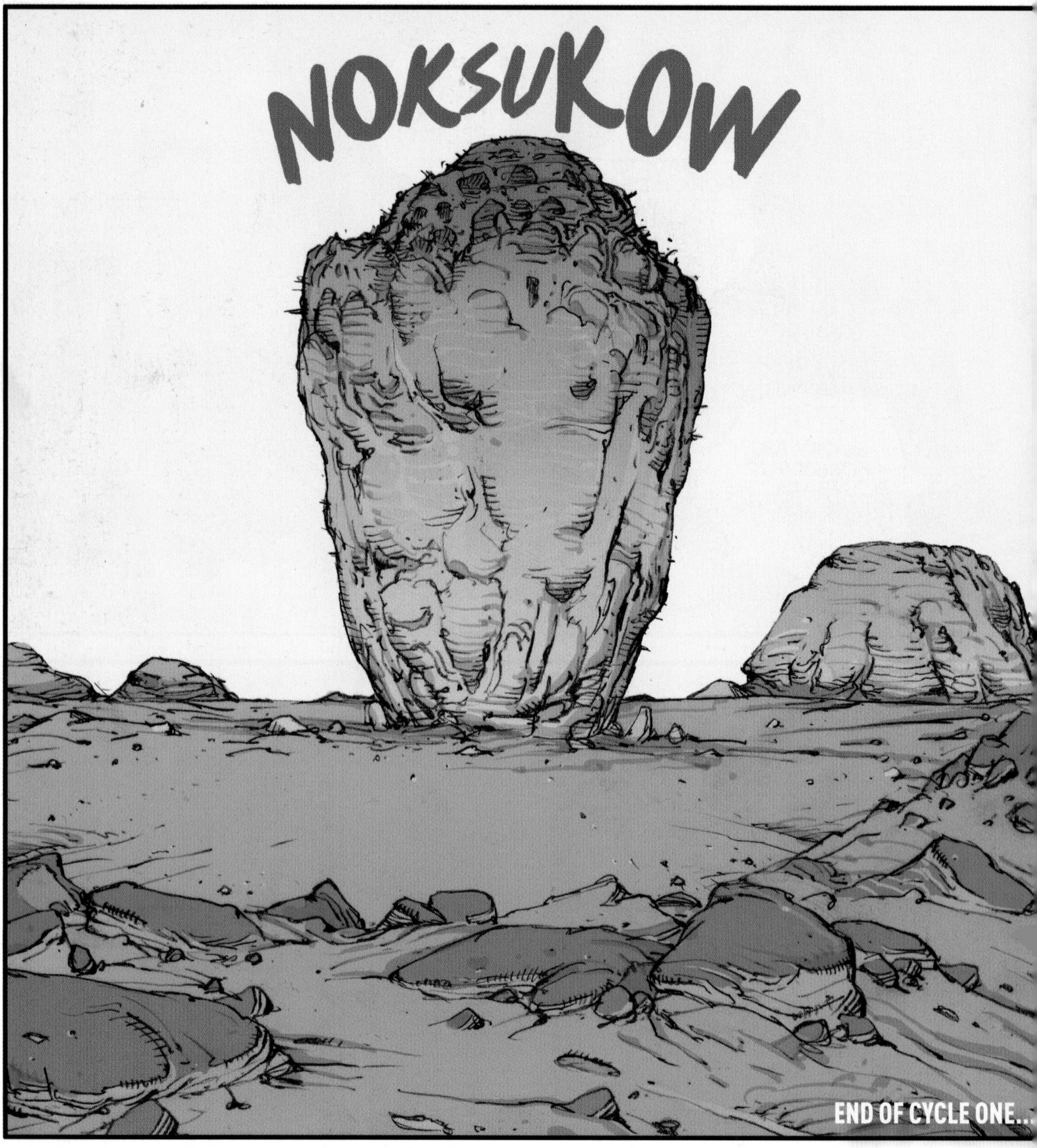
NOKSUKOW
END OF CYCLE ONE...

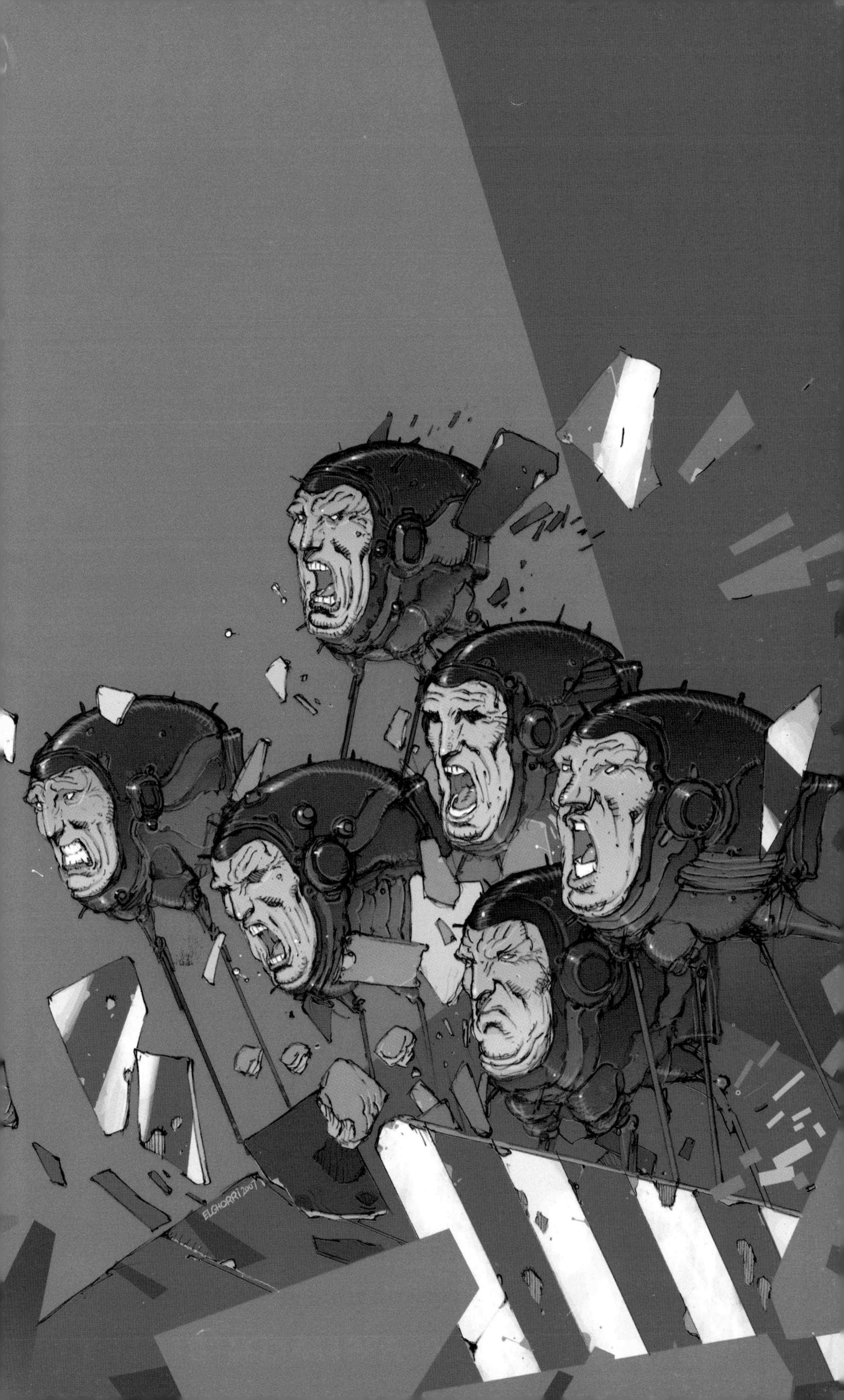
ELGHORRI 2007

COVER GALLERY

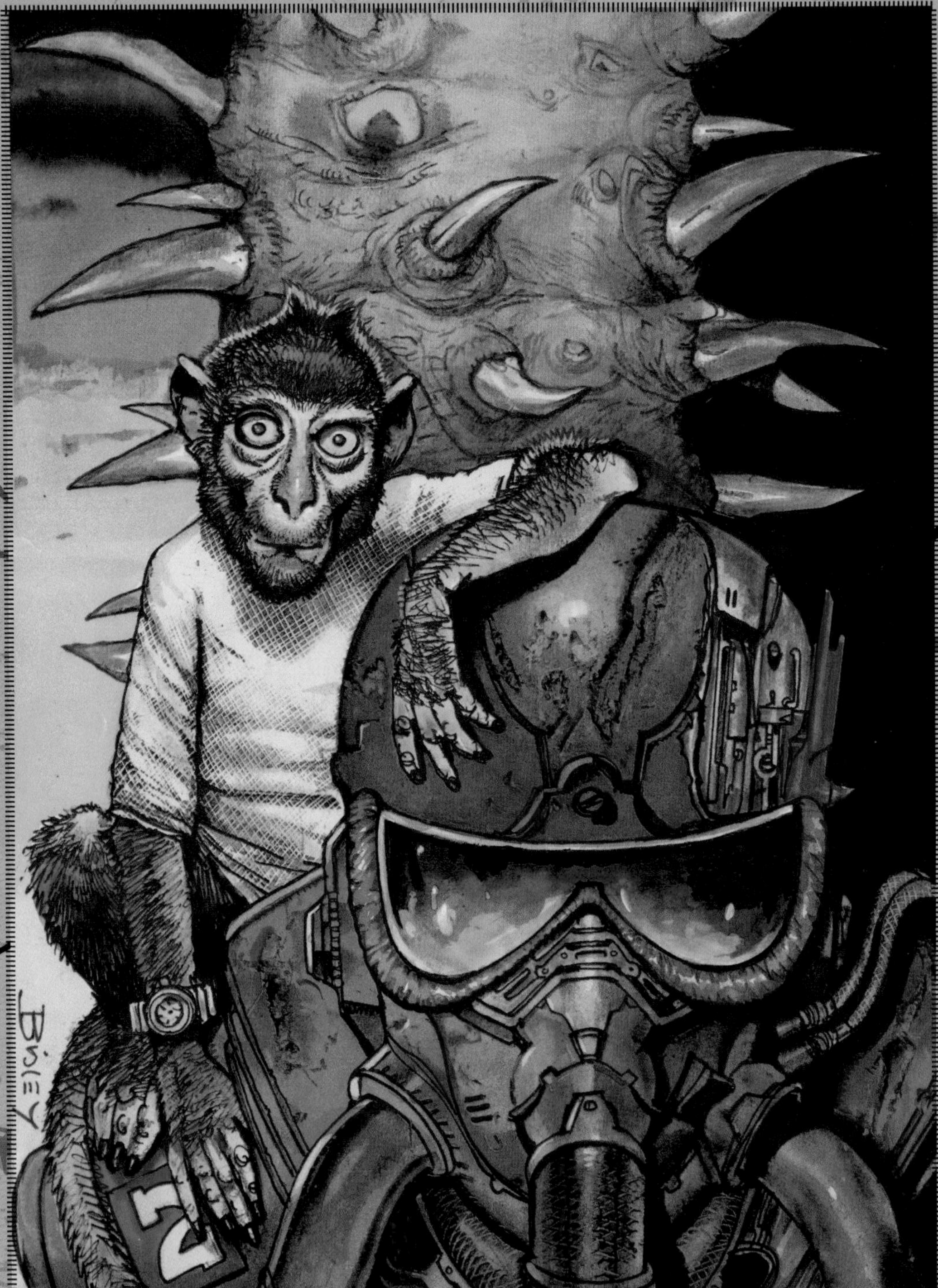
BISLEY
2

ISSUE#1 COVER A **SIMON BISLEY**

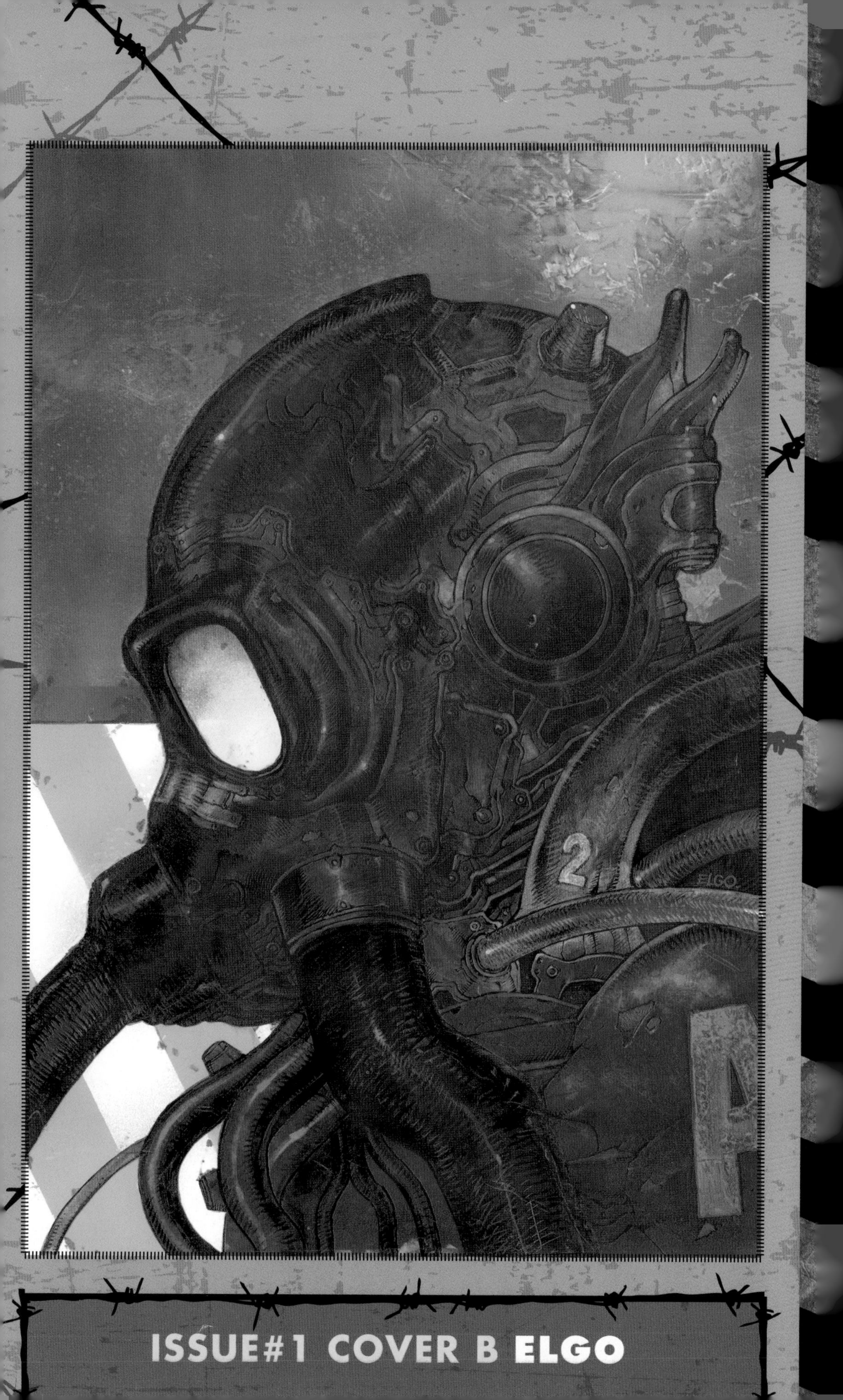
2
ELGO

ISSUE#1 COVER B ELGO

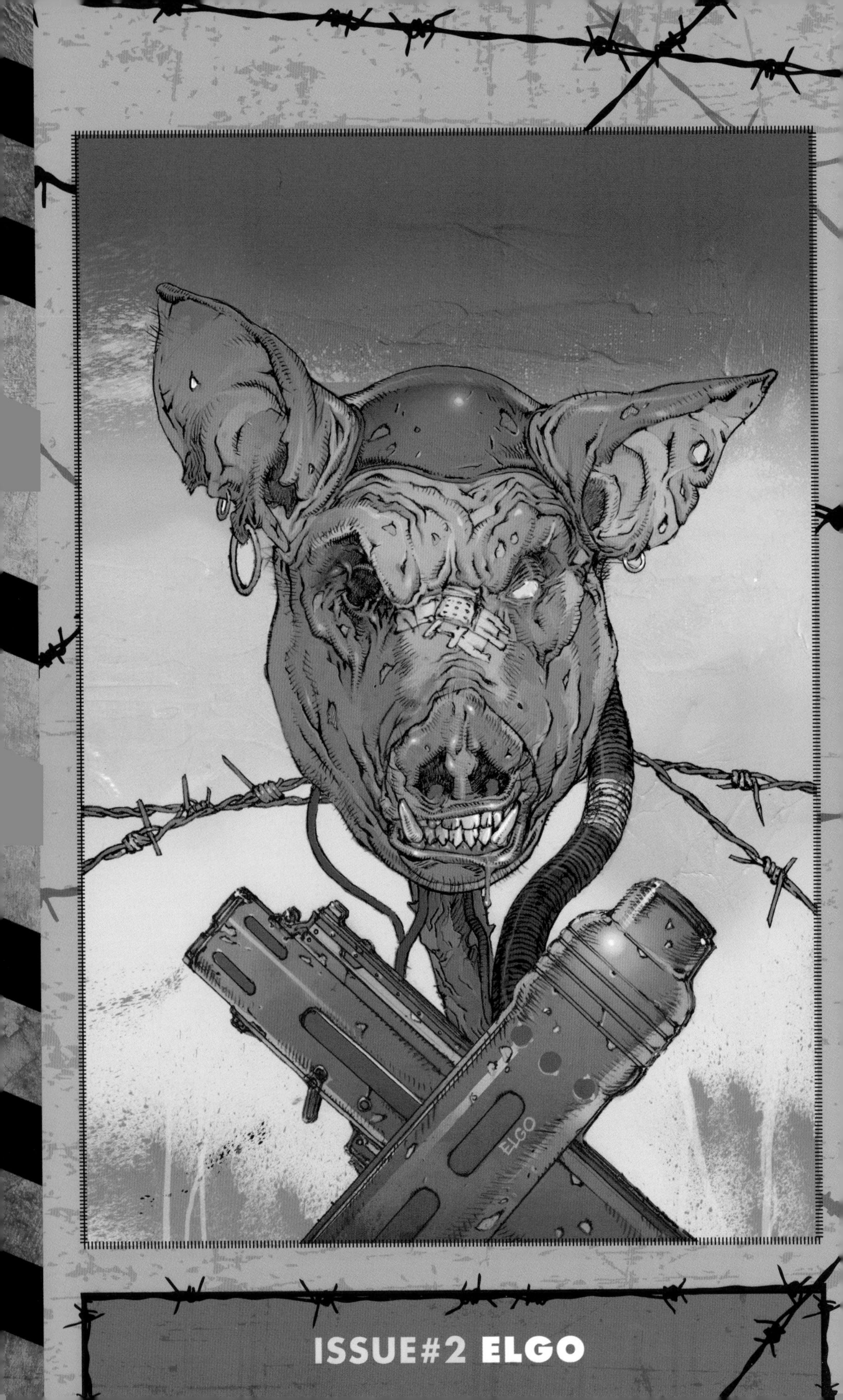
ELGO
ELGO

ISSUE#2 **ELGO**

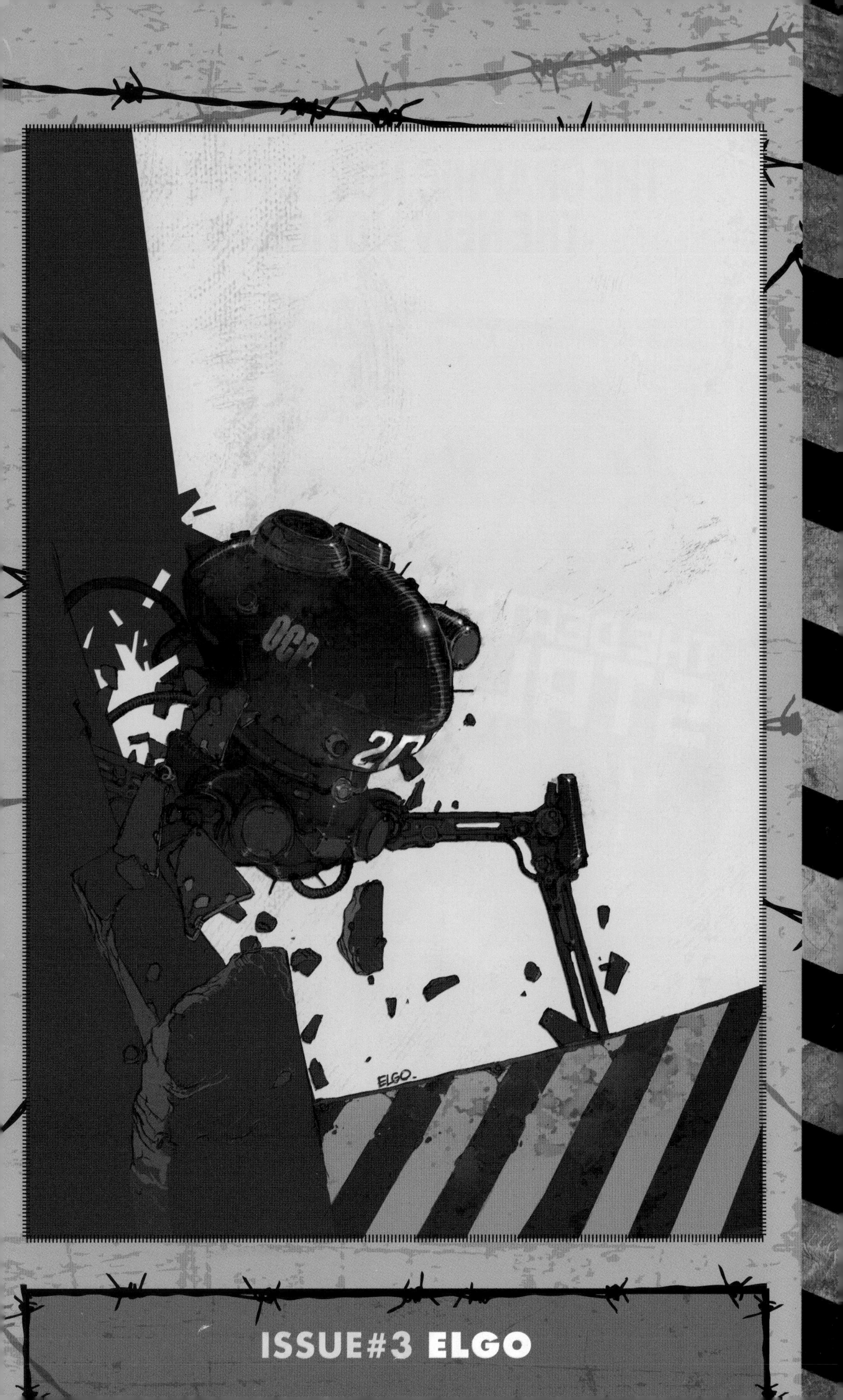
OCP
2
ELGO.

ISSUE#3 ELGO

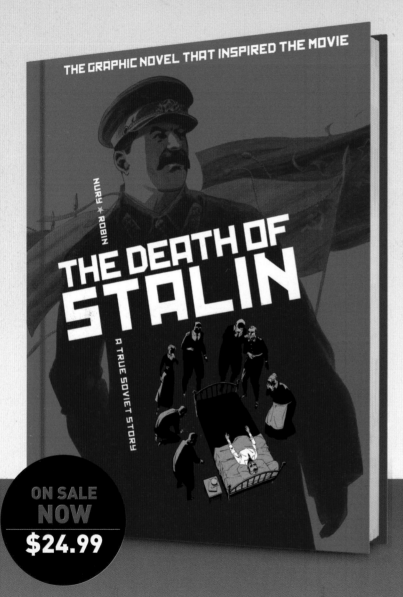

AVAILABLE NOW

THE GRAPHIC NOVEL THAT INSPIRED THE MOVIE
DEATH TO THE TSAR

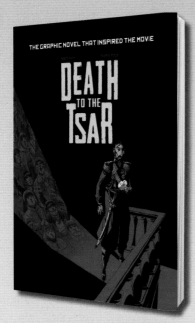

DEATH TO THE TSAR
ISBN: 9781785866418
Hardback Book

MATHIEU BABLET
THE BEAUTIFUL DEATH

THE BEAUTIFUL DEATH
ISBN:9781785861345
Hardback Book

JOMORVAN
LOOKY
THILL
HERCULES
WRATH OF THE HEAVENS

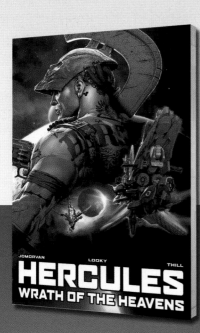

HERCULES: WRATH OF THE HEAVENS
ISBN: 9781785855863
Softcover Collection

STEFANO RAFFAELE / CHRISTOPHE BEC
UNDER
SCOURGE OF THE SEWER

UNDER: SCOURGE OF THE SEWER
ISBN: 9781785864834
Softcover Collection

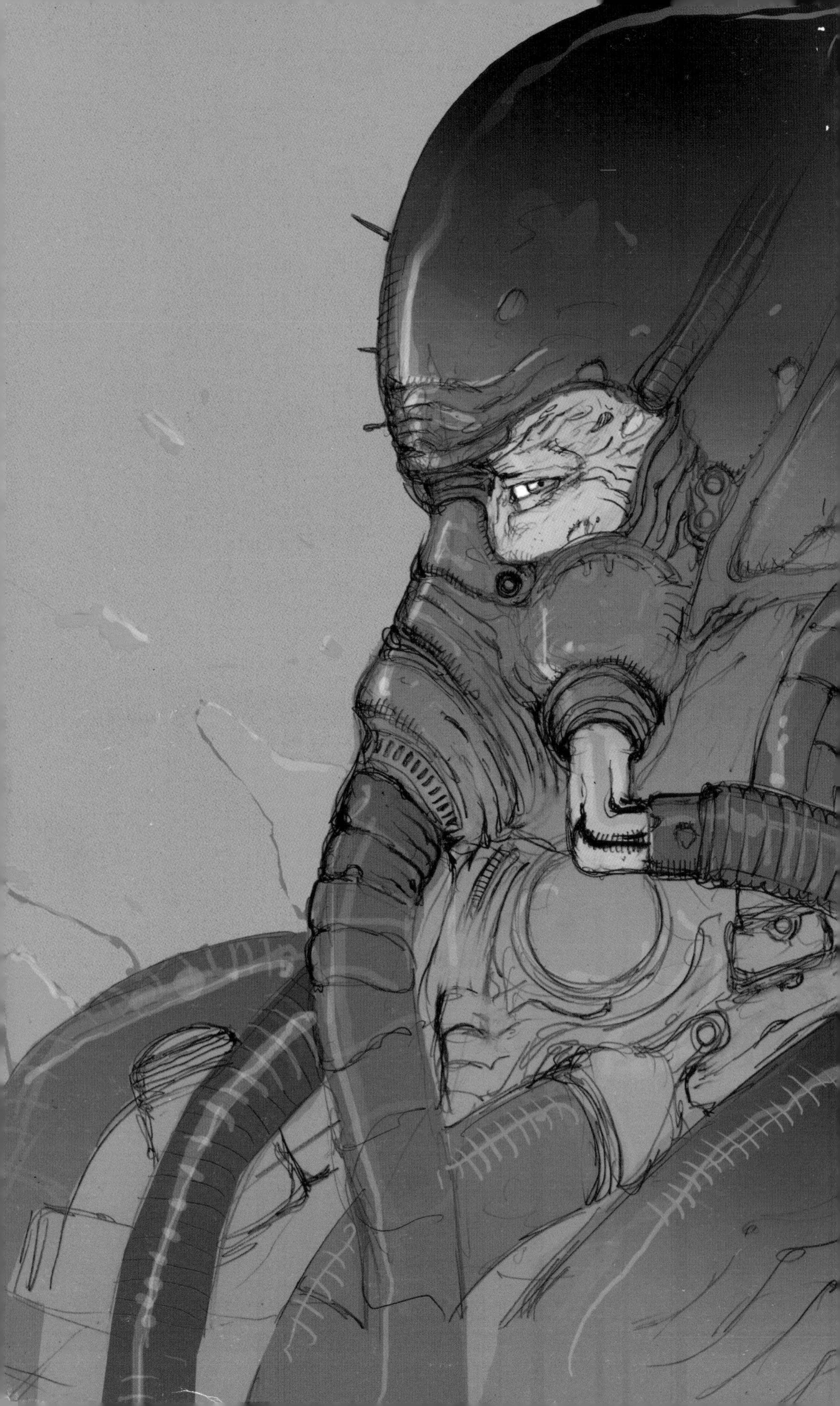